THE HOUR OF THE POOR, THE HOUR OF WOMEN

THE HOUR OF THE POOR,
THE HOUR OF WOMEN
Salvadoran Women Speak

RENNY GOLDEN

CROSSROAD • NEW YORK

1991

The Crossroad Publishing Company
370 Lexington Avenue, New York, NY 10017

Copyright © 1991 by Renny Golden

Printed in the United States of America
Typesetting output: TEXSource, Houston

Library of Congress Cataloging-in-Publication Data

Golden, Renny.
    The hour of the poor, the hour of women : Salvadoran women speak / Renny Golden.
      p. cm.
    ISBN 0-8245-1088-7
    1. Poor women—El Salvador—Interviews. 2. Feminists—El Salvador—Interviews. 3. Women in community development—El Salvador. 4. Basic Christian communities—El Salvador. 5. Church and social problems—El Salvador. 6. Church and social problems—Catholic Church. I. Title.
HV1448.S2G65 1991
362.83'08'6942—dc20   91-15140
                                                      CIP

Grateful acknowledgment is made to Orbis Books for permission to reprint the map of El Salvador from *The Religious Roots of Rebellion* by Phillip Berryman.

It is late
but we ourselves
are this late hour.
　　　—Pedro Casaldáliga

Now is the hour of God,
now is the hour of the poor,
and we are discovering
now is the hour of women.
　　　—Venancia

Contents

Foreword

This is a book of testimonies about women in the war zone of El Salvador. The stories testify to the extraordinary faith and courage of these Salvadoran women. They also testify against the governments of El Salvador and the United States, which have waged unrelenting war against the people whose aspirations are the legitimate aspirations of all people, to land, daily bread, and dignity. In our admiration for the positive witness of these women's words and lives, it is well for North Americans not to forget the negative testimony. The conduct of our government toward the people of El Salvador is ongoing war crime, one that should be arraigned before the court of heaven and human history.

What is so extraordinary about the lives of these women in the war zones of neocolonial war against the poor? We might begin to answer that question by exploring how patriarchal militarist societies have seen women's relation to war. Officially women have been excluded from war. War is men's business, and women should stay out. This, of course, does not mean that women have not always been deeply affected by war. It has been their sons, husbands, lovers, and fathers who have been sent to fight or have directed the fighting.

Women have always been prime victims of war. They have been the vulnerable recipients of "collateral damage." Their bodies have also been the terrain on which men have acted out their contempt for other men, by showing the helplessness of conquered men to protect their women from outrage. Unthinkable that women themselves should be protagonists in battle. For those sorts of women particular kinds of outrage have been reserved, for the double insurrection against conquering power, both as members of the conquered community and as women "out of their place."

Patriarchal militarism has always had its exemplary role for women in relation to men's wars, as cheerleaders, sending their men off with kisses and flowers, welcoming them home again with bands playing, holding the family together while men fight, weeping at gravesides. Men become heroes by having women reflect back to them their uncritical support of their military feats, at twice their normal size.

Today patriarchy pretends to be egalitarian by sending some women off to war as well. What a tender scene it is as the mother kisses her toddler goodbye and loyally heads off to do her "duty" in the service of her country. Perhaps after the carnage is over she too will have a few medals on her blouse. Uncle Sam is an equal opportunity employer in the patriotic work of protecting our "national security." But these token gestures do not really change the gender division of labor in war, his to fight, hers to nurse and weep and cheer.

In the Salvadoran people's army there are women fighters too, the *comandantes* — *muchachas* alongside the *muchachos*. Here the equality is less of a sham. The women really do shoulder the risks alongside the men. In the government of the liberated nation, these women may take their place in democratic national assemblies, if they survive. They show that they too can die, as men have died, in battle, with a gun in their hands. Women are no longer to be regarded as helpless victims or uncritical standers-by. In the ranks of the martyrs women are more than amply present as well.

But the women *comandantes*, while an important part of the story of the people's resistance to injustice, point to a different role played by many other women who carry no weapons. As Renny Golden makes clear, the central drama of these women's lives is not about how to die, but about how to live. They witness to the insurrection of life in the midst of death, of compassion in the midst of hatred, of truth in the face of lies. Theirs is the witness that can carry us from death to resurrection and to a new earth.

As the Sandinista leaders so often declared (and were so sadly prevented from living out), "the revolution begins when the war is over." The revolution is not won by war. War is the cruel necessity imposed by governing elites that refuse to change and who force their people to unseat them from power. Victory in that war to unseat genocidal elites simply clears the way for the real revolution to begin, the building of a new society where justice might prevail, where the true bonds of community are respected.

The *comandantes* help to win that war, but the leaders of base communities, the peasant leaders and organizers, women who hold together the bonds of life in the midst of death, they are the ones who carry the principles of the true revolution, the revolution that can begin only when the war is over. It is that witness to revolutionary life beyond war that is what this book is all about. As North Americans we need to hear these stories, in shame and sorrow for who we are in this drama, but also in solidarity with a people who continue to point beyond our system of violence to a new humanity.

ROSEMARY RADFORD RUETHER

Acknowledgments

This book does not belong to me. It feels paltry to thank the authors whose story and history the book encompasses. So many of those responsible for the book's construction must remain anonymous to protect them from reprisals. Gracias, *compas*, I offer back this gift that your histories have given.

To Mary Ann Corley for her unfailing generosity in typing and editing the manuscript; without her advice and friendship this book wouldn't have been possible; to Secundino Ramírez for inspiration that has lasted this last decade; to Michael McConnell for a writer's wisdom and a friend's encouragement; to Lorna Stone and Allen Schwartz for editorial help when I was stuck. Thank you, my friends.

I especially want to acknowledge the primary translators of the women's life histories, Yvonne Dilling and Scott Wright. Although I speak Spanish, my level of proficiency is below that needed to translate these interviews. Equally important, I believe Yvonne's shared experience of war and commitment invited the women's confidence in ways that I could not. Yvonne has recounted the year and a half she spent in Mesa Grande refugee camp and her experience of swimming with children on her back across the river Lempa during a helicopter machine-gun strafing in her book *In Search of Refuge*.

Scott Wright, who also spent a year in Mesa Grande, and the years since 1981 in war zones of the Salvadoran countryside, translated interviews when Yvonne could not. Scott is a pastoral worker whose sense of "accompaniment" has placed him at the side of *campesinos* fleeing the 500- and 750-pound bombs that U.S. taxes have paid for. His presence, along with that of people like Dr. Charlie Clements and many less famous North American pastoral and humanitarian workers in the resettled areas, witnesses to another type of U.S. presence: one that stands for life.

Yvonne and Scott's assistance was invaluable because of the esteem in which they are held by the Salvadorans who knew them. An example of the people's confidence was demonstrated to me while attending a celebration liturgy in the Santa Marta resettlement in Cabañas. The visiting celebrant, Fr. Jim Barnett, asked the *campesinos* if they remembered certain *gringo* church workers from their years of exile in Mesa Grande refuge camp. The *campesinos* nodded politely but impassively to acknowledge a priest's name he mentioned. Then he asked if they knew two other friends — Yvonne and Scott. At that, the somber chapel broke into smiles and a great applause. Indeed, the people remembered Scott and Yvonne.

Acknowledgments

To Nancy Jones and Dan Dale, missionaries in El Salvador who housed me, fed me, and worried about this project as much as I did. Without them I wouldn't have made it through.

Lutheran missionary Bill Dexheimer translated Reina's testimony. Bill collaborated with *campesinos* in compiling their testimonial tribute to Laura López entitled "The Life and Testimony of Laura," which he translated. Bill's overall editorial advice on the manuscript was invaluable. Additionally, Bill and Jim Barnett, O.P., offered a place to stay and generous assistance during my trips to El Salvador. Minor Sinclair and Margaret Lyle shared their translations of interviews that Scott Wright had taken of Emilia and Venancia. For their collaborative spirits I am grateful.

Thanks to Adrianna Plasse for her translation of Rebecca's history; to Kathleen Lynch for much shared work and information about women's organizations of El Salvador; to Peter Hinde, O.Carm., for pinchhitting as translator for Scott during lengthy interviews. To Mary McCann I owe a great deal for her support and forbearance in seeing me through some logistical stonewalls and for her translation of Gladis Sibrián; to Jenny Smith and the U.S.–El Salvador Institute for Democratic Development for providing the interview with Comandante Rebeca Palacios, as well as for arranging our meeting with Gladis Sibrián; to Micaela Barg of Co-Madres for translating América Sosa's life history; to Ed Dunn for Lupe's translation and for his great stories; to Barry Shelley for leading me to Cristina Gómez's sons; to Lee and Marsha (Sfier) Cormie for challenging and supportive manuscript advice; to Jim Harney whose photos inspired the cover design and to Salvadoran artist Alejandro Arévalo for his beautiful work; to Betty Campbell, R.S.M., for first telling me about Silvia and other heroines; to Gary MacEoin, Scott Wright, and Tom Montgomery Fate for generous editorial help; to Rosemary Radford Ruether for continual generosity and for affirming this work at a critical moment; to Elisabeth Schüssler Fiorenza for support and advocacy for this book; to Dan Hartnett and Mary Ann Corley, who encouraged me to accept the fellowship to write this book at a time when I hesitated; to the Chicago office of the American Friends Service Committee and the Chicago Religious Task Force on Central America for continued support, solidarity, and encouragement.

To Frank Oveis and John Eagleson, editors at Crossroad/Continuum, for valuable help. A special thanks to the Southwest Institute for Research on Women (SIROW) at the University of Arizona for awarding me a Rockefeller Humanities Fellowship to write this book. SIROW and the Women's Studies Department bring together a wonderful array of gracious and challenging women scholars who did much to support and encourage this effort. To my friends Susan Gieger and Michele St. Germain for manuscript advice and personal support while I was in Tucson.

ACKNOWLEDGMENTS

To my school, Northeastern Illinois University, for research support. To a friend in El Salvador, whom I cannot name, whose work and support for this project, as well as his committed life, remain for me a source of inspiration. Finally, thanks to Penny Lernoux, who told me early on to avoid scholarly language and to trust stories.

Excerpts from poems used in epigraphs are from the following sources: Roque Dalton, Gilberto González y Contreras, Chan, Marcelino H., Cutumay Camones, from *El Salvador at War: A Collage Epic*, edited by Marc Zimmerman (Minneapolis: MEP Publications, 1988); Pedro Casaldáliga, *In Pursuit of the Kingdom* (Maryknoll, N.Y.: Orbis Books, 1990); Claribel Alegría, *Woman of the River* (Pittsburgh: University of Pittsburgh Press, 1989); Ariel Dorfman, *Resistance Literature*, edited by Barbara Harlow (New York: Metheun, 1987); Mirna Martínez, *Ixok Amar Go*, edited by Zoe Anglesey (Granite Press, 1987).

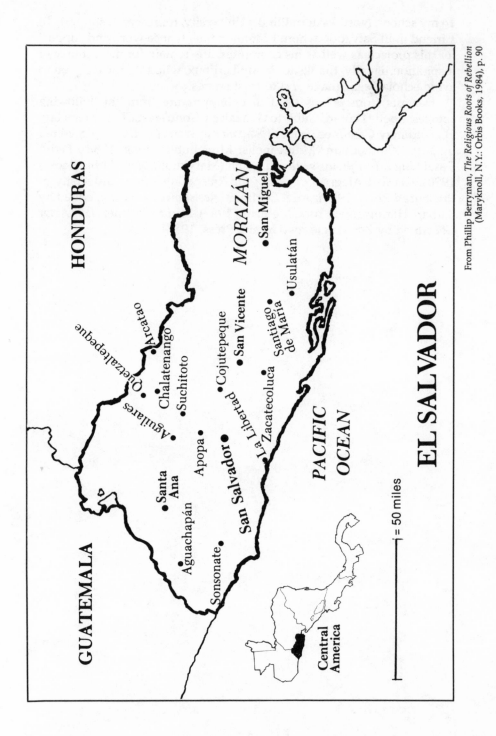

GUATEMALA

HONDURAS

Quetzaltepeque

Arcatao
• Chalatenango
Aguilares • Suchitoto
• Santa Ana
Apopa •
Aguachapán •
Sonsonate •
San Salvador •
La Libertad •
Cojutepeque •
San Vicente •
Zacatecoluca •
Santiago de María •
MORAZÁN
• San Miguel
• Usulatán

PACIFIC OCEAN

EL SALVADOR

Central America

| = 50 miles

From Phillip Berryman, *The Religious Roots of Rebellion*
(Maryknoll, N.Y.: Orbis Books, 1984). p. 90

Introduction

When I was five years old, my grandfather, Dinny Murphy, sang "Macushla," a lament for leaving one's beloved and one's Ireland. He cried. Then he dried his eyes and taught me an Irish rebel song. It was my first lesson in sentiment (and a good deal of sentimentality) that was larger than family; it was my first lesson in the solidarity of the dispossessed; and it was my first lesson in dangerous memory.

My grandmother told stories of an enchanted Irish village underwater in a forest near West Meath, about the necessity always to walk a horse or dog on the bog at nightfall because animals sensed evil or devilish spirits. She also told me of the time Black and Tans (British security forces) rode over their fields and beat her brother Jack with a riding crop because he objected. I was six and I learned my first lesson in resistance. I understood intuitively that moral responsibility demanded historical choice. Though I didn't know the meaning of the word I knew "solidarity" meant choosing a side.

Neither of my grandparents ever told their own stories, only snippets of their people's. Pity. Their stories *were* the story of a colonized people. My grandmother's story was the story of the most oppressed, the most invisible of the Irish nationalists, Republicans, and resisters. Life histories are texts that recover history and culture, not in the words of scholars, but in the words of the colonized. This book tells the life histories of Salvadoran women in the midst of a war against their own neocolonial elite and the captains of U.S. empire. The metaphor that people's historian Eduardo Galeano uses to describe the history of Latin America's resistance and conquest is "memories of fire." This book recovers the memories of women who are a hidden center, the blue flame, within a fire that has swept Central America in the latter part of this century. To speak of the liberation occurring among peasants, workers, the base Christian communities, the popular organizations, or the guerrilla forces without reflection on the experience of women within that process is to speak abstractly and, therefore, erroneously about a new social creation. El Salvador's liberation process seeks a new model of popular governance.

In the current international crisis old models of government have given rise to uprisings of the people of Central Europe, the Middle East, Southern Africa, and Central America. These movements seek models of governance that reflect and are accountable to popular will. Popular will cannot be collapsed into the category "proletariat," as Marxist theorists have advanced, without ignoring the cultural, ethnic, racial, and gender

15

experiences of the majority. Analysis of class oppression within national liberation struggles is insufficient without descriptions by poor women* of their own experience within that process.

Those of us who have travelled to El Salvador and encountered community *(comunidad)*, sustained primarily by women, have discovered a new possibility for social life. *Comunidad* is reminiscent of the fading experience of extended family networks in the U.S., and the communal ideals reclaimed in the social movements of the 1960s and 1970s. *Comunidad*, however, contains dimensions of social life that transcend U.S. experience politically and spiritually. Salvadoran community is created by the *base*, those who in U.S. culture are the most marginalized and ignored — the illiterate, the homeless, the destitute, the hungry, the dirty, the women. *Comunidad* is neither anarchic nor mystical but highly organized, disciplined, and democratic.

Popular democracy, the PPLs *(Poder Popular Local*, Local Popular Power) created by peasants in the war front of Chalatenango, and Cabañas in the early 1980s, reveals a model of political governance that reflects the radical mutuality demanded by the base Christian community as well as the collectivity instilled by agricultural cooperatives.

Comunidad is the spiritual infrastructure of the popular church. The Salvadorans have created a new church that has incarnated God's generosity and compassion. The spiritual and political "lessons" that Salvadorans have taught each other are for us also. The world is hungry for popular democracy that transforms the cynicism of a "democracy" run by elites to benefit the rich or a "social democracy" orchestrated by state bureaucrats. Equally urgent is the need for economic models that practice justice for the poor as a first priority.

In the First World the hearts of youth ache for a life of meaning, a life worth struggling for. Colonized youth die in wars, but the colonized children of Empire die in gang or drug wars. The psychic deprivation of alienated middle-class youth is so accomplished that they cannot name the source of their suffering. Our cultural "priests," the psychologists and social workers who seek to heal these wounds, are themselves without maps to guide them out of the despair that lurks beneath the surface of U.S. social life. The longing for connection is immense.

These women's life histories reveal the creative power of shared life, its capacity to heal the broken heart and body of a people. There are lessons here for our people, so lost, so cut off from the restorative bonds of communal life.

---

* The term "poor women" used throughout the book describes the majority of Salvadoran women, most of whom are homeless, landless, and unemployed.

Bread and Word

> *Revolution, revelation, of those who believe and create; not infallible gods of majestic stride, but ordinary people, for centuries forced into obedience and trained for impotence. Now even when they trip they keep walking. They go in search of bread and word.*
>
> —Eduardo Galeano, Memory of Fire

Bread and word. That is the daily search of Salvadoran women, for enough corn to grind into tortillas on the *metate* and for words for a new voice in history. Nothing impedes their walking, not charred villages, not centuries of silence. On the deliverance road they discover their words, they share whatever bread they can, and they find themselves.

Each woman's voice breaks a silence. "This people forced into silence seemed dumb; but when it opens its mouth, it says no. The silence of these years has been so deafening that the military took it for resignation."[1] Eduardo Galeano is speaking of Uruguayans, but he could have been talking about Salvadorans. Or of the most silenced Salvadorans — the women. Recovering their stories imitates a practice of the base Christian communities: stories of those who were *entregados* (completely given over to the people) are presented to the community as a means of evoking dangerous memory. Recovering dangerous memory creates new human identity by providing exemplary actions that tell the people who they are and who they might become. Memory saves threatened identity. The "new person" being created has lived in countless thousands who have gone before, giving history a new meaning by their resistance. Through the lives of ordinary people who refused to betray the community, collective remembering discovers what it means to be human, not in theory but in history.

The people are no different from people of other cultures, but suffering and a capacity to hope imbue them with a depth that must be experienced to be communicated. *Mística* is how Salvadorans name this profound dimension of their struggle. This quality is not "owned" by the church of the poor. Rather it is a constitutive element of insurgency, an element that is particularly Latino and indigenously Salvadoran. It is as ordinary as sacrifice for others, and as inexplicable as the appearance of insurgent hope in those moments when Western psychological development theorists would predict despair or paralyzing grief. *Mística* is not mystical in a wafty, metaphysical way. It breaks through clouds of passivity and individualism. It is always historically embedded.

Though the spirit of *mística* is acknowledged by male militants and strategists as well as pastoral workers, the men most able to cherish this revolutionary ingredient are those who can embrace women's specific contribution to the liberation struggle. *Mística* is the soul of the poor, uniquely revealed in women.

17

Introduction

Nothing so demonstrates the new flesh of a people rising from the dry bones of the old as the history of their leaders, who are so often women and so often invisible. Ethnography should begin here. It rarely does. From the furnaces of war it is still men's words that burn. Yet in the war zones depleted of clerics, of males, and of the educated, necessity has given rise to a transformed community that reveals women's capacity to preserve life amid genocide.

Threaded throughout these stories are three themes. First, with a few exceptions, women identify their Christian faith as an initial and sustaining source of commitment to the liberation process. Their consciousness of themselves as the church confronts theological models of a church *for* the poor. Their faith demands a church constructed *by* the poor. Such a model radically challenges virtually every First World model of church, including those of feminist and liberation theologies. Invariably such models are, at best, adversarial options *for* the socially dispossessed classes of women and peoples of color. Few models present marginal women in the U.S. *speaking for themselves* in religious communities or congregations.

Nor does this book propose to offer such an undiluted model. Rather, it represents an effort to allow Salvadoran women to speak for themselves while recognizing that another voice, the author's, the voice of a First World white professional woman, has constructed a framework for the reader's receiving that word. In a section on methodology and personal history that follows I elucidate my motivation for electing this role and the contradictions and possibilities it imposes.

The second theme revealed in these testimonies is the historical significance of women's contribution to liberation. Liberation theologians have used the category "the poor" to locate God's action in history. This term is gender neutral and, therefore, obscures and universalizes specific experience. The 1968 Medellín Conference of the Latin American Bishops spoke of a "preferential option for the poor." Such an option demands a conversion, not only to the side of the poor struggling for liberation but to women's struggle within that process.

What does it mean for women to be self-determining within national liberation struggles? What dangerous memory of *pueblo* (the people) in solidarity and resistance do women bring to the creation of a new history? Until women have recovered their voice through the revelation of experience, a profound dimension of the process will be invisible and silent. The absence of this voice, as the absence of the indigenous, black, or mestizo voices, impedes and misrepresents popular will and the meaning of the people's identity. These life histories make one contribution to an emerging discourse that reflects women's practice in revolutionary movements.

Feminists, womanists, and *mujeristas* have produced gender theory that has affected Salvadoran women's consciousness of themselves as historical subjects and historical force. Salvadoran women are applying gender theory within a context of insurgence and genocide. Moreover, the experience of Salvadoran women challenges First World women theorists. Women ethnographers and anthropologists interviewing and documenting women's voice in "postcolonial discourse" are methodologically rigorous in examining the power relations of interviewer and interviewee. Although this self-conscious critique of First World scholarship is critical, it does not address the demand for commitment to and practice of solidarity. A preeminent lesson of these life histories is that commitment calls forth solidarity, while the practice of solidarity inspires deepened commitment — thus producing the liberation process and "postcolonial discourse."

This leads to the third theme contained within these life histories: the lessons of death and resurrection. The practice of solidarity in El Salvador leads to death. But death is not the last word. Life is. Resurrection is not simply symbolic or disincarnate. The dead do rise and continue in the liberation struggle. Over and over in these testimonies women recall the assassination of a relative, community member, or leader, and insist that their *compañeros* will have died if they do not lift them up by continuing on the liberation path.

These stories present insights into the nature of hope and suffering. In learning about the life of *campesinas* (farmworkers), organizers, martyrs, and militants who struggle to create a new history, a new woman, a new popular church, we learn about our own reality that we cannot see. Solidarity, which theologian Jon Sobrino calls the people's name for love and commitment, is not simply a moral category. Solidarity is the process of carrying forward the revolution. What does this tell us about the shape of the world, the face of American empire, about methods of restructuring the world? The lessons are less prescriptive than inspirational. They call us to hope, to a recovery of a nonimperial history — those dangerous rivers that run beneath our ship of state.

Methodology

Urged by Salvadoran refugees in sanctuary to go to El Salvador and see the "face of war" personally, I began travel to El Salvador in 1985. I have spent up to six weeks in Central America each year until the present. Even during the height of the Sanctuary movement's national publicity, it was rare that Salvadoran or Guatemalan women refugees offered public witness. Meetings with women in Salvador, and a brief visit to Nicaragua, made it clear that women's experience was different from men's but rarely recorded or shared. Furthermore, in the Sanctuary movement the national spokesmen in the U.S. were male clerics, while women sustained the daily work. This use of voice and public space differentiated by gender was apparent in the religious sector in both First and Third world countries. Meetings with Salvadoran women organizers and especially a meeting with a leader of the base Christian communities for the entire Usulután area led to an invitation to document the life histories of the women.

These are the motivations that led me to the project. The theological and political significance of the project emerged as I heard the testimonies. For two years before I began interviewing women I had doubts about my right as a foreigner, safe from the ravages of war, to publish these stories. The task belonged to Salvadoran women, those so long silenced and unacknowledged. I expressed my reservations (cultural, linguistical, moral) to Reina, a leader of the base Christian communities in the coastal region of Usulután, one of the "hotter" areas of the war. Reina is wary of *gringos* and so sensitive to security issues that I awaited a rebuke. Yet, with exquisite patience, this woman twenty years my junior absolved me. "Look," Reina said, "we have no time to write anything down. So much history, the precious stories of our women, are lost in this war. You have this opportunity we don't have. Take our stories down. Share them with your people. *No te preocupes* [Don't worry so]." Five months after this conversation the health clinic attached to Reina's church was raided by the military, and she has been underground ever since.

So I have written the stories down. These women's lives provide a lens for seeing the liberation movement of the base communities as a social process. The focus is on female agency in the construction of the new community of the disenfranchised and, concomitantly, on how such an experience creates the new woman, the new humanity.

The interviews are divided into sections: Base Christian Communities, Peasants, Organizers, Martyrs, and Militants. These sectors are representative of women's participation in the national liberation process but they do not represent all women, nor by selecting these sectors do I propose to present a comprehensive sociological overview of Salvadoran women. The stories do present a social chronicle that uncovers a substratum of history — women's role as animators of community and as architects of the social cohesion of the base. These narratives were gathered clandestinely. In every case the women agreed to meet with me because a contact from a base Christian community or a popular organization had made arrangements guaranteeing my trustworthiness. The people's openness was the result of the *confianza* (trustworthiness) of others — Salvadorans and North American missionaries — who are part of the *comunidades de base* (base communities) or popular organizations. My friends' confidence in me was not based on my professional skills or even "personal" trust understood in U.S. terms. The *confianza* (which includes personal trust) was based on my work, which over the years involved solidarity organizing and support of refugees, as well as commitment as a writer.

Each of these interviews represents a gift given and a risk taken. What in other circumstances might have signified an individual woman's interest in self-reflection through interview or in having her story published was not the case for these women. Public figures like María Ester Chamorro, who is the wife of Rubén Zamora, the vice presidential candidate of the Democratic Convergence (a coalition of opposition groups), Gladis Sibrián, U.S. representative of the FMLN-FDR, and Comandante Rebeca Palacios and Ana Guadalupe Martínez, commander and FDR-FMLN peace negotiator, are identified by their own names in this book. The only other actual names I've used are the names of the dead. But even with pseudonyms women fear recognition. For women organizers and religious women used to daily risks, taking time out from their work with the base communities or popular organizations was a political choice and a gift of their time. Clearly they understood the need for women's voices to be heard, for North Americans to learn how Salvadorans lived under the "democratically elected" government of ARENA. But they had spoken with North Americans for years, pleading, as had Archbishop Romero in his letter to President Carter, for an end to all U.S. "military, political, or economic aid." At the time I interviewed them in July 1989, ARENA, the party U.S. Ambassador Robert White held responsible for Archbishop Romero's murder, had been in power for four months and U.S. aid to continue the war poured in at a rate of $1.5 million per day.

It was a tense time. Catechists had been picked up from their parishes; the offices of one of the refugee organizations had been raided and arrests ensued. With inexhaustible patience they found time to meet. I sat in a church with two missionary friends and talked until nightfall with Matilde, a sister who is *quemada* ("burned," or marked by security forces). Though it is dangerous to go out after dark, "night is the only free time we have," Matilde said. "The days belong to the people." Our cab dropped her off a block from her apartment; a cab driver informant might note her address because she had been seen with North Americans. Her "home" was one of two apartments she moved between now that her community house was no longer safe. I watched the slight women disappear into the shadow of the projects, aware that the night's risk was as ordinary in El Salvador as breath and, for the committed, as necessary.

I interviewed another religious sister, Ana, in a pickup truck, which she drove through checkpoints on the way to Aguilares. Accompanying her on pastoral "rounds" was the condition she set for an interview. "To understand me you must meet the people."

Getting past checkpoints in the countryside often feels less dangerous than making connections in the city where speaking with a North

Introduction

American journalist could greatly endanger an individual or organization. When meeting women to be interviewed at organizational offices or
parishes I usually took two cabs to allude *orejas* ("ears," i.e., informants).
By July 1989 foreign nationals could be deported for entering the offices
of the nongovernmental Salvadoran Human Rights Commission or the
Mothers of the Disappeared.

Access to the countryside had become almost impossible. For that
reason I could not conduct an interview with Emilia in Chalatenango.
Members of the base Christian community, however, were willing to
pass army checkpoints with interview tapes concealed on their persons
in order for "the lives of women to be heard."

I managed to get into the countryside for two interviews. The interview with Lupe, a *campesina* woman with seven children, occurred
while she made *atol*, squeezing liquid maize through porous cloth as
her children and chickens scurried underfoot.

An unsuccessful interview with Olivia in Santa Marta, a resettlement
site in Cabañas, thirty kilometers from Honduras, was conducted a day
after hand grenades had destroyed village huts and soldiers had sprayed
the area with machine-gun fire. No one had been injured, but the people
were terrified. I have not included Olivia's partial interview from that
night because I could not get the male leader of her pastoral team to
stop talking and to let his "assistant" speak. The women later explained
that Olivia organizes and inspires the community while acquiescing to
Jorge's demands. "He is an old man," the women said, "and he was very
brave at the Lempa river massacre in 1981, but he talks too much."

The "Light of Ocote" document is not an interview but a text produced by the base communities; Scott Wright interviewed Venancia in
Morazán; the interviews with FMLN combatants Rebeca Palacios and
Clelia were conducted by friends who used my interview questions to
frame the life histories.

I have usually eliminated the general questions because they were
repetitious. In many cases the woman had their own sense of direction
in storytelling. Occasionally I've included questions that elicited specific
responses. I have edited the women's texts and occasionally, though
rarely, rearranged the order of the telling. The general questions I always
included were the following:

Can you tell me the story of your life beginning with your childhood?
What special problems have you faced as a woman?
What is the source of your faith and hope?

In interviews with militants or some women organizers I asked some
form of the following questions:

You have been able to develop your own sense of confidence, your own
identity, and you are a recognized leader of the FMLN. How have you

22

been able to break out of the role restrictions placed on Salvadoran women?

Five years ago there were few women's organizations in El Salvador. Now there are nine, some like CONAMUS naming themselves as feminist, organizing for an end to rape and women abuse in the midst of a struggle for national liberation. Can you explain this sudden growth of women's organizations fighting for women's rights?

Your great poet, martyr, and revolutionary Roque Dalton said during the 1970s, "When a woman takes her gender as a political category, she begins to stop being simply a woman in herself and becomes a woman for herself." Do you agree with this? CONAMUS, for instance, believes that what Roque said is still not accepted, that is, that gender is still subordinate to class. What are your ideas?

Form and Voice

I have chosen personal *narrative* as a form that reveals these pastoral workers and political organizers as agents for a new humanity. Women's narrative allows the story to be told from the experiential view of those who, in the selective act of narration, construct three critical histories: that of the new *comunidad*, of the new woman, and of the individual woman's own selfhood. Narration, grounded in the woman's self-description and ordering of events (or in the case of the martyred women, the community's collective memory of her) presents a history developed in process, faithful to the Latino notion of history-making expressed in the popular poem by Antonio Machado: "Walker, there is no road, the road is made by walking."

A woman telling her story is the subject of her own history, one who sees her life and confers meaning upon it. As texts, these life histories deconstruct church and state canon on the role of lay people, women, and the poor. Life history as text was chosen in order to remain faithful to Salvadoran women's voice and form of social and self-revelation. This deviates from the normative literary form, which submits the subject's text to the author's. In contrast this book presents the women's narrations as text, which in turn shaped the writer's contextualizing of them. The individual stories, not their collective summary, contain the people's history. Over and over, sometimes eloquently, sometimes timidly, never easily, the women choose *life* over death, *pueblo* over diminishment. In a certain way the reader takes the journey with each woman and is confronted with her choice, is confronted with the crossroads that Salvadorans have faced for ten years: despair or hope, life or death. It is a repetition ancient as war, as women's hidden life in the heart of wars, in the heart of life.

Introduction

The testimonies that follow speak of a new hour in history. Venancia, a *campesina* pastoral worker from Morazán, is history's bellringer, tolling the hour of the silenced: "Now is the hour of God, the hour of the poor, and we are discovering now is the hour of women."

1

THE HOUR OF GOD:
THE BASE CHRISTIAN
COMMUNITIES

Photo by Jim Harney

*The breath came ... that brought us the light that broke the night.
And our communities became a live church. How did the breath get
there? ... The word of God came to us and the poor began to have faith
in other poor people.*

—*Christian Base Communities of Morazán*

Here, in the language of *mística*, is a distillation of the base Christian
community's history. When the poor evangelize the poor, a new church
is born. The Salvadorans' history of the Christian community movement
is imbued with metaphor, as the social history "Light of Ocote" in the
narrative section that follows will demonstrate. To understand the Salvadoran *comunidad* as both an embodiment of spiritual liberation and an
effective counterinsurgency tactic requires the language and inspiration
of *mística.*

Mística has everything to do with history and is, according to Sister
Rosa, "practical" as opposed to "too spiritual, too outside of humanity."

Sister Rosa works with an urban parish in San Salvador, part of the
base Christian communities, "the church of the poor that has been developing a completely new conception of faith, not only in the theological
sense but also in the practical, starting from the presence of God acting
in history, in a world where to give testimony of our vision of faith has
a different matrix." For Rosa and the base Christian communities:

> faith impels you to commit yourself to the concrete situations of
> daily life, ... to those who suffer in factories with a salary of hunger,
> to students in the university with overwhelming money and family
> problems, to displaced thousands without anywhere to live. ... In
> a country at war such as El Salvador, this commitment implies
> putting your own life at risk, ... to take on the problems of others,
> not only in the theoretical, romantic sense, but to really assume
> others' problems as if they were your own.

Sister Rosa is a member of a base Christian community that has
had 620 members killed or "disappeared." Without an understanding
of the base Christian communities one lacks adequate tools to analyze
or explain the social cohesion of a revolutionary process that has neutral-
ized a U.S.-sponsored counterinsurgency war that has cost $4.5 billion
since 1980 — one of the world's largest military assistance aid packages.
Mística is part of that social cohesion.

Ignacio Ellacuría, S.J., president of the University of Central America until his assassination, reflected on the often repeated Central America slogan, "There is no contradiction between faith and the revolution":

At times it would seem that only the masses have faith and that the leaders have science. But there are two indisputable facts: first the majority of the people have come to the revolution out of a need for justice that was awakened and encouraged by the new preaching of faith, and second, some of the most important leaders of the new stage of the revolution were also profoundly Christian. . . . Committed Christian faith not only did not impede the revolutionary movement but advanced it. Living praxis overcame theoretical prejudice.[2]

Father Ellacuría explained his discussion of this "tension" with Joaquín Villalobos of the FMLN High Command. Villalobos agreed with Ellacuría's summary "that Latin America's masses are profoundly Christian and at the same time . . . profoundly revolutionary. The faith comes from Christianity and the revolution comes from Marxism. But the two meet in the people."

Such a consensus between a church leader and a military leader is the result of the people's action, regardless of the ideological insights of either of the leaders. The people's decision in the El Salvador process cannot be underestimated or else the trap of writing history based on interpretations of national leaders, invariably educated males, is inevitable.

Commander Villalobos and Father Ellacuría argue persuasively that the locus of both Christianity and Marxism is the people and that "faith comes from Christianity and the revolution comes from Marxism." But even this assessment is still too disembodied. A historical materialist position would argue that the revolution comes from the people's revolutionary practice and that incarnated faith comes, not from "Christianity," but from a Christian people's practice.

Villalobos and Ellacuría's synthesis came twenty years after the birth of the base Christian community movement and almost twenty years after the Popular Forces of Liberation (FPL) were formed by a baker and a union organizer. Twenty years of struggle and blood. In 1989 Father Ellacuría mixed his blood with that of the martyrs of El Salvador, savagely massacred with five other Jesuit professors of the University of Central America, along with their housekeeper and her daughter, by thirty uniformed soldiers.

Base Christian communities provide an extraordinary application of the principles of the Latin American Bishops Conferences at Medellín, Colombia, in 1968 and at Puebla, Mexico, in 1979. These watershed conferences challenged the Latin American church's historical alignment

27

with the oligarchy by affirming the church's obligation to "defend the rights of the oppressed" and to make an "option for the poor."[3] Pope John Paul II made this declaration at a meeting of indigenous communities in Oaxaca at the time of the Puebla conference:

> You have a right to be respected and not deprived of the little you have, often by methods that amount to plunder. You have a right to throw down the barriers of exploitation.
>
> [To the landowner's he said,] "You have . . . left the land fallow, taking bread from so many families who need it. Human conscience, the conscience of the people, the cry of the destitute, and above all the voice of God and the church repeat with me: it is not right, it is not human, it is not Christian to maintain such clearly unjust situations.[4]

Within a year, Archbishop Romero expressed the Salvadoran church's witness to these principles:

> I rejoice, brothers and sisters, that our church is persecuted, precisely for its preferential option for the poor. It is the glory of our church to have mixed its blood — the blood of its priests, catechists, and communities — with the massacres of the people and ever to have borne the mark of persecution. A church that suffers no persecution, but enjoys the privileges and support of the powers of this world — that church has good reason to be afraid![5]

The Eloquence of History

If the history of the people's church and the archbishop who defended it were a painting, the artist would be Picasso capturing, as he did in Guérnica, the blood that unites innocence and marks history with its unforgettable spilling. Romero said that blood speaks "the most eloquent of words."[6]

The *matanza* (massacre) of 1932, like its terrible rebirth in the 1980s, is the word of blood that speaks today in El Salvador. Its eloquence is in the defiance of the people; the intended effect, defeat and compliance, has not marked the Salvadoran inheritors of that memory. The 1932 insurrection against a military dictatorship was spearheaded by Farabundo Martí, a Marxist, and Feliciano Ama, a religious leader of the Indian masses. The rebellion was doomed from the start. The peasants had centuries of rage in their hearts but only machetes in their hands. The Salvadoran military had machine guns, rifles, and the leadership of Maximiliano Hernández Martínez and General Ochoa who, according to survivor Miguel Marmol, had profound hatred of the insolent masses. Sitting in a courtyard, Ochoa demanded that the captured crawl on their knees to where he was seated:

He said to them. "Come here and smell my gun." The prisoners pleaded in the name of God and their children, having heard the sound of intermittent shots.

But the General insisted. "If you don't smell my pistol, then you are a communist and afraid. He who is without sin knows no fear!" The *campesino* smelled the barrel of the gun, and in that instant, the general would put a bullet in his face. "Bring the next one in," he said.[7]

If the Indian men "deserved" their fate for the audacity of fighting for corn and a piece of land to sow it, the fate of women, like "Red Julia," who led the peasant revolt in the town of Sonsonate, can only be imagined. The impudence of women "sins" twice.[8]

Salvadoran elites see the masses as a personification of sin against God and nation. The ruling elites' clash with the church represents a power struggle, grounded in their defense of economic control of the land and production, but ideologically cast in the struggle for "democracy" and "Christianity" against "godless" communism and a "subversive" church. Although the 1932 insurgents killed only one hundred soldiers, the Salvadoran oligarchy and military decided to teach a lesson to the rebel masses. During the month following the uprising they systematically killed thirty thousand. The Indians did learn one lesson — the price of resistance. They never again wore their *trajes* (traditional dress) and they stopped speaking Nahautl. For years organizing lay dormant. But memories of fire and freedom would burn again.

General Hernández Martínez, who had himself elected to rule for twelve years following the *matanza*, offered the following insight into national social problems in the 1940s:

It is good that children go barefoot. That way they can better receive the beneficial effluvia of the planet, the vibration of the earth. Plants and animals don't use shoes. It is a greater crime to kill an ant than a man, because a man who dies is reincarnated while an ant dies forever.[9]

Following another uprising in 1944, the eccentric Hernández resigned, ushering in a transition period from the mid-1940s to the mid-1970s that institutionalized military leadership determined to modernize the economy. In collaboration with U.S. policy strategies, forty-four multinational corporations came into the country during the 1960s. By the end of the 1960s the capital-intensive industries displaced workers, export prices fell, reform was rejected, and labor militancy grew.

In 1968 labor militancy intensified. The National Association of Educators of El Salvador (ANDES) led a nationwide teachers' strike. *Campesinos* organized into farmers' collectives: the Christian Federation of the Peasants of El Salvador (FECCAS) struggled for land reform.

The state's answer was more repression. General José Alberto Medrano, head of the National Guard, formed the paramilitary group known as ORDEN, a precursor to today's death squads; it was patterned on the Vietnam counterinsurgency model that created a civilian network linked to the army.

During the same period, two events occurred that would alter the course of Salvadoran history. The Latin American Bishops Conference at Medellín in 1968 would legitimate the church of the disenfranchised, an invisible majority in Central America, and, in 1970, a baker named Salvador Cayetano Carpio broke away from the Communist party of El Salvador because of its rejection of armed struggle in order to form the Popular Forces of Liberation (FPL), the first of five revolutionary organizations that later joined to form the FMLN.

That year, when a conference was held on land reform, the archdiocese of San Salvador (then under the leadership of a moderate, Archbishop Luis Chávez González) sent a young priest to present the church's position. Father José Inocencio Alas, one of the first priests to work with base Christian community groups in Suchitoto, delivered a talk that affirmed land reform as a moral imperative and requirement of justice.

In the oligarchy's mind, land reform was blasphemy and communist inspired. Father Alas was abducted as he walked to the parking lot after his talk. He was stripped, tortured, drugged, and (only because of an international outcry) abandoned still alive on a mountain outside the city.

In June 1970, two hundred clergy and lay people met for a Pastoral Week and declared that Alas and his *campesino* pastoral team would no longer stand alone. The church, too long afraid or protective of its privileges, would support the formation of base communities (*comunidades de base*) and would support the *campesinos'* struggle to unionize.

Rome was not pleased. But for the *campesinos* the declaration was "good news." Pastoral centers were opened that trained fifteen thousand catechists and *delegados de la palabra* (delegates of the word) between 1970 and 1976. A nonclerical church was in formation, fanning into the countryside with its gospel message. The message was simple: that in God's sight peasants were equal to the *hacienda* owners; that the peasants' suffering was not God's will, but a result of unequal distribution of land and power; and that throughout history God defended the cause of the poor and downtrodden.

In the minds of the elite minority these ideas were bullets aimed at *their* nation's heart. For the majority, this gospel was a resurrection. Those who were historically buried walked out of tombs of nonexistence into history. Sister Joan Petrick, a Maryknoll sister who worked in the mountains of La Libertad for seven years, could walk into villages and identify people who had been involved in a base Christian community simply by their physical bearing: "They walk upright, their heads held high, with self-confidence," she noted. "The other peasants shuffle along, their heads bowed."[10]

The history of these communities reveals the process "by which the Salvadoran people — that oppressed, scattered people, prostrate with despair — got up and walked." That is how a priest, whose pseudonym is Pablo Galdámez, described the effects of base community formation between 1970 and 1980.[11]

It all started in the early 1970s, those nights of "demolishing the dark by sheer patience and light, trying to clean up the messy faces of all those men and women, all those victims of misery and despair." The process of transforming a slum of dejected, isolated individuals, families plagued with alcoholism, domestic violence, prostitution, violent *machismo*, and malnourishment into a community began in nightly meetings of small groups reflecting on their lives in the light of Scripture.

By the mid-1970s they were confronted with a theological problem. How would they respond to the newly forming popular organizations? The community was divided. Would support of the popular organizations still constitute pastoral work? What about spirituality? Eventually they decided that spiritual conversion implied social commitment. Notions of faith separate from social struggle seemed naive, even selfish. They were walking new paths, expressing with their lives a faith that Archbishop Romero would defend to his death in a few short years.

One can only imagine what a gift Romero was to a people whose prelates cavorted with their enemies:

> Our faith was still weak and immature and we took scandal when we saw pictures of the pope's ambassador, the nuncio, drinking champagne with the generals, or one of the bishops wearing a colonel's uniform for the Feast of Jesus our Savior.[12]

The base Christian communities of the countryside, despite massive land dispossession, flourished. The best known of these communities was in Aguilares, the fruit of Father Rutilio Grande's pastoral work. From 1972 until 1976 Grande and a pastoral team undertook evangelization work, organizing ten urban communities and twenty-seven rural ones. Grande's communities were similarly confronted with the question of their relationship to the popular organizations. FECCAS, a Christian peasant league, prepared for demonstrations a year after the National Guard rolled out tanks against peasants occupying lands in San Vicente in 1974. By 1975, over 40 percent of the rural population was landless and 96.5 percent of those with land had under seven hectares, the minimum subsistence needed for a family of four.[13] The Christian communities of Aguilares reflected on the meaning of accompanying the

31

people: how far should they go? What should be their relationship to FECCAS? Grande clearly tried to maintain a distinction, although he believed that "as a result of the dynamism of conversion and growth in faith" Christians "would normally become agents of change working for unionization and the defense of labor rights."[14]

Such distinctions didn't interest the Salvadoran right. Grande's final "error" was a sermon he preached in Apopa in 1977 after the parish priest, Father Mario Bernal, was banished from the country by security forces.

Ana, a nun who worked with the Aguilares pastoral teams, was in the church the day Grande preached. She feared for him as did the community who saw strangers tape-recording Grande's prophetic denouncements. Calling the nation an "established disorder," he said:

> I'm afraid that if Jesus of Nazareth came back, coming down from Galilee to Judea, that is, from Chalatenango to San Salvador, I dare say he would not get as far as Apopa, with his preaching and his actions. They would stop him in Guazapa and jail him there.[15]

"One month later they assassinated Father Grande," Ana concluded.

In February Oscar Romero became archbishop; by May 1977 security forces or death squads linked to the military had killed Father Alfonso Navarro; catechists were "disappeared."

The Other Church

In a culture defined by male power (*machismo*) and a feudal awe of clerics, the targeting of priests was both a symbol and an attempt to cut off leadership of the base Christian communities. The mistake of the right was to misunderstand the democratic infrastructure of the *comunidades* and the bonds of faith that gave them cohesion. When violent repression eliminated priests and army invasion with full-scale bombardment drove whole villages to hide in the hills, it was women who accompanied the communities, taking on leadership roles never before possible.

In the 1970s religious women had, by virtue of their marginality, some protection in doing pastoral work. By the end of the 1970s, however, religious women were taken more seriously and murdered along with men, as the murders of four North American women demonstrated. Most of the religious sisters who volunteered to go into the countryside were themselves from peasant roots. Living in religious orders had elevated their class position but it had not erased the memory of their *pueblo* whose meager harvest feeds the children so poorly that four hundred children die of malnutrition per week.

Sister Ana, a Carmelite for twenty-five years, was one of seven sisters who went into the villages (*cantones*) to work in the 1970s. In

1972 she worked in an outpost in Ciudad Barrios, where Archbishop Romero was born. "It was the most powerful experience of my life," she said. "I went to help the people but the people showed me the path." In 1976, she went to Guazapa to form pastoral teams and coordinate with the pastoral teams in Aguilares. Many of the peasant leaders they trained were killed along with their communities when the military occupied Aguilares in 1977 two months after Rutilio Grande's murder. Five hundred *campesinos* were killed in this purge.

Ana would have to leave her order. The mother superior issued an ultimatum to the band of seven Carmelites who continued pastoral work with the base Christian communities. It was then that the new archbishop, Oscar Arnulfo Romero, who had become the sisters' confidant, went out to the *cantones* to receive the religious women into a new "order," the *comunidades* of Guazapa. In a ceremony attended by the base Christian communities from the *cantones* where each sister worked, Archbishop Romero received their renewal of vows made to God present in the people. Ana describes receiving a new habit as a symbol of the community's reversal of the world's standards, those of both church and state:

> Until then we had worn full Carmelite habits. But the women from the communities had made us clothes and we took off our habits that day. I had been in habit from 1960 to 1979. That day I was at a fiesta for the first time in street clothes — the clothes of my people.

Bishop Pedro Casaldáliga of Brazil has said that "the history of the church of Latin America is divided into two parts: before and after Archbishop Romero."[16] Yet Romero's international status is not why the Salvadoran people loved him. It was the man himself, an archbishop who confessed to being too impressionable. It stuns one familiar with Salvadoran *machismo* to consider a male, one with some power, who could admit to such vulnerability. If Gustavo Gutiérrez is correct that true conversion involves an embrace of the radically *other* in history, and he is referring to the poor, Romero is the "new man" because he embraced the poor, and because he regarded women as pastors. Here was a male cleric who was shaped relationally. Rather than a weakness, his impressionability was an invitation. He learned to be prophetic from his people. "I've never felt I was a prophet," he said, "in the sense of being the only prophet of the people. I know that you and I, people of God together, compose the prophetic people."[17]

Romero's identification with and legitimation of the people's liberation was so complete that he was accused of being a "dupe" for the left. According to theologian Jon Sobrino, accusations that Romero was manipulable are political efforts by state and ecclesial authorities to reduce and therefore suppress his prophetic word. It was the people's suffering and initiative, says Sobrino, not political pressure, that "manipulated" Romero. Romero could not have misunderstood the political impact of his defense of the people's right to organize themselves. He was proposing, as had Padre Alas ten years earlier, that the people had a right to popular power when he asserted in February of 1980: "I believe more than ever the popular organizations are the social forces which are going to push forward and achieve an authentic society with social justice and liberty."[18]

It is a disarming portrayal of a church based in the authority of its people, not its princes. Archbishop Romero is revealed as a shepherd of the lost sheep: the invisible *campesinos* already the targets of massacres in Aguilares and Guazapa and the forgotten women of church history who stood with them. With Archbishop Romero the authority of the *comunidades de base*, of nonclerics, of uneducated masses, and of women is authenticated.

A prophet speaks the truth, and Romero was simply stating the facts. He was not being mystical (though he was a mystic and an activist bishop) when he predicted that if he was killed his spirit would rise amid the people. He simply understood the people as the prophetic word of liberation that would continue to be heard. That was his faith: he believed in the poor and the voiceless. This accounted for his radical openness. It was the people who gave the world Romero. He was, after all, the right wing's candidate for archbishop. To turn his back on his former allies and fellow bishops, to reconstruct his theology, and to do this at fifty-seven years of age at the apex of his ecclesiastical career can be explained only by a radical conversion to a prophetic people.

Prophecy, like the slain Romero, lives on where the struggle for freedom continues. The liberation process is not carried by theologians, intellectuals, or the powerful of church or state, but by the people and especially their leaders, by women like Ana and the community who are bearers of prophetic hope. Today Ana lives on the outskirts of San Salvador, one of the shanty neighborhoods bombed by the Salvadoran Air Force for seven days during the FMLN offensive in November 1989. It was not the first time she held the hands of dying children. During her years in Guazapa she blessed two of her bravest fourteen-year-old catechist leaders three days before their bodies were found eaten by dogs, their tongues and eyes cut out. She said goodbye to Laura López, her best "pupil," who was martyred in Guazapa in 1985. She didn't know then that an "option for the poor" would cost everything: her order, her sisters, her privileged life. She didn't know, either, that she would find in the rubble, amid impoverished, toothless farmers and illiterate grandmothers, a new humanity and a church that would be a "sign to the world." She didn't know that this church would withstand a technologically advanced, mammothly financed war, which would explode into the next decade, bringing to power the ARENA party, the very party that "kills for God."

Still, "It's all light," she says. The dark night of the soul during her years as a Carmelite when she "did not feel life among the community" gave birth to her work in the rural village where she found life. "I discovered the life of God in the people. It was a resurrection amid so much death. Now I don't feel sadness — fear yes, but no more sadness."

The "people" who were the occasion of Ana's conversion were mostly women, all who were left in the war zones. The popular church is distinctive because it is a church of nonclerics, of the poor, and most of the local pastoral leadership is women. This inauspicious people's church has transformed church history.

The Church of the Poor: Revolutionary Ecclesiology

The convergence of the popular church and revolutionary vanguard has less to do with shared ideology then shared class solidarity. What the Medellín Conference called an option for the poor takes on revolutionary dimensions when the poor opt for themselves, for their freedom and self-determination. For the FMLN, a revolution in which peasants and workers have leadership accomplishes the liberation of the poor and oppressed. If the party fails that commitment (by "absolutizing" itself, for example) it fails its revolutionary goals. Revolutionaries promise a new social order that transforms hierarchies of power and privilege. But what, or whose, standards hold them accountable? Equally important, but less scrutinized, is the question of accountability of the church. When has the church failed and when has the church been faithful to all its people, even the least powerful? Two ways to evaluate both the church and revolutionary organizations are (1) to ask to whom they are accountable (2) to examine their practice.

Theologian Pablo Richard develops an analysis of church-state relations to determine church accountability. In Richard's framework, evaluation of the church involves an examination of the church's practice in relationship to authoritarian states: is church practice supportive, accommodationist, or in prophetic opposition? Also of critical importance is the need to examine ecclesial practice in relationship to social classes: is the church opposed to or supportive of the "interests, projects, values, and strategies of different social classes"?[19] Such an analysis uncovers the church's actual relation to social classes and asks the critical question: *which* social classes does the church support; *which* class interest does it oppose? If the church attempts neutrality in a military state, a state existing to support elite interests, the church *de facto* supports elite class interests.

The question of whether the church is supportive of or in opposition to the state is usually the only critical question North Americans pose in evaluating the authenticity of the church's "option for the poor." However, Richard shows that the church's ecclesial practice in relation to social classes may undercut (or reverse) the church-state relationship. Richard poses three types of church: the conservative, the social-Christian, and the popular. These three formations can coexist and are all related to the same formal ecclesial structures, but they each represent different visions and practices of what the church should be.

The conservative ecclesial model that governed the Latin American church from 1870 to 1930 supports the authoritarian state and opposes the participation of the people in church or state governance. The social-Christian model, which influenced the Latin American church between 1930 and 1960, takes an oppositional stance in relation to authoritarian governments (dictatorships, military regimes backing the oligarchy). It opposes violation of human rights, impoverishment of the masses, and suppression of freedom.

The social-Christian practice is liberal, seeking representative democracy and supporting industrialization and a "developmentalist" economic model of change. This reformist church is aligned with the interests of the middle class. Its challenge to the authoritarian regime is to uphold constitutional guarantees of rights, implement economic "development" projects, and reinstitutionalize democratic principles of government. This position of the social-Christian church, historically aligned with the Christian Democrats, thus legitimates the authoritarian state by proposing conditions of reform that, if met, allow the state's primary oppressive role to continue.

This church's intention is to humanize the state, to divest the state of its repressive hold on dissent, to liberalize the hardliners in the military. But the social-Christian church misunderstands "the class nature of the state [and] the political role of the armed forces in an authoritarian state."[20] Church opposition is to the military regime, to the civilian government front, but it does not challenge the state. "At no point . . . is the system of capitalist domination, the capitalist model of accumulation, the rule of the bourgeoisie over all the exploited classes, and so forth, called into question." In summary the social-Christian church has no political analysis to reveal its own class privilege afforded by capitalism.

Richard's critique of social-Christian church practice also recognizes the contribution this church makes to liberation. The church offers material aid and political legitimation to the programs (both political and ecclesial) of the democratic opposition. Further, the social-Christian church facilitates democratic consensus between the poor masses and middle class against military dictatorships. Finally this liberal-populist church defends the church of the poor and its institutions: clinics, schools, cooperatives, etc.

According to Richard, the social-Christian church, unlike its thriving social-ecclesial counterpart in the U.S. (the liberal church), is doomed. The popular church, the church of the *comunidades de base*, stands in contradiction to the social-Christian church (as well as the conservative church). The church of the poor opposes the authoritarian state *and* aligns itself with the interests of the poor. Reina, a pastoral worker directing the base Christian community coordination of Usulután, describes class identity with the poor in this way:

> You see, there's a definite reason for the growth of the *Iglesia Popular* [popular church]. If it exists it is for a reason. In the first place it exists because we want to be one with the people. Second, it exists because we are Christians who want to have a living faith, that is, a faith manifested in concrete acts, walking with the people in their struggle for liberation. So when you have decided to take that road, there are definite consequences.
>
> Perhaps we wouldn't have these problems if we did otherwise. We would be a church working among the poor, but if we didn't take positions, things would be calm for us. . . . We cannot be part of the *Iglesia Popular* unless we are completely identified with the poor. Otherwise, it's a charade; we might dress poorly or eat sparingly, but that means little if we are not seeking the liberation of the poor, working for the day when they will no longer be poor.

The *Iglesia Popular* announces the good news of liberation for the poor while denouncing its enemy — the military state. The social-Christian church simply has no good news of a new creation to announce, at least no good news for the poor who seek a life without exploitation, a life not possible under an economic system in which their cheap labor is essential to the accumulation of capital.

Giving birth to this church, as Reina implies, has been enormously costly, not simply because of the efforts of the state to abort its birth, but also because of the conservative church's opposition. Reina describes this opposition:

> Our dream is to see the birth of a different kind of church, better yet, to recover the church of Jesus. So there's a lot of opposition; the hierarchical church has maintained its opposition for years, and will not so easily want to lose it. They engage in a scheming just like the U.S. embassy — devising counterinsurgency plans. They make plans to crush us, to destroy us, to make those seeds of a New Church disappear, the church that is being born among the poor. They try to impose their own ideas of what pastoral work should be, a way of working that is alienating and lulls people to sleep. It's not just alienating; they turn out Christians almost dead — about as lively as a stone.

So within the gasps of colonial Christendom and the ebbing New Christendom of the social-Christians, a birth is taking place, the birth of *Iglesia Popular*. Like any birth it is messy, painful, and ecstatic. There is a surprise in this new creation, one that Pablo Richard did not anticipate because his evaluative and descriptive categories are based on class and do not include gender. The surprise in the birthing of *Iglesia Popular* is that the midwives are women. Just as the social-Christians lack a political analysis to reveal their own class biases, so too male interests are invisible without an analysis that identifies the distinct interests of women, as women, among the peasants and working classes.

If God's revelation is discovered amid the poor struggling for liberation, is it not a still greater scandal to discover God as woman? Hidden in history is another depth of the struggle of the poor. This is *mística's* biology: women embodying God. How is woman to be taken seriously — she who has so little skill, so little political experience? Perhaps if she were trained analytically, were more articulate, ... but as it is, can she be God's expression?

This is the epiphany, the moment when everything is turned on its head, when God is revealed anew — not the expected Father God, but a vulnerable, tenacious God broken and bloodied in Morazán, Cabañas, and Chalatenango, yet full of hope. What a surprise, an assault really, to discover that this God

> is not a Jesuit,
> not even educated,
> not ordained
> not inevitably a male militant,
> this God is not an individual,
> but a people,
> this *pueblo* who are
> peasants and workers,
> women, and anonymous,
> who are mostly
> all there is of God.
> This obscure God who seeks
> solidarity,
> who makes everything
> new in history,
> everything possible.
> This God who announces
> the audacity of women.
> What a surprise!

38

Light of Ocote

We struggled precisely so a love such as ours
could become the most common
and usual kind of love in El Salvador,
almost the only kind.
—Roque Dalton, "Third Love Poem"

This text is a production of the base Christian communities of El Salvador
north of the Torola River in Morazán. Here is a history of the church of the
poor as told by the creators, using the language and metaphor of mística.

Around here we are all Christians, we are all poor, and we all go about living in the middle of a war. We all have these three trademarks. Our tree is made with these three woods.

We are all poor. We lack food, education, health — the most basic things that one needs to live. Some of us know why we are poor; we have a highly developed sense of awareness. Others are just as poor, but they don't really know why they are that way or how it is that they got that way. Anyway, everyone, whether we know it or not, is equally poor.

And we are all suffering from the war, including those who say that they have nothing to do with it or that they are in the middle and not with one or the other side. The bombs kill us all, the threats afflict us all. This pain of war is not a question of will.

The church that is to the north of the Torola River, in Morazán, El Salvador, Central America, has a history. This church was not always as it is now. And it is a little of this history that we would like to tell you. We explain and understand many things by using dynamics. To begin, let's imagine one of those dynamics.

There are a few coals on the ground. Yes, they are lit, but so little that they don't make a fire. Actually, they seem extinguished. But if we put a branch of ocote [a type of pine] near the coals, the ocote begins to smoke, it throws out its smoke until the smell of wood is noticed. But it doesn't do any more than that. There is not enough strength in the coals to light the ocote.

Then someone comes and blows a few times until the coals begin to get stronger and they manage to light the ocote. Once it is lit, the fire grows until it is huge.

This is what has happened among us. Those coals, that ocote, those puffs of breath are very similar to what our history has been like in recent years.

When the Coals Didn't Make a Fire

Life has always been a heavy load for us. Life was very hard. It was not life, it was agony. Everything was a constant battle to survive death, which surrounded us on all sides. When it wasn't the droughts, it was the heavy rains that ruined the crops. If not that, it was the diseases that fell like flies over the children. Since there were no medicines, any of these diseases killed. There was once a meeting of Christian mothers and they asked: "How many live children do you have and how many dead?" Everyone had one dead child, many had two or three, some had up to six little ones dead from hunger, from not eating right, from those diseases.

There was no school or even the dream of having one. And if there was one, then the teacher never came. And if the teacher came, it was because he was being punished and he was soon sent somewhere else. There was no horizon in the world, there was nothing ahead but death. We lived in order to die. After the war began there was even more death. Then death arrived with bullets and bombs. There were massacres, slaughters, and fear.

In the midst of this affliction, praying made life more bearable. In the middle of the *cantón*, the little village, the chapel that we had all built with our sacrifices and our love waited for us every Sunday. We all filed past the statue or the picture of the saint. Everyone murmured petitions or desires: that the child would be cured, that the man would not come home drunk, that the crop would turn out well, that it would rain, that the girl would marry well, that the son would return, that life would be better, that this would change, that would change.... We lit a candle to give more force to our prayers and we made promises to give it even more of a push. All of this was our religious belief and ritual and it was a great relief.

The priest was not necessary in the chapel. We saw the priest only once each year for the fiestas of the patron saints and sometimes he would charge us a pretty penny.... Since some of us had the intelligence to learn some prayers or even the entire rosary or some other celebration for all of us to get together and pray together, even if the priest didn't arrive, it was still nice to go to the chapel. The chapel was the place for complaints. Everyone could tell about their troubles there, about the load that they carried and about how difficult life was. There was no other place where we could express these complaints with the confidence that they would be heard. Who but God...? Since we didn't make a good impression or express ourselves well, no one listened to us *campesinos*. Nobody. Not even the priest with all his grandiosity, or the mayor with all his authority, or even less someone that was high up. In the chapel, alone, without a sound, God listened to the words that we said and those that remained embedded in our hearts. Nothing changed, everything

40

continued to be just as ugly, but it made things more bearable to tell God our troubles and things seemed to get at least a little better.

The chapel was a place for women. We came together, men and women, but the women had many more troubles and pains to talk to God about. The misery is the same for everyone, but women live with it day and night, seeing the children cry from hunger, watching their stomachs swollen with worms. To them falls the care of the children with diseases that can't be cured, to them falls seeing the children die without being able to do anything. The women are the ones who know every day that there is not enough, that there are only tortillas and salt. And to them belong the complaints of the husband who comes home hungry, and not knowing who else to blame, he blames his wife. She feels more deeply all the bad things and even ends up feeling guilty about them. And other days there is the drunken husband who spends everything on drink, out of desperation, because he can do nothing. And later he comes home and hits her and there is the shouting and the beatings. Sunday, in the chapel, everything could be forgotten.

The men were always quicker with their prayers. Yes, they greeted all the saints, but they would soon go to the plaza to talk with their friends. The women, no, they stayed longer, their prayers were longer. They had more complaints to present, more petitions. They also had to beg God to change the hearts of their husbands and ask God to heal them. They had much more to ask for. The chapel was a place of parties. Sunday was a happy day. We saved our best dress and new hat for Sunday. We saved our most attractive things for going to the chapel to pray to God. At times there were songs in the chapel, there were happy celebrations. And afterward you could have a drink, and in the plaza they sold cinnamon, fat peppers, and linseed, which is good for aches, and even some aspirin. And the neighbors talked about their sickness and about their remedies, and that also made the aches and pains hurt less. And in some corner somebody would be selling bread or something else and we would all buy some. The children always got candy or something. And it was a great joy for everyone to meet together, to pass along news, to talk about life, to greet our friends and to see each other.

The fiestas of the patron saints were the very best. More people came, people from far away, and there were more people selling things and even sports events and a dance. The unfortunate thing was that the party ended in drunkenness and then the machetes came out and people would be injured or even killed. The blood was a signal that it was time to return home before some worse mishap occurred. The fiesta was over. The next day life began anew, the everyday struggle and suffering.

In the midst of the complaints and the fiestas, that is where our firm faith in God was, our faith that our God has ears for the poor. If a visitor came by, a stranger to our parts, perhaps he would say, "And what good does so much praying do?" The stranger didn't understand the deepest parts of the well of faith. It was difficult to understand the world, but things didn't change and not even the authorities of the church paid any attention to us; instead they would put us to one side, just as the worldly authorities did. But it wasn't a matter of understanding, it was a matter of believing: we always kept our faith in God, in the God of the poor, in the God who would put a hand into our life and would perform the miracle of opening up a way out. What this hand would be like nobody knew, but we never doubted God. That trust, that love. And the fiestas were like a little sign that God would act.

The coals seemed to be a little bit of ash and nothing more. You couldn't see the fire that they guarded inside. There seemed to be nothing. But in the coals there was a hidden fire. When the ocote got nearer to the coals, there was the proof: the ocote smoked and there was even the smell of a burning ocote. Because there was fire. All the ocote had to do was come closer. The fire was possible.

How the Ocote Caught Fire

Someone blows a few times on the coals that seemed dead and they begin to glow and the puff of breath brings the flame to the ocote. That's what happened in our lives. The breath came, the new wind that brought us the light that broke the night. And our communities became a living church.

How did the breath get there? By two means: the word of God came to us and poor people began to have faith in other poor people.

We believed in God, yes, but we did not know God's word well. Perhaps the greatest fruit of the Second Vatican Council was to put into the hands of the poor what was ours, though we did not know it: our book, the Bible. The council opened a window to the world and let in fresh air that healed the church. And it was also the occasion for us to read the Bible for the first time. Before, on the other side of history, the Bible was not known by us or read by us. It was even a prohibited book.

With the council that changed. This book of God is subversive because it turns the tortilla over, because it throws down the order of kings and empires and it puts the poor on top. This book with its stories of liberation, with its message of the prophets, with the life of Jesus that conquered death, with the stories of the first Christian communities, changed our life. This book taught us that we, the poor, are the preferred ones of God, that God wants the poor to stop being poor and that God calls us to work to change things. Our finding the Bible was like an earthquake. It changed the way things are, it changed the way of our thinking, of our doing things. It was the first breath that made the coals turn red. And in what seemed to be only ashes there was born a fire.

The coals became redder. Now it was only a question of blowing hard. Priests and religious people and new pastoral agents brought us the Bible and the documents of the council. Catechetical centers opened that prepared us to be catechists and celebrators of the word in our own communities. Puffs of air and more puffs of air.

After that Archbishop Romero arrived, who preached the word of God in the midst of repression. His prophetic voice fanned a flame in the ocote. The red coals became fire. It was he who did this. Through him we were able to understand what God told us, we were able to understand that the word of God spoke about our own life. We began to see that the Christian faith was a task and an obligation. And that is how we, poor men and women, began to stop believing in the false promises of outsiders, the great and powerful, and we turned to our neighbors to reflect with them, and to organize with them, and to believe in them. "When the poor believe in the poor then we will be able to sing freedom. . . . " We began to believe and to sing. We the poor turned toward the poor, God's preferred ones. And our neighbors, who had nothing and could do nothing, became our brothers and sisters in the faith. And believing in God and believing in our brothers and sisters we began our journey.

The communities were born, the base Christian communities, communities of the church and of this base of poor Salvadoran Christians, thirsty for justice, hungry for bread and peace with dignity.

Many Christian organizations were also born. From among us came pastoral workers and community directors. Community organization was born. We were no longer alone. The coals were afire, the flames were rising. And in the fire no flame is separate and you cannot distinguish one from the other. Where one ends the other begins and all are light.

Sparks of Fire Everywhere

The fire has its history. There is the example of one of the new organizations: the Congregation of Christian Mothers. In 1985 the community of Carrizal, in Perquín, was compelled to leave by the Arce battalion. When they arrived in Tejera the air force bombarded them: two were killed and several wounded.

A group of people from Perquín went to see them. But they didn't have even a first aid kit to treat the wounded. Life spoke there, in that pain, in that impotence of not being able to do anything. A group of women reflected on the gospel: "I was hungry and you gave me to eat, I was naked and you clothed me. . . . When you refused to do this for my brothers you refused to do this for me." Then they felt that they were being challenged by the same God, speaking to them through that act of life, fresh and present.

They decided to form an organization to defend life always: the Congregation of Christian Mothers. Soon other women from other regions did the same. It was the first organization of women to the north of the Torola River. The word of God and faith in one's neighbor, just as poor as oneself, lit the fire of the ocote. In that way the groups of literacy teachers and health brigades were born, and community organizations and cooperatives grew. Projects and more projects. All of them were signs of life, signals of hope that were also acts of liberation. Other women organized to seek out food for the children. When they decided to do this they didn't know that they were going to have to confront the army, which had them under siege and would not let them pass.

These women, who before had gone no further than from the grinding stone to the well, suddenly were seen fighting for their rights in the very offices of power. They fought hard and they returned victorious. The army had to lift the siege and the food arrived for the children and for everyone. From that victory more projects were born: chicken farms, bakeries, tailor shops, bread and milk for the children. Each project was a sign of life, another announcement that freedom was arriving.

The communities flourished and the pastoral organizations multiplied. Who didn't want to be one of "the mothers"? Some joined to go along with the crowd and others to see what was happening, but everyone joined. In short, it was a miracle. Before, if any one of us, man or woman, had gone to the departmental capital, it was only to resolve our own problem or that of our family. And now we were going not only for ourselves but for the whole community. Never before had such marvelous things been seen, never before.

Prophetic actions were born, like those that we had read about in the Bible, because we also had to be prophets of the God we believed in, the God of the poor, the God who goes with the "least of these."

We had learned to love ourselves, to consider ourselves brothers and sisters. And so we had to defend ourselves. When any brother or sister was captured, when there was bombing, when the army came and mistreated us, there we would go, all the neighbors together, to report whoever did this deed to the humanitarian organizations that had been flourishing at our side and helping us to defend life.

"Solidarity" is the new word that we use for love. Solidarity is to share our fate, the fate of the self-conscious poor, and to have a stake in our liberation, risking, entering into history and doing so on the side of the downtrodden, on the side of the poor, which is the side of God and the side of life.

After the bombing of Torola, the other communities went to visit them with food. And that community, so poor and afflicted, became happy. From the poverty of these people went beasts laden with help for others poorer than they. We gave the community of Jocoaitique a

44

symbol. Because of the bravery of this Christian community that has been punished so much, in prison and under torture, but firm like a rock, we all agreed that we should give them only one symbol: flowers. We gave them flowers to congratulate them for their strength, because their bravery makes us all strong.

In daily life we have seen that this action of God, of raising up the poor and giving them life, clashes with the powerful in this world. At first it didn't seem so clear to us, but now we know it well.

When the light came to the world, the world did not accept it: we read that in the word of God. Not everyone likes the light. The life of Jesus was like that also: he made signs of life, but in doing so he contradicted the plan of those who loved death. He clashed with their interests. So Jesus ended up on the cross. The life of God, God's salvation, knows no other road than the cross.

In our lives we have already felt this. Our projects seem to us to be so good and so just, but they prohibit them, they want to destroy them. They continuously attack us and accuse us of being subversives. They threaten us. Every one of the organizations that were born of the light of the ocote is persecuted and slandered. Every catechist is accused, every director is watched by them. And they kill and torture them.

These difficulties have frightened off some, because we have not all realized that we would have to fight a lot with those who are not friends of the light and want to get rid of the ocote and the coals and to level the ground that we walk on. We have been afraid to die. We have not thoroughly read the word of God. But when we have continued to read it we see that the path lies there, by way of the cross. Through this death, that of the life that is given up, we arrive at the light, at more light.

To defend life and to continue to raise up the light, our people have had to take up arms to fight to hasten the day of justice for all and the day of true peace. They pushed us into this violence, they forced us into it. In this process toward peace our church of the poor lives now. In the midst of this just and necessary war we proclaim the word of God. In this war we announce that the Day of God is near and that the promises of God will not fail: the lowly will be raised up to occupy the places once occupied by the mighty, the humble will be lifted out of the dust, and the powerful will be thrown from their heights, just as the Virgin Mary sang when she was waiting for the birth of Jesus.

We are like a lit ocote illuminating the world. It was the puff of God's breath that gave us that light. And the Sunday celebrations in the chapels are today this firm faith, faith in the God of the poor and faith in other poor people, in the brothers and sisters that we have at our side. They used to take our lives away and we didn't know how God would act to change things. Now we give up our life and we already know that God is on our side, that God is with us and that we are going to win.

Matilde

Our hope is greater than their death.
                                    —Matilde

Matilde is a slight woman. Her dark eyes have the look of an alert, startled innocent. Everything else about her is focused, intense, ready for anything — for eventualities that wound the mind. The woman has walked through fire. To survive, she has neither turned her heart to stone nor left it on the killing floors of the campo. *There is a depth one experiences in her presence, and a hard-won practicality. There was no chatting or small talk. Matilde used time as if it were a gracious but dying friend. She began our interview, lit candles when the church fell dark, had a community member serve us pupusas knowing that we would talk through the dinner hour and that we would have to travel after dark with no opportunity to buy supper.*

Matilde is one of the founders of a new religious community. The community, unlike traditional religious congregations or orders, is not canonically linked to Rome. Community members are, therefore, not officially "sisters." Nevertheless, they are vowed religious who effectively live out vows of poverty, chastity, and obedience to and for their base Christian community.

I am a *campesina*. I was born in a *cantón* in Cuscatlán. My family had thirteen children — three were adopted. There were fifteen of us. I feel grateful that I was born into a stable family. My parents still live together. Despite the lack of formal training, because we were poor, I never saw my father mistreat my mother.

Though we were poor we owned a piece of land, although later a dam broke on the river and water flooded our land. There were no schools in my town near Suchitoto. So, I didn't go to school until I was nine years old. However, my mother taught us all to read and write. I received my religious training from my mother, who was a catechist. She prepared us each for First Communion. My mother was very religious. Each night we said the rosary and each child would take turns leading the prayers. My mother was also very service-minded; she had an attitude of service to neighbors. Once when a poor neighbor woman was sick, my mother went to the woman's house to do housework for three months.

We had lots of fruit trees. My mother gathered fruit and gave it to neighbors rather than sell it. My mother and I were very close. She listened when I talked about religious life. I never knew any religious nuns. But when I was thirteen the person with whom I shared my longings was my mother.

My mother helped me with a decision. There is a saying: "A resolute decision, a happy life," So when I was nineteen I entered the convent, the Oblates of the Sacred Heart.

When I was a child in the 1950s and 1960s we'd hear about persecution in the city. I remember in the countryside occasionally bodies were discovered decayed in a sack, the bodies mutilated, the faces disfigured, strewn along the banks of the Río Lempa. My father served in the civil patrols and he'd come across the bodies and report to the judge. But the judge would say that these people were common criminals, just bury them. Others said no, they were leaders of the people!

I remember during election time that the parties would come to our *cantón* to make propaganda, but they would never come again during the year. We had no schools, no clinics, no good roads. We felt deceived.

My motivation in becoming a nun was to be of service to others. But I didn't find that possible with my order. Now the order has changed but not back then. It was a shock coming from a *campesino* home to find myself in an order dedicated to educating wealthy children. I wasn't all that clear but I knew I didn't want that.

I remember going with another sister to an evening class and seeing people sleeping in the streets, under bridges. This affected me deeply. I began to ask what response religious life had to this suffering. I was convinced a comfortable, protected life, separate from the people, was not what I wanted.

I worked in the congregation's clinic, which allowed me to be in contact with the poor in Mejicanos [a town on the outskirts of San Salvador]. But the clinic was basically for emergencies. I wanted to give my life to the people more completely. The poor have always been an important factor in my faith. I stayed in the convent only three years. I didn't leave to study or better my life. I still was committed of service to others and wanted to realize my ideals in the context of a religious vocation, but I didn't know how that would happen.

In December 1970 some of us became the Pequeña Comunidad [small community]. There were three of us — one of the others was a sister, the third was a servant in our religious congregation. We lived together and studied and worked to earn a living, doing pastoral work in Zacamil on weekends. I've worked here since 1968 with the Padre [Galdámez, the pseudonym for the priest and author of the book describing work in the "slum gullies" of San Salvador]. We rented a room in San Miguelito where the market now stands.

We wanted to form a religious community life without legalistic limitations, a life creative and open to the spirit. At this time each of us had a sector for our pastoral work. But we were learning everything from the people. I owe my faith to the people. The marginal communities were our teachers, showing us what faith is. The people were the source that gave us life and encouragement in our small community.

I spent twelve years, beginning in 1968, working with the communities not only in San Salvador but in San Marcos, Santiago, and outside the city.

December 1980 marked a new stage in my life. This was a period of tremendous persecution. Our catechists were killed. We faced a new challenge. I had worked as a secretary for Archbishop Romero, and Silvia [another sister, Silvia Maribel Arriola, who was killed in 1981] worked as his secretary. When he was killed in 1980 we were without work.

At the end of 1980 Silvia and I made a decision to accompany the people at the front. I went to San Vicente on June 5, 1981, five days before the offensive. Silvia went to Santa Ana.

I was three years in San Vicente. At that time the civilian population of twelve thousand people lived in nine *cantones*. During the early years of the war the army directed operations against civilians, not just the FMLN. They considered the people like animals. During the invasions thousands of us would flee through ravines and hills. A simple two-hour walk would take an entire night because so many were walking. It was totally an exodus experience. This happened countless times during those early years.

During forced flight [*guindas*] I was struck by how many children died. The bodies of the children would swell from malnutrition during the month-long marches. Mothers couldn't even stop to bury their children except to push them aside under the brush and leave them there.

In March 1982 the army ambushed the civilian population near Apastepeque near Cantón Laguna Ciega, and 156 were killed, the majority children and elderly who were riding mules.

At that moment I experienced a crisis of faith because I had believed in the God of the poor and oppressed. But I saw it was the poor and oppressed that always died. Where is God? I asked. The poor are always near the door of death, submerged in poverty and misery, and when they do decide to struggle, they die in war. The question remained: "Why does God allow the poor to die?"

In August 1982 I witnessed two more massacres — the first at Santa Rosa near Santa Clara and the second at Amatitán near San Esteban Catarina in the Department of San Vicente. It was a crisis of faith and also a crisis of my own humanity. In Santa Rosa there were five different groups of civilians surrounded by the army. The groups from Tecoluca, where David Rodríguez was ministering, were fired upon with grenades. People were literally blown to pieces. I found pieces of flesh in the trees, in the bushes. The children's screams were engraved in my memory. Our group was not detected, but to stay undetected, the mothers had to cover the mouths of their babies. The operations went on for days. We walked through the night in silence, but all I heard were those screams and in my mind I saw again what had happened. I wondered if I could ever forget what rang in my ears, what played before my eyes. Would I ever be the same again?

Two days later there was a massacre at Carraboza in Amatitán. We walked all night until 5 A.M. We arrived at Carraboza and we heard voices of people bathing in the river. It was soldiers, so we decided to send out a group to identify who they were. So four of us, two women, a man, and one child went to a high place to see what was going on. But by the time we reached the hill, the massacre had begun below. They killed 179 people. Only our group was still alive. The man I was with lost his entire family: his pregnant wife, children, mother, fourteen in all. He saw them die.

In the midst of this crisis of faith and my humanity, while experiencing this death and bloodshed, I also knew that the suffering was not only crushing but somehow transformative, somehow I gained strength. The memory of death and blood, of those I've known, has been transformed into faith. But I was indelibly marked by this memory.

The persecution against the churches, the vigilance we're subjected to daily, has made me afraid. But the hope I feel is in the people and in the cause of liberty. Our people have a prophetic faith and courage. Even if they killed all of us, they could never kill the cause of our hope or God's presence among us. Our hope is greater than their death.

Ana

What path will you take to heaven
if you don't go along the earth?
For whom are you climbing Mt. Carmel
if you go up and don't come back?
—Bishop Pedro Casaldáliga,
"Questions for Climbing and
Descending Mt. Carmel"

A friend of mine who works with the Lutheran Church told this story about Ana. When Lutheran Bishop Medardo Gómez went out to Aguilares to administer the "laying on of hands," he called forth from the assembled congregation a woman seated among the people. The woman who walked to the altar that day was Ana, a minister who had worked with those communities for almost twenty years. In recognition of her ministry, the bishop asked if she would join him in administering the blessing.

49

The Hour of God: The Base Christian Communities

When my friend Dan tells the next part of the story, he cries. "There they were, a Lutheran bishop and a Catholic sister laying hands on the heads of campesinos whose faith had already endured all that the blessing prepared them for." Ana's summary of that day was typically simple and brief: "The spirit of God has lifted up this community." Ana often recalls those pastoral workers, so many of her friends, who gave their lives that the spirit of God would be lifted up among the people. She is fifty-two years old and she has been responsible for the formation of hundreds of catechists. Yet she is rarely mentioned in church history accounts. When her name is brought up, however, people invariably refer to her with deep respect, often using the adjective humilde (humble). This characteristic and women's social dispensability account for her invisibility. Ana's humility is partly campesina reticence and partly due to twenty-five years of Carmelite discipline. Mostly, however, Ana's humility is tied to her conviction that the "people are my teachers."

The first half of the interview is choppy because I was writing in a pickup truck as we traveled to Aguilares. The noise level didn't permit using a tape. The last half, and most personally and politically revealing, took place in the parish house of a North American priest who is a friend of Ana's. When Ana began to speak about "women's issues," he asked if he should leave to provide greater space for her disclosure. She declined. Later he said that he had not realized how disregarded women, even those such as Ana who are so deeply integrated into the "process," must feel.

Like Matilde, Ana is a founder of a small community of vowed women. Her community, however, has encountered setbacks and disruption of the base community work, leaving her group of sisters in a less cohesive phase. In a new adaptation, however, single mothers involved in pastoral formation live with Ana's small group at different times. The sisters live and work in the countryside and city.

※

There were two young catechists I worked with from Guazapa. Cecilia was twenty-seven and Sonida was fifteen. I worked with a pastoral team in the same place that Rutilio Grande worked. These two young women were friends of Laura López [a pastoral leader who was killed in 1985]. Another member of our team was Cristobel, who was killed in 1982. Each week in the *cantón* of Santa Barbara they celebrated the word. Each of them was an example of commitment in their own family lives as well as in the community. They began the base Christian community meetings with a prayer they had learned from the sisters who had been their formation team. They always met even during the most difficult times for this reflection.

Each *cantón* celebrated a fiesta for the founding of their base Christian community. In Rutilio Grande's area, Cecilia and Sonida helped prepare the community for those celebrations. In Guazapa at the end of 1976 the pastoral teams worked with the communities to discover their most basic needs after a period of reflection on their situation. The people didn't own their own homes; they worked on the sugar plantations and had to rent land where they planted their corn. Most of the harvest had to be given back to the landlord. Our reflection time helped us discover that this was not the work of God.

[*At this point our truck arrived in Apopa to pick up some women catechists. Ana pointed out the surrounding hills, called El Chapines, as "our beauty."*]

In 1977 Father Mario Bernal, the parish priest from Apopa, was expelled from the country and Rutilio Grande denounced this. He gave a very strong homily in which he said, "Our brother Cain is still alive in this country." One month later Rutilio was killed.

[*We now picked up three women and some children while avoiding* orejas *(spies). In June and July of 1989 in Apopa eight youths had been captured by the army. One was found mutilated in a field and another was tortured in an army barracks.*]

In 1982 Cecilia and Sonida were both killed. Three days before they were captured they visited me, and during our liturgy we reflected on those who had been killed. Cecilia said to me, "Ana, I feel afraid but this reflection has given me new strength."

The soldiers had forced families to lie on the ground with guns pointed at their heads. They bound and gagged Cecilia and Sonida. Then the National Guard grabbed them by the hair and pulled them into a pickup truck. At the command post in Aguilares they were tortured for five days. We found their bodies along that road. Their eyes and tongues were cut out, their feet were broken, and dogs were eating them. Sonida's mother and father went to recover the bodies. When they failed, they went to Msgr. Urioste, but the monsignor couldn't talk. The mother had to give consolation to Msgr. Urioste. She quoted Psalm 91 to him. It is a psalm of someone in danger asking God for strength.

Three months later our community reflected on the strength of those two young women because they remained faithful to the end and never revealed anyone's names. I think they died August 4 and their anniversary was yesterday.

[*We pass an area where the two women lived and Ana comments on how humble and happy Cecilia was.*]

There were sixty in Cecilia's Christian youth group. After her death many joined the guerrillas in the Guazapa mountains. Many others who stayed working as catechists in Guazapa were killed.

Another catechist leader that I worked with was Cristobel [Rufina Guevara]. She was part of Laura López's coordinating team. She was from the *cantón* of Loma de Ramas. She was very dynamic. She and her husband were responsible for her *cantón*'s pastoral team.

After Rutilio's death all the priests were thrown out of the region, so another sister and I coordinated the work with Cristobel and Laura López from 1977 to 1980. The people's suffering motivated Cristobel to go to Usulután in Tierra Blanca in 1981–82. In August of 1982 Cristobel left Usulután to meet me so we could attend a pastoral workshop in Costa Rica together. But on the way she was killed.

[*Now we arrive at the farm collective called Buen Pastor (Good Shepherd). The community of Buen Pastor sits in the middle of cane and corn fields. Women in their best dresses await Ana and her North American companions. They have prepared* rigua/hilote (*a corn with cream dish*) *for us.*

On the trip back to the city I asked Ana what it means to be a good teacher. She pointed in the distance to the village of San Jerónimo, where her "student" Laura López had lived, and then she gave these characteristics of a good teacher.]

Good teachers have these characteristics: (1) They are able to listen; (2) they have humility; (3) they can enter into the concrete situation of those they teach; (4) they can help people analyze the root causes of their problems.

Vows to the People

Our home was very religious. My mother gave us a lot of encouragement to persist in our faith. We never saw our parents fight. If they disagreed we didn't hear it. In my town the people were very respectful of religion.

Each year a woman named Visitación prepared the children for First Communion. This happened even though our town was practically abandoned by the church. We almost never had a priest.

My father bought a book about Maria Goretti [a young Italian martyr] and read it to us. My mother was a woman of the hearth. There were ten of us and I'm the last of the girls. My father was a *campesino* who worked the land. He had a special love for children.

I came to San Salvador when I was fifteen. It was my first visit. I came to study at Bethlehem School in Santa Tecla. I graduated from high school there.

In 1960 I entered the Carmelite novitiate of St. Joseph. My first years there were normal. But in 1972 they asked me to work in a little mission outpost in Ciudad Barrios where Archbishop Romero was born. Those years formed me, working in different villages. It was the most powerful experience of my life. I went to help the people but the people helped me to grow.

In 1976 the sisters asked if I wanted to work in Guazapa. This was the second most important experience of my life. There the pastoral team helped us to take the work out into the *cantones*. These were important years because we developed a whole new method.

We began to hear about massacres. Then we reflected on our daily lives and our pastoral team became one with the people. It was a process that united us with the people. The examples of those people who gave their lives still inspire me today.

On September 25, 1980, when we were preparing for the patron saint's day, the *muchachos* [guerrillas, literally "boys"] took over Guazapa. The mayor's office and military command post blamed us. They subsequently placed a bomb in the convent but we weren't there. Then the community sent us word not to return. The house was burned down and the civil defense patrols had stolen our things, including money for church repairs and the cooperative.

At that time there was a massacre near Guazapa. Because of all that we left Guazapa. Although the work had fallen off, we began again in 1982. I was invited to work with the pastoral team that was there in Apopa. There were only fifteen of us.

One was a beloved old catechist who disappeared in March, then another catechist disappeared. But those who continued were able to inspire the work in the *cantones*. Some of the catechists who began those small reflection groups were the women from Apopa who drove with us to Aguilares today.

From 1985 on our work took off in Apopa. We have a sewing collective, a mechanics' collective. We're working on an agriculture project. Then last August the bishop took away our parish priest. The new priest isn't progressive. He discourages our work. He wouldn't accept well-trained communities because they challenged him too much. Because of him the world fell apart again. Still the people at the base continued to work. Currently we're working on an infant and child care center. Also we're trying to keep up each other's spirits.

A group of us left our congregation in 1979. We had been doing pastoral work and I think because of this we developed a new perspective about our congregation. Our congregation was open at first, but when the massacres began they recalled us all from the work. But we went to our base communities and they helped us understand that the role of a religious is among the people, not away from them. The congregation, little by little, was closing doors to us.

We met with Archbishop Romero to discuss our work. He said we needed to be light and salt within the congregation. He said that only we could decide what we must do about the congregation's recall. However, he said, the poor must be evangelized.

So we returned to our congregation and asked for a dispensation to work in the *cantones* for some time, and then we would meet with the congregation's administration to decide together our fate. But the congregation said no, decide now to continue in the order or continue working in the *cantones*. So we returned to speak with Archbishop Romero. He said again that only we could make this important decision. However, before we left he gave us the documents of the bishops' conference at Puebla and asked us to read them before we decided.

Perhaps we knew all along we would never leave the people.

Archbishop Romero went out to Guazapa to celebrate Mass and we brought the communities together. He asked everyone gathered there if we women had been a witness to them. The people said yes. Then he asked them to share their ideas about what kind of religious life they preferred. The people said that until then they had never known nuns to be in the *cantones*. "You aren't nuns anymore," they said to us. "You have no habits, but you're the same people to us."

After that Archbishop Romero had us renew our vows to him in front of the community. Then he thanked the community for who they were and we had a great celebration. When he was eating he asked them if they missed nuns without habits. They said to him "Archbishop, the habit doesn't make the nun." Until then we had worn full Carmelite habits. But the women of the community had made us clothes and we took off our habits that day. I had been in a habit from 1960 to 1979 and that day I was at a party for the first time in street clothes.

We moved into the convent in Guazapa. When the bombing happened the deepest loss was losing the cassette with Archbishop Romero receiving our vows.

The woman who made my clothes that day was Cecilia, whom I told you about earlier. I still have one red dress she gave me. A special part of that day was that Archbishop Romero asked us to bring all our families for the renewal of our vows. We renewed vows of obedience, poverty, and chastity that day.

One of the sisters who made her vows works in Santa Tecla today, another is here in our *barrio*. It's a little painful that some have gone now.

You have trained many people, yet you don't think of yourselves as priests of the new church?

To serve the people doesn't require a title or having a high role. In fact, our purpose was to be one with the people, never distinct from them. When we worked with the young people and asked them to deepen their commitment, they said, "Why?" "You nuns have never done it." They challenged us. When we talked to them about getting more training to serve the people, they challenged us to bring the seminary or convent or school to them, to train them out there in the *cantones*.

We have offered sacraments in those areas where the people have no priests. *¿Cómo no?* [Why not?] I want to be very honest with you. Yes, I celebrate Mass. We have brought a tortilla, blessed it and shared it with the people. I want to be honest, but if the bishop finds out we'll be excommunicated at once.

[*At this point the parish priest who had been listening couldn't restrain from commenting: "But, Ana, there is no need for any official to give this permission. No bishop, no prelate has this power. No, only God's spirit can do that. This breakthrough is happening all over the world. I'm angry at the church." "For good reason," Ana answered. Then she continued.*]

I've always thought the church was very *macho*, and there is no room for the Spirit of God in *machismo*.

How do you work with priests who are very committed, revolutionary priests who are still macho?

This is one of the hardest things. This limits our ability to feel the Spirit of God working among us. Even if they have all clarity in their political, economic, and social thinking, they still aren't willing to accept women's criticism of their work. Only a few have been able to accept that.

Are there any priests who have changed? Is there life after machismo? [*Ana was silent for a few minutes, pondering the question. With a sigh and visible heaviness she finally responded.*]

No one I can think of.

Have you experienced the dark night of the soul that Carmelite mystic John of the Cross talks about?

I feel it today when there is a lack of understanding especially among my brothers. Just the other day I was reflecting on a passage of St. Teresa, and we asked ourselves about the dark moments of our lives.

In the Carmelites the darkest night was not feeling life within the congregation. Working with the people in the small villages was where I discovered the life of God in the people. It was a resurrection amid so much death.

Now I don't feel sadness. Fear, yes, but no sadness.

Reina

The words come to us burning
from the wombs of strong women.
—Gilberto González y Contreras,
"Here We Are"

Reina is responsible for the pastoral work of the entire Usulután region. She has a teacher, she says — the people and the liberation proceso itself. What makes her exceptional is that she is in a leadership role as a young woman. Even though women are the sustainers of the base Christian communities, they are rarely directors of entire regions. The national and regional leadership of the base Christian communities is primarily male.

Unlike most of the other interviews, taken "on the run" in 1989 after ARENA's triumph, Reina's narrative took place in 1988. We had a few hours to explore questions. It was the last time I saw Reina. When I returned in 1989 she was underground and still is.

⚜

My work consists of accompanying a number of pastoral teams that have ministries in rural communities. I visit and encourage the *catequistas* [lay pastoral ministers] working in war zones, especially among the *desplazados* [those people displaced by the war]. Of course, my work is but a tiny grain of sand amid the work of all the pastoral teams.

Our long-term vision is to contribute to the renewal of the church, that is, so that the Catholic Church in the diocese where we work will be more in tune with the needs of the people. You see, in the dioceses of El Salvador the direction given to pastoral work by the bishops is not at all consistent; in fact, it takes many different directions all at the same time.

We do not have, for example, anything like we had before 1980, when Archbishop Romero spoke to all of us in the archdiocese of a *pastoral de conjunto* [unified pastoral strategy]; now each parish acts according to its own criteria. They can decide to do whatever they wish — the pastoral decisions they make, the direction they give to their work, their methods. That is, everyone decides on their own the direction their program of evangelization is to take. So they can decide whether they will promote human development or if they will speak of human dignity and rights or of the relationship between the human person and God. Until last year [1987], there has not been the least amount of pressure from our diocese on parishes to carry out pastoral work that combines evangelization with social development.

I have been working in this region since January 1985. I started with two colleagues, both of them also *catequistas*. Up to the present time

56

our objective has been to carry out a different kind of pastoral work, and we have always tried to unify the network of pastoral teams that have been developed. Also, in the last two years a number of nuns have joined our teams.

Here in El Salvador we are living a process of communion and participation of grassroots pastoral workers; a new church is being born from the people, with equal participation of laypersons, nuns, and priests. Also, it's important to point out that we work not only at the local level; we try to serve the needs of all the communities with which we work in various parts of the country in a supportive and ongoing manner. One of the services that we feel is most necessary is the formation and training of new *catequistas*, new celebrants of the word, and new communities. In this formation process, we would like to be able to help each member of a Christian community, each Christian community itself, to live out a process of reflecting upon and maturing in their faith. We want that faith to grow to the point where our people are able to attain moral maturity, to face life with strong moral and ideological values, so they are able to discern the difference between the way we live today and the way we would like to live in the future, to ask, "What can we do to transform our situation?"

We believe it's important to set our sights high. There's no reason we should set limits to our actions. We can look at our situation and judge whether it is in accordance with what we believe to be just. And once we have made this judgment, there's no reason for us simply to stop in our tracks. We all have the capacity to transform our world. We have the ability to *act*. So we move forward, always trying to discover new alternatives for responding to the situation we live in.

What does it mean for you to be entregada *[totally committed, literally, handed over]?*

First, it means to respond to a call. Traditionally it's been thought, and some still believe this, that this is a direct call from God. But I believe you shouldn't make such an unquestioning affirmation. Why couldn't we better say that it's a call from our fellow human beings? It simply means to give the necessary response to a situation that you may be facing at any given moment.

I grew up in a working-class *barrio*. When I was fourteen years old I started teaching catechism, not long after my First Communion. Really, until that time I had never suffered much in my personal life, nothing that marked me in any way. But, yes, later on our family was touched in a very concrete way by the violence the poor have always suffered here. So gradually my thinking became clearer; I knew *why* I was doing what I was doing, for example, why I had to leave my family.

I left home when I was seventeen, and even if I could have had the opportunity to continue studying, that was no longer attractive to me. What really attracted me, what motivated me, was the possibility of being able to contribute to the creation of new Christian communities, to help others see that we needed a change in our country. So I felt that one of the things I could do with my life was to help others to become conscious of their situation, and then to take a stand. You feel like you can help others to start walking down that road, and that's why it makes sense to make a total life commitment, to "hand over" your life, to give of your time, not to waste your time doing other things. For example, that might mean not to want to have a family, or a paying job, or to better your living conditions.

What is the commitment that goes along with your work, in practical terms?

I think that's something that we shouldn't try to answer for ourselves. I shouldn't try to say what percentage of my potential commitment I presently give, or whether my commitment is total or not. Often the demands are *much* greater than what you are able to give in practice. A number of us do dedicate ourselves full-time to the work.

I believe that a person's personal life might limit what that person can do, so if I should ever get married I would want my companion to have a strong commitment to the people. And I wouldn't want to have children for a number of years, because they limit what you are able to do. They limit your level of commitment, because you have to dedicate a lot of time to taking care of them. The other day a woman was talking to me about this. She said, "I feel bad when I have to leave my children. But by myself I can go every which way, and if I eat, fine, but if I don't, well that's not so bad either. . . . " If you're alone you don't have to worry about others so much, but the limitations of having a home are quite substantial.

What does the word "commitment" mean for you in terms of spirituality?

I believe it means trying to find where God is working in history. At times we have said it means trying to make Jesus come alive here on earth: his life and example, his teachings, and also his liberating actions. You can read the Bible and find that Jesus tried to address the concrete needs of the people, that he felt deep affection for the most needy. He always *acted* in their favor. When the lepers came to him, he didn't turn them away.

We have come to realize that Jesus' teachings did not bring death or condemnation. He did not teach suffering just for the sake of suffering. On the contrary, he *lived* and brought signs of life that engendered life and strengthened the faith and hope of the most afflicted. He showed them a different side of life — less dark, less oppressive.

The other day we were having a study session with some foreign church volunteers, and we talked about the question "What is our role here, in this specific situation?" We tried to come up with an answer based on the teachings and practice of Jesus, because almost all the volunteers who are working here were motivated to come by their faith. So we discussed the difference between a theology that gives life and one that brings death. We spoke of how we feel a great distance between the way we would like to live the gospel and the way many of our bishops and pastors live it. They are very, very far away from what our people are feeling and suffering. We realized that they have tried to avoid conflict at all costs, whatever might cause problems. They try to separate out any part of Jesus' message that is liberating. It's like they want to cover it up.

How do you define ministry?

Really, I don't know how to define it. I don't have a definition for the work that we do. But the fact is, for many years, perhaps for centuries, the church has blocked all opportunities for ministry for those who are not consecrated as priests or nuns. They took away the people's right as children of God to share the gospel, their right to be in positions of leadership where they could orient the people — and this is their right as given in baptism. They never gave the people the sense that they had these rights. The people always have to be led by a priest or a nun, as if they had a monopoly on religious sentiments, the religious beliefs of the people.

So our ministry consists first and foremost in helping people understand that we all have this right, to open each other's eyes, to announce the good news of hope and liberation. We are all capable of this, in spite of not having studied a pile of books. I believe that's one of our worst problems, that over the years everything was handed down *to* us; we would go to church to listen to the homily, and then we didn't return until the next Sunday. And that's how the faith was lived out by our people, at least until about ten or fifteen years ago — a completely traditional way of living the faith.

We used to go to church like water jugs, just waiting to have water poured into us. Our faith was a "borrowed" faith; the priests allowed us the privilege of understanding the gospel in the manner that *they* explained it to us. They never explained the things that really mattered. So, it's only been with the passing of the years that more and more laypersons have become clear about these things, often with the help of one of the priests who had a different vision of what pastoral work was all about. We learned that we have a treasure within us: the life we have lived. And if we take that lived experience, and reflect on it collectively, taking into account of course all our errors and limitations, still we see that we ourselves have something to share with others on the journey toward God's Reign. We can take the message and give it life.

Archbishop Romero used to say, "And who is the church? The bishops are not the church. Neither is the cathedral. It's not even the pope. The church is the people of God, the place where Jesus became flesh and blood." The people are the church.

So our ministry is to identify with the people, to live and share with the people. And I believe it is less difficult for those of us who are not living on the fringes of people's lives. We *are* the people. Perhaps it's more difficult for those who have so much education but are not firmly planted among the people.

What is the role of women in the church here in El Salvador?

The first step for women to take is to become aware that we have our own unique identity, not only within the church, but also as women in our Salvadoran society. But we have not yet lived this new identity. Many older women with children — our own mothers are the best example we have — lived a life that they themselves didn't choose. It was the kind of life that most women were forced to live. Perhaps if they had had other opportunities to choose from, they would have chosen a different life. So that's the first thing we need to realize, that as women we are not living a complete life; rather we are only living *one* part of our lives. For many women the only option is to be housewives and mothers, to take care of their children and their husbands, that is, those who have their husbands at home.

Women have to confront doubly miserable conditions of exploitation and are always among the poorest of the poor. They are exploited by the government, by the business where their husband works, or by the landowner. It's a system that at times encourages the woman to buy things she doesn't need. Her husband also exploits her, not appreciating her dignity as a woman. He often uses her like a piece of furniture, something that you use as long as it serves you. And at times even the woman's children don't appreciate her, relegating her to second-class status.

A while ago we were meeting with a women's group from one of the repatriations [communities of returned refugees who have come from the camps in Honduras], and we talked about a lot of different issues together that had to do with our situation *as women*. We tried to create an atmosphere of trust among ourselves, dropping our defenses, taking off our masks. We asked ourselves, "What is our living situation really like? Are we in agreement with the way things are — or not? Does it appear to us that it's just to continue living in this manner — or not? Could we possibly live in a different manner? And what is it that puts up obstacles in the way of our living in a different manner?" In other words, we tried to see what it is that makes us live like we have to live.

Afterward, we were analyzing how once a woman has become conscious of her own situation, she usually comes to the realization that her mission is to be within the process of transformation of social structures that is taking place right now in our country. This change of consciousness especially happens with those women who are active in an agricultural cooperative, a women's association, a community council, or a pastoral team. We're talking about much more than simply changing things in the family or community. What we want is to join with the men of the communities in a process of transformation of the economic, social, and political structures, so that we have a society where *no one* is looked down upon, a society where all — men, women, and children — are able to develop their own gifts and abilities, to put them at the service of the whole community, and not just to serve the interests of a minority.

But there are many women who didn't pass through that phase of reflection, but simply became involved in some type of work. That might entail working to better the living conditions of the community, or becoming part of the revolution going on in our country, or joining a pastoral team. The difference is that some women have been able to reflect deeply upon their womanhood, while others have not been able to. They very naturally became part of a process of collective change. The ideal would combine the two: to reflect on our role as women, what we want to do with our lives, independently of what our husband, the children, the neighbors, or the boss want — but at the same time to become part of that history that we are all making together. We should do this with the men and with the rest of the community, and with all our people.

It could be a danger that women might want to raise the concerns of women to such a high position that women's rights are given priority over anything else. But women won't be able to gain those rights, nor will we be able to change our lives in a definitive manner, unless there are profound structural changes in our society. I believe a woman should not see her *own* needs as fundamental, but rather the needs of the people, the life of the people. Our struggle today is for the freedom of the people, the dignity of an entire people. In the future we will be able to dig deeper into those issues alongside our male *compañeros*. We're not talking about a problem that's solely the fault of the husbands; it is the result of oppression that comes from above. The situation of women is the fruit of a system that's like a bad tree that produces only rotten fruit. The society in which we live engenders this adverse situation, something none of us want to live.

I understand completely what you've said, except at one point you said that a woman's task is not to think of herself, but of the people, so that her task is to have humility. But the church has always told the people that the greatest sin was pride, but that sin was a sin of men. The sin of women is not to have pride, is not to speak their word, is to remain humble in a false sense. Women should not be afraid of the men saying, "You're not thinking of the people." They should speak for the people, for the people to have the voice of women, not always the voice of men. For example, in my country the compas [political militants, in this case male], when the women disagree with what they are saying, will often say to them, "You're not thinking of the people" — as if they are.

No, I definitely believe that this is something that you can't erase so easily. We've been living like this for thousands of years. History tells us that in primitive societies men and women lived alike — equality of rights — and, yes, it was ideological influences that made things change. The equal participation of men and women in primitive society began to change.

Many of us would like to see things like that again, but at the same time we question what our priorities should be as women. In this phase of the struggle shouldn't we be working first for the triumph of *all* the people? We can be working toward this goal, while at the same time analyzing these kinds of questions whenever we have the opportunity.

You see, the roots of the problem go deeper. For example, we women don't want to enter into continual arguments with the men, or with our male colleagues, or with our husbands, just because they act in a *macho* way. We need to be somewhat open and understanding of them, because their problem is systemic — the result of a corrupt history.

It's true that even though many of us have this level of consciousness, we still don't appreciate our own gifts, and many other women don't help us much to appreciate ourselves. We can see this in the communities themselves, for example, in the communities of *desplazados*. When they are electing their community council, which is the group of people designated to work out the problems of the community, the women often get left out.

So one day we were analyzing this situation with a group of about thirty-five women of one particular rural community. They were asking, "Why are there eight men on the community council, and only two women?" Some of the women said that in fact the majority of those proposed for these positions by the community were men, even though the majority of people are women. So you see, the women themselves don't assign difficult or important tasks to other women, that is, positions of leadership. The women don't have confidence in their own ability to be in leadership positions within the community.

That's why we think it's so important for women to become more conscious of their need to get more involved in community tasks. Wouldn't it be quite different if in a community the majority of the women would nominate other women? In most communities, of every one hundred persons, eighty are women and twenty are men. What could the men say? But, if women don't appreciate or value themselves and so they don't nominate women, well then the men certainly aren't going to nominate women.

They will remain invisible. It's because a woman's work is hardly ever compensated financially. There is no established price for her work, but nevertheless it's work. And she's there, even though she might not be continually talking, but she exists, she is present.

Yes, that's all true, but when the female slave of the male slave speaks her word, then there is a revolution that goes deeper than just structural changes, that is, deeper than in a society where this is not possible. One theme present in the works of Gustavo Gutiérrez is that when the poor evangelize the poor, this is the liberation process. But I believe this revolution can go even deeper when the most oppressed, the most invisible, are able to speak their word. Some compas from Nicaragua were speaking to a group in Chicago, and they said that many times the struggle demanded that they not deal with their own empowerment, and after the revolution, which continues, they still are confronting deep and profound problems. That's why I think the Salvadorans, particularly in the countryside, have a unique opportunity, because even now they're confronting the problems earlier than the Nicaraguans did, the problem of women finding their voice....

I believe that here in this country the war is very, very complex — so difficult to understand, or to live. Perhaps not even half the women who should be participating are actually involved. Still you can see a notable increase in women's participation.

In many poor communities, especially in the countryside, women are taking on important leadership responsibilities. And in many communities they are starting daycare centers, so that the women can be freed up from having to care for their children during the day. This opens up the possibility of other work, such as food production. Being involved in production helps women to feel more secure, that they are doing something important for the community, and that they are as capable as the men. Women are also leaders in the workers' organizations, developing policies and doing other sorts of work. They are present. They act.

Also, many *compañeras* have been very involved in pastoral work, and they have helped make a valuable contribution to the *proceso* [revolutionary process] the people are carrying out.

When the Iglesia Popular [People's Church] experiences repression, can it count on the protection of the institutional church?

It doesn't have any. Not only does it not have their protection, the bishops virtually disown it. They try to delegitimate it as church. They wash their hands of any problems. They become indifferent, and at times they even become the accusers. In those cases they're responsible for what might happen to the communities or to the *catequistas*.

In the first place the church exists because we want to be one with the people. Second, it exists because we are Christians who want to have a living faith, that is, a faith manifested in concrete acts. The *Iglesia Popular* has problems because it is conscious of its duty to be clearly identified with the people, and not just with words, but with acts — walking with the people in their struggle for liberation. When you have decided to take that road, there are definite consequences. We need to be clear about the possible consequences when we take these positions.

I say this because I really believe that you have problems here because of the way you do or do not act. Take the example of Archbishop Romero. He came from a *campesino* family, but one that was not very poor. He went through a long seminary formation process, which put him in a different social class, giving him more power in the church. What caused problems for Archbishop Romero was his taking a certain position. He became a part of the *Iglesia Popular*, even though he himself was not poor.

What gift has the Iglesia Popular *given to the world?*

I don't know ... perhaps the gift we have given to the world has been to show that it is possible to make something *new*. If you combine collective grassroots effort with a faith that doesn't give up in the face of problems, then you can do *great things!* You can do things you never thought possible.

Another gift has been the recovery of an authentic church, a church of the people. Jesus came for a specific purpose: to announce the good news to the poor and to live among them. He spent most of his life with them. So, this is the recovery of a church that doesn't fully exist at the present time; it's being built with the efforts of thousands of people. In a certain way, all of us are contributing ideas and content to this new church, with all our experiences.

The other day I was at a study session concerning the present situation in the country, and a Jesuit priest was speaking. He said that for many the teachings of the church are immutable dogmas. They are self-evident truths, set in stone, that no one can change. We don't believe in unchangeable, absolute truths. World history — the history of nations, of human development — is always in flux, and it is that unfolding history itself that helps clear up things little by little. The church of the poor is a church that is always *creating*. It's not satisfied to remain stuck in the past. So that's our contribution.

How do you understand "revolutionary hope"?

I believe it's the ideal of seeing our condition transformed, the profound desire to be persons with the possibility of developing our capacities to the full, persons who have had, and still have, their rights trampled on. So it's the hope of securing those rights, that they might really be ours, that they won't be snatched away. The right to life, the right to sufficient food, housing, to be able to read and write, and finally to be able to determine our own destiny.

That might seem almost impossible in such a tiny country, a country dominated by a superpower that's part of the world capitalist system — I'm talking about U.S. imperialism — but we believe it can happen with the united efforts of all the people, with their ever-increasing consciousness that this war is not one of just a few, but rather of a whole people. It's a war of the weak against the strong, the pint-sized against the same giants as usual. But the small are not alone. They're united among themselves, and they can count on the support of people from other parts of the world.

That gives you confidence, the solidarity we have that we didn't experience before. For example, we have big gatherings and interchanges with people from other Latin American countries. And then there's the support we receive from the people of the United States. I'm not at all sure what the percentages would be, but certainly a good part of the people in the U.S. are becoming conscious of the things their government does to the other countries of the world, how it exploits and bullies the smaller countries. And they're seeing that it's important to make an option in favor of the poor people of the world, against the violence their own country is imposing on us, against the war being waged on us. That also gives us hope. We really believe that in the long run more and more people from other countries will be struggling alongside us.

We know that this revolution has indigenous roots. It has not been imported. It's not the work of Russia or Cuba. And it's not being directed from Nicaragua. It started here, and it started with just a few. It was just a handful of workers and students who created the first political-military organizations, who said that armed struggle was necessary here if there is to be any possibility of radical change. They took that route because the previous decades had shown the electoral route to be bankrupt, the same with coups and mere changes of governments. Those types of changes were merely cosmetic; nothing really changed *structurally*.

But I get a lot of hope from seeing so many people making this revolution, from realizing that these people are motivated by their faith, and have deepened their faith to the point that they make an explicit political commitment to the liberation of their people. This makes us feel that whatever country becomes conscious of its own situation, and determines to change it — like Vietnam, for example — then that country can withstand any invasion. In the end they will be victorious.

Solidarity among the peoples of the world plays such an important role. It's really a determining factor, because the people of other countries have the role of telling the truth to their own people. They can tell others what's truly happening here, to help them understand the legitimacy of this struggle. So all this moral and political support from outside helps strengthen the *proceso*, and will contribute greatly to the triumph. But our hope is that more and more of our own people will become organized and will join the struggle.

What makes you afraid the most?
    Jail, interrogations . . . I'm afraid that I'll be afraid, and that this fear will make me weak. You see, it's not like you're afraid all the time. You just take it for granted that when you are fully involved in a process such as the one we are living, then your life is never guaranteed. But one never knows. When the difficult and painful moments come — alone, face-to-face with an interrogator — you never know if you'll hold up physically or psychologically, whether you'll be capable of resisting the interrogations and the tortures. There are some who drop out because of this fear. Their work loses effectiveness.
    The repression is rising. More people are showing up dead. They explode bombs in trade union offices. They're constantly spying on people around the parishes and following people. Because of all this you feel a lot of tension. And that's exactly what they want. They're escalating the war, the repression, so that our work will diminish.
    So that's something I also personally fear, and along with my colleagues I hope we can overcome this fear — not only us, but all the people. I hope we can all overcome these problems, that they won't weigh heavier than our love for our people. Our convictions and our faith must overcome them.
    You know, we're human, we have weaknesses, and at times we don't give it all we've got. So that's a fear we have, of not giving all we might give, of preserving our own personal interests and always thinking about defending our own life, protecting ourselves. So that's something we're all up against.

How old are you?
    Twenty-three years old.

2

THE HOUR OF THE POOR:
THE PEASANTS

Photo by Jim Harney

> *Until now the only thing that no tyrant has managed to overcome has been dreams. And there are dreams which last for centuries.*
> *—Manlio Argueta*

Dreams outlast tyrants. The first dreams, the Indian dreams, belonged to peasants. The first defeated were peasants, and the first to remember are peasants. This is their danger.

The ocote becomes fire from ashes. Peasants smolder, remember the offenses of centuries; remember land, volcanoes, and *pueblo.* How do symbols carry the sparks of resistance and, most importantly, how do *campesino* leaders translate symbols to action, to the power to create history? What forms of political and ecclesial practice are faithful to the peasants' cultural ideals and symbols? In summary, what was the process that impelled Salvadoran peasants toward a popular revolutionary movement?

> We must sharpen . . . our analysis of how power is contested at the grassroots level. If we reject the notion that peasant movements must inevitably be led from above or outside, we have to be able to explain how rural communities with limited resources organized themselves.[21]

Dependency theorists have explained Third World nations' impoverishment as resulting from the world capitalist system's ability to use the abundant cheap labor and resources of poor nations, as well as their control of the world market, terms of trade, and "development" funds. What few theorists have explained, however, is the persistence of the peasants' resistance to their exploitation. Peasants are seen as victims, forced to bend to international and oligarchic oppression. If insurgency develops, peasants are depicted as supporters of the liberation struggle but never initiators. Many leftist theorists see peasants as victims of false consciousness who are led to critical consciousness and revolutionary actions by the liberating ideas of a vanguard party. More recent social theorists, however, argue that the intervention of the military state (for instance, in El Salvador, the *matanza* of 1932) is more determinant of *campesino* unification and resistance than the influence of political parties or church leaders. The *campesinos*, then, responding to state repression, developed their own sense of class oppression and cultural opposition. Bill Dexheimer, a missionary who spent three years in El

Salvador, sees the peasants' allegiance to a particular party as practical rather than ideological. The peasants ask, "Who was it who protected us? Who broke the army's siege?"

Two catalysts crystallized *campesino* resistance, transforming resistance into a revolutionary popular movement. The church and the revolutionary organizations joined their paths to the peasants' cause — a cause steeped in the deprivations and endurance of centuries, as well as an ancient refusal to be conquered. Initial efforts to organize peasant cooperatives in the 1960s, though partial and weak, had been "coals" lit in a semifeudal darkness. When priests and sisters, many born in the countryside, reentered the lives of their peasant communities, armed with a new method of reading the gospel, the flickering burst into flame. The *campesinos* read the gospel with a new method that simply asked the poor the meaning of the word of God in the light of their experience. Church and party leaders fanned the flames, but the peasant's solidarity was the fuel.

The peasants of Suchitoto answered when Padre Alas brought the message of Medellín to his parish of forty-five thousand in 1969. Alas describes a training session for peasant leaders who then formed Bible reflection groups. All the groups gathered in a closing plenary session for common sharing. To break the customary sacerdotal privilege and affirm the emerging authority of the peasants, Alas was not the liturgical officiator. Instead, the community elected a secretary who presided. The people's authority was authenticated in the *comunidad* and established the basis for new organizational forms that were radically democratic.

Alas describes an early reflection of the children of the communities, a force that pulled their parents deeper and deeper toward communal solidarity:

> The children, who were always present, came and said to me, "We have also studied the text of the Bible, and we think that here in our village it's not like it was in the first Christian communities...."
> I asked them why: "Because our parents continue fighting over their things, my mother says the chickens are hers, and my father says the cows are his; all this means is that they don't own things collectively. We would like... to put things together, own them collectively, and we would help [our parents] with it, too."[22]

A new conception of authority and leadership was developing. Those who considered others, who sought no advantage over others, who shared out of their poverty — these were the exemplary persons. If goods and work were to be shared, so were decisions. *Responsables* (persons responsible for some aspect of communal work) were people capable of facilitating this democratic process that sought the contribution of all.

Democracy, as a political formation, grew out of the *campesino* construction of *comunidad,* the social practice of becoming a people spiritually and nationally. *Comunidad* as the symbol of a new people — those who stand for each other, committed to uphold and cherish the lives of all, even the weakest — demanded a transformation from egoism to a love for others. Such love is expressed in a commitment that leads to becoming organized.

Venancia, a *campesina* who lived in Villa Rosario in the department of Morazán, speaks of a new awakening for the peasants:

As Christians what did Jesus say to us? Do we continue in this passivity and death and poverty or does Jesus invite us to raise ourselves out of this situation? That's how in the middle of the 1970s, the communities began to take more and more seriously their Christian role and also their political role when the popular organizations and the political organizations appeared in this area.

The necessity to make love efficacious politicized the communities. As the *campesinos* applied the demands of the gospel to their situation they moved beyond the notion of *comunidad* as a description applying only to their lives as Christians but also to their lives as farmworkers, as mothers, as youth who needed to organize themselves against the mounting persecution.

In Chalatenango the opportunity to unite and organize presented itself in a farmers' union. Caravina describes the evolution from base Christian communities to a farmworkers' union:

[*Comunidad*] gave the peasants a sense of identification, of security and unity in what they were doing. No longer did they conform to what the boss or dictatorship said. But the peasants, the people, had to liberate themselves. What kind of liberation? How? When? Who was to lead it? This was a problem . . . but the first step had to be an organization which encouraged the peasants to participate. . . . In this way we moved toward the formation of the UTC (Union of Rural Farmworkers) . . . in November, 1974.[23]

In those early farmers' meetings the *campesinos* remembered who they were as a people — descendants of Indians whose communal lands were stolen by the Spanish, then appropriated by the oligarchy.

We always oriented ourselves through the UTC. We realized that without an organization we were worth nothing against the oligarchy. We had a very clear idea of why we were fighting: we used to talk about "primitive" society, how the Indians had lived, the arrival of the Spanish, and then how, over time people had developed. We wanted to understand our history.[24]

History, like the gospel, had become dangerous in Chalatenango, as well as in Aguilares, Guazapa, and Morazán. The *comunidades de base* could not have developed without the people as communal bone and muscle. Nor without a *campesino* social base could the revolutionary organizations have organized a social infrastructure capable of mounting and sustaining a political insurgency that would last into the next decade, and remain unbroken even after massive, hideous repression. Anthropologist James Scott summarizes this dialectical relationship: outside leaders (party or intelligentsia) may be needed to transform resistance into revolution but "it is largely a matter of taste as to whether we see subordinate classes as helpless without a radical intelligentsia or the radical intelligentsia as helpless without an insurgent mass."[25]

Campesinas: Yeast Rising

Although this democratic practice had yet to transform gender politics, the *comunidades* did challenge *machismo*, especially irresponsibility toward the family. Drunkenness, infidelity, and abuse were acts of the "old man"; faithfulness and love, characteristics of a true Christian. Women's leadership as delegates of the word in the community's formation process was an initial step toward a social transformation of women's lives.

It was women who encouraged women to become community leaders. From 1975 to 1977, Sister Asunción directed CEPROR, a rural development center that offered community leadership courses to two thousand women. One of the courses questioned the social and sexual division of labor. According to Sister Asunción the course questioned why "men are always seen to be intellectuals" and women feel that "community action is a mystery to them and that the only thing they really understand is looking after the kids."[26]

Such efforts of women in pastoral work preceded the formation of a national women's organization. AMES (Women's Association of El Salvador) which was affiliated with the Popular Forces of Liberation (FPL) would not come into national existence until 1978. When AMES and the Association of Progressive Women of El Salvador, AMPES, which organized women workers, were forced underground by government repression in 1979–80, AMES was able to continue in the liberated zones.

By 1987 another women's organization, the Association of Salvadoran Women (AMS), was founded; it continues today in the war zones of Morazán, San Miguel, San Vicente, and Usulután. AMS was also preceded by a Christian women's organization motivated by the work of women leaders in the base Christian communities. Venancia, a pastoral worker from Morazán, describes the beginning in 1983 of the Congregation of Christian Mothers for Peace and Life:

We felt it was possible to develop a pastoral program oriented toward women. We began to form small groups made up entirely of women. . . . There was no education, no health care, no means to work on behalf of life. The basic causes of this situation were the repression, including bombing, illiteracy, and hunger. We met to reflect on the word of God and to see what it was saying to us.

Not only did the Congregation of Mothers set up food and health care projects; they were the resurrecting force in Morazán after an air war offensive against the communities that decimated the material and social infrastructure of village life. Venancia describes the mothers' role in reinspiring the communities after the terror and devastation of those years. It was women who called the men to resist. If the people rising toward freedom are the bread of life, the women, in Venancia's metaphor, are the yeast:

When the Congregation of Mothers began, the atmosphere of repression was still very much present; that is, all that had taken place in 1980 and in subsequent years had been done, so that the people would not get together, so they would be afraid to hold any type of meeting. I feel that one of the great things the women have achieved is to have raised the people's spirits and to have increased their courage to struggle. . . . In all the communities the men were the ones who were persecuted the most by the armed forces and, therefore, it was they who were afraid to get involved in doing anything for the community, because it tended to be dangerous. So when the women began to struggle to do something for the community, for example, to start a school, to organize a community supply of medicines, to begin a small baking or sewing workshop, all this was dangerous. But when the women started doing these things, by their actions they spoke to the men, telling them that united it was possible to overcome repression. . . . As the women were confronting even the armed forces and demanding their rights, the men began to discover that they, too, could do something in their communities, and that is how the community *directivas* ("councils") were born.

One of the things I came to admire is that these women, in their unity and their willingness to confront repression, have caused the men to stand up, too. . . . It was like a yeast that raised the whole community.

FECCAS was one of the first peasant unions organized by the Christian Democrats in the mid-1960s. Peasant hopes in this reformist but ineffective organization had all but vanished by the mid-1970s. When Rutilio Grande and the people's pastoral teams began Christian community formation in Aguilares at that time, the people resurrected their moribund organization, breathing new life into FECCAS as they discovered faith in themselves.

At the same time, the UTC was formed in Chalatenango with such enthusiasm that the majority of *campesinos* had joined before the year was out. "It was easy to organize the people," says Evaristo, because "many village committees ... were organized through the celebration of the word, where we used to discuss our (suffering) situation, whether it was the will of God or not.... Five of the six [executive founding members] were *celebradores*."[27] "The priests preached the gospel but it was the peasants who set up our organization."

By 1975, FECCAS and the UTC had joined to form the FTC (Federation of Farmworkers) which then became part of the People's Revolutionary Bloc (BPR), called the Bloque. A united national farmworkers' organization had formed. In 1977 they organized peaceful land invasions of *haciendas* where owners had evicted peasants and refused to rent idle land to *campesinos*. The army moved in.

The counterinsurgency efforts of ORDEN (a paramilitary right-wing organization) and ANSESAL (Salvadoran National Security Agency) had been unable to thwart the new defiance of the peasant organizations. Both security organizations grew out of U.S. fiscal aid and advisory assistance dating back to 1957. A young Salvadoran lieutenant, Robert D'Aubuisson, distinguished himself in the coordination of ANSESAL, which centralized information coming from ORDEN in the countryside. ANSESAL operated out of the presidential palace and answered to the president.

The terror and destruction wrought by ORDEN and ANSESAL are documented in the testimonies of Lupe and Ana. No historical overview or analysis can touch what these voices reveal. The *campesinas'* testimonies reveal the cost of peasant struggle and remember those who died, refusing by the retelling to let death be the final word. These memories confront U.S. complicity and present to the world the horror of U.S.-supported counterinsurgency wars in Central America. Through mothers, wives, and sisters, the fallen *campesinos* still speak. Survivors carry history in memory like a hidden wound.

When the united peasant unions intensified their struggle for land, the answer was unimaginative but predictable — death. In San Vicente seven *campesinos* were killed in 1974. In May of 1978, fifty *campesinos* were killed by the army in Cuscatlán. In San Pedro Perulapan, FECCAS leader Tránsito Vázquez was taken out of a worship service by ORDEN members. His head was later found impaled on a tree. Soon after, delegate of the word Felipe de Jésus Chacón, a leader in the popular church, was captured by the National Guard. As a warning to the peasant church, Chacón's scalp was cut off, his face peeled of its flesh, and his body drawn and quartered. His son Juan, also a leader in the base Christian communities and the Bloque (BPR), would follow his father in death. Elected a member of the Democratic Revolutionary Front (FDR), the political opposition party affiliated with the FMLN, Juan Chacón was assassinated with five leaders of the FDR in 1980. All were tortured, but Chacón's body was found with his left arm in a *¡presente!* salute.

By 1977, peasants had joined their cause to the struggle of workers in San Salvador. An alliance of peasants and workers peacefully occupied the Ministry of Labor, seeking negotiations with factory owners and increased wages for farmworkers. Even then, the new archbishop's intervention on behalf of the *campesinos* was not enough to stem the mounting violence in the countryside. Nevertheless, peasants risked capture in order to support workers' strikes in the city. Solidarity was no longer a political word, but a deed of the nation's organized poor. Factory occupations and land takeovers erupted, as did retaliatory attacks by ORDEN and the National Guard. Leaders in the popular church, in FECCAS, the UTC, or BPR were "fingered" by ORDEN and eliminated or captured by the National Guard.

A moment of truth for the institutional church, the church of the social-Christians of Pablo Richard's typology, presented itself. The government considered the farmworkers' unions to be communist organizations, and several bishops — Aparicio of San Vicente, Barrera y Reyes of Santa Ana, Alvarez of San Miguel, and Révelo of Santa Ana — agreed with the government. Archbishop Romero could have been expected to take the usual moderate position of neutrality. But Romero turned his back on his own conservative model of church, as well as the social-Christian model of the few bishops who supported him. He was converted to the church of the poor. In defending that decision, he hammered a manifesto on the door of the New Christendom of the social-Christians. This declaration came in the form of pastoral letters.

Romero's third pastoral letter was called "The Church and the Popular Organizations." In it he defended the people's right to organize even though popular organizations in El Salvador were illegal at the time and considered fronts for the guerrillas. The relationship between the base Christian communities and FECCAS and the UTC were so deeply forged that Romero's pastoral letter cautioned against the fusing of the base Christian communities and the popular organizations. Faith and politics are united, the pastoral insisted, but they aren't identical. Nevertheless, he identified the action of the Spirit as informing the popular organizations' struggle for justice. Romero's pastoral also addressed the formation of government-sponsored peasant organizations, such as ORDEN, which did not defend the rights of the people but persecuted the *campesinos*, especially those who were organized.

Archbishop Romero's next pastoral was written amid the mounting violence of 1979. It was his last pastoral letter and the one that would shape the Salvadoran liberation process most deeply. "The Church in the Midst of Crises" made three profound declarations. One was an admonition to popular organizations not to "absolutize" their organization, holding its life above the people's cause. Second was an endorsement of the people's right to defend themselves through "insurrectional violence" if necessary. Quoting the text of Pope Paul VI in the encyclical *Populorum Progressio*, Romero said: "When a dictatorship violates human rights and attacks the common good of the nation, when it becomes unbearable and closes all channels of dialogue, of understanding, of rationality, when this happens, the church speaks of the legitimate right of insurrectional violence."[28] Third, he legitimated pastoral work with the popular organizations by calling such work "accompaniment" of the people. Accompaniment very often meant a willingness to encounter the forces of terror that were unleashed against the rural poor.

On October 15, 1979, a military coup of reform officers backed by the U.S. installed a civilian-military junta. By December, the entire civilian government had resigned, convinced that the democratic sectors of the country were being used by the military. By January 1980 demonstrations drew two hundred thousand marchers. Proposed land "reform" in the countryside became a means to identify and then eliminate or neutralize *campesino* leaders. The army declared a state of siege and moved to the countryside to take over 250 of the large plantations as a protection against appropriation by the guerrillas.

By 1981 the FMLN had captured large farms that they gave over to the peasants in Chalatenango to be run collectively. In these zones, schools for children and literacy centers for adults were established.

The most revolutionary institutions that developed in Chalatenango were people's popular government (PPL) and people's community councils.

The popular governments in Chalatenango and the community councils in Morazán were composed of women as well as men. Women in the PPL's were instrumental in developing a daily "glass of milk" campaign for all children — a nutritional breakthrough. At that time, women represented "50 percent of the [popular organization] rank and file, 30 percent of the FMLN combatants, and 40 percent of the revolutionary leadership."[29]

The popular governing councils developed initially in Chalatenango, but fanned out to the FMLN-controlled zones, so that by 1982 people's councils governed in Cuscatlán, San Vicente, and Usulután. In the urban neighborhoods, the people's self-governance infrastructure was composed of popular committees, but these councils were clandestine.

Is it any wonder, after people have tasted collective governance, which affirms *campesino* dignity and authority, that the U.S.-Salvadoran counterinsurgency efforts to win the people's "hearts and minds" was never effective? This form of direct participatory democracy was based on the ideal of radical mutuality upheld in the *comunidades*, not on a Western notion of liberal democracy preoccupied with electoral, representative politics. It is difficult for North Americans to understand radical democracy, where the poor masses collectively decide their fate.

Peasants Counter Counterinsurgency

Massive repression following the 1981 FMLN offensive and the air war offensive beginning in 1984 drove civilians out, many fleeing on *guindas* (rapid community flight from approaching patrols or planes), living for years as displaced persons. Others fled to the camps in Honduras and still others fled to distant lands, including the U.S. In spite of the Sanctuary movement's success in giving fleeing refugees a public platform on which to witness to the atrocities they had suffered under low-intensity conflict, the U.S. public remained ill informed about the actual nature of the war in El Salvador. The U.S. media blackout regarding genocidal military campaigns was simply a well-orchestrated aspect of the psychological operations of low-intensity conflict (LIC). A U.S. "psych-op" objective is to avoid the "Vietnam syndrome," in which growing segments of the American public express sympathy with (or worse, solidarity for) the enemy — thus eroding national consensus for continued U.S. aid.

The Salvadoran military's application of "psych-op" objectives has been a failure. Salvadoran "psych-op" counterinsurgency goals are to win the people's "hearts and minds." But if the people's heart and mind is undivided, if the masses have understood themselves as a people, the U.S. and Salvadoran military has to match that commitment with more than sacks of beans or rice, even for starving communities. The condemnation of LIC's ineffectiveness, especially in winning over the peasants, was not made by critics of U.S. foreign policy but by U.S. military officers. In a study by four lieutenant colonels of the John F. Kennedy School of Government in 1988, the officers concluded that the "U.S. has yet to grasp fully what it will take to win . . . popular support, . . . the ultimate strategic aim in counterinsurgency."[30] The U.S. project to train the Salvadoran military to use AID-funded projects in civic action programs in order to win the *campesinos* over "sputter along ineffectually. . . . Millions of dollars are poured into economic support programs that do little to advance the interests of U.S. policy."[31]

Counterinsurgency was "countered" by the *campesino* population in numerous ways. When they could no longer stay in their villages because of the military depopulation strategy, they began an exodus;

before leaving, they buried some of their tools and utensils, so determined were they to return to the land, to the dream of corn and freedom. The military objective in bombing their villages (a flagrant violation of UN protocols and the Geneva Convention) was to destroy any infrastructure that could sustain the FMLN. Saturation bombing sweeps sought to drive civilians, whose homes and crops had been destroyed, into government-controlled camps (called strategic hamlets in Vietnam), where they would receive food and shelter. In this way the FMLN would be isolated and the civilian population pacified.

The intensive bombardment of the countryside had displaced almost eight hundred thousand people by 1988, and this did not include the one million in exile. By 1985 the problem of displaced *campesinos* had overwhelmed the archdiocese of San Salvador, as well as the Lutheran, Baptist, and Episcopal churches, which had provided shelter and food to the *desplazados* (the displaced) in San Salvador and surrounding areas.

The military cordoned off the countryside, blockading food and medicine shipments to areas where whole villages and encampments of displaced refugees were starving. According to a priest working with the Social Secretariat of the archdiocese, "The children are dying of malnutrition, malaria, diarrhea; of very common diseases that shouldn't kill persons. We cannot get medicines up there; the armed forces say the medicine and aid are for guerrillas and they confiscate the supplies."

To counter this plan and break the military blockade of the countryside, the displaced formed their own organization, the Christian Committee for the Displaced (CRIPDES), which found ways to reach peasant communities in the countryside. Necessity invented openings in the armed "wall" blocking off the countryside. With strategic ingenuity *campesinos* slipped through the ravines, trails, and fields.

An alliance between peasant organizations, such as CRIPDES, and North American religious groups, particularly sanctuary congregations who had come to know Salvadoran refugees, led to a new tactic for countering counterinsurgency. The *campesinos* offered the *gringos* an opportunity to practice the spirituality of "accompaniment" by journeying with them into the countryside to get medicines and food to the people. For the North Americans, the opportunity to be socially useful to peasant communities seeking to feed the displaced was unique and compelling. Both groups understood that North American usefulness was in the protection their privileged citizenship provided Salvadorans and the truckloads of food.

The North Americans' act of accompaniment was to take on critical strategic importance both spiritually and politically when peasants decided to resettle the countryside. Tres Ceibas resettlement took place in May 1985, and Tenancingo was also resettled in 1985. U.S. delegates in the later resettlements* focused international pressure on the armed forces' determination to seal off the countryside and disrupt civilian peace initiatives. In June 1986, 125 *campesinos* traveled back to their land in San José las Flores, Chalatenango, with 16 U.S. religious workers. In spite of captures, interrogation of children, bombardment, and injuries, the residents of San José las Flores reconstructed their town; they built a school, a children's center, and a clinic. The El Barillo resettlement of six hundred peasants took place in July 1986.

The last resettlement before the grand exodus of eleven thousand from Mesa Grande beginning in 1987 and ten thousand from Colomancagua in 1989 and 1990 took place at Panchimilama and was accompanied by the Salvadoran Lutheran Church with Bishop Medardo Gómez and six U.S. religious workers.

Each resettlement was coordinated by the Christian Committee of the Displaced of El Salvador (CRIPDES) or the Committee for National Resettlement (CNR), another peasant-initiated organization, which grew out of CRIPDES. Once communities were settled on their land it was essential to send seed and medicines to the area until the first harvest. Delegations of U.S. religious groups traveled into war zones with supplies and backup letters from U.S. senators in order to get access to the countryside in the "democratic" country the U.S. was supporting.

Low-intensity Conflict (LIC) and *Comunidad*

Santa Marta and Segundo Montes are transformed communities that exemplify women's role in reconstructing and maintaining *comunidad*. The two communities were formed by *campesinos*, mostly women and children, who fled across the Honduran border in 1980. The Santa Marta residents were survivors of the Sumpul River massacre where six hundred were killed, many shot by helicopter gunships strafing the swimmers carrying children on their backs. Salvadoran high command General Blandón referred to the military strategy behind that phase of the war as "draining the sea to catch the fish." The metaphor is precise, though horrifying. The "sea" is the people. The "fish" are the guerrillas.

The Santa Marta villagers, along with other refugees, formed the Mesa Grande refugee camp of ten thousand. Refugees from Morazán fled to Colomancagua, a camp of about ten thousand, with a thousand refugees going to San Antonio camp. The camps were composed mostly of women and children on foreign soil, barren dust really. There were no anona and conacaste trees, no wild gajardo blossoms. In that desert bowl they began to pull together the fragmented mind and spirit of the

---

* The English term "resettlement" is used throughout to refer to the Spanish *repoblación*, which refers to a conscious, collective decision of the people to reestablish their villages in areas ravaged by conflict.

most traumatized, the mothers who lost children, the orphans bereft of playfulness. They opened collective kitchens where *abuelitas* (grandmothers) pounded corn into thick tortillas. Those who could read set up schools. Everything was faced collectively. The men formed shoe and construction collectives. The women's sewing collectives clothed thousands. They distributed sacks of grain and beans given by the United Nations High Commission on Refugees (UNHCR) according to each family's needs.

The catechists from different villages formed pastoral teams that worked in small base communities during the week, then formed a larger congregation for Sunday liturgies. A church of nonclerics was organizing itself and that church was women. Usually the *delegados de la palabra* (delegates of the word) who took leadership roles were men, but it was women who had become the social infrastructure of the *comunidad*, organizing themselves into a community of mothers and serving as the *directivas* of the camp. Women took on a new role. If the war had torn children and husbands from them, closing off parts of their lives forever, it opened doors too. The necessities of survival opened the doors of history to women.

By 1985 life in Mesa Grande had become dangerous. Honduran soldiers, always an unpredictable, menacing presence, had entered the camp, shot three *campesinos*, and wounded children in a raid to find FMLN guerrillas. The refugees understood, moreover, that the military policy of depopulation, which drove them out of the country, was a counterinsurgency tactic that could be countered with resettlement; and they came up with a daring plan of mass resettlement. Together, in their base communities, they sat in candlelight talking into the night, calculating the risks. They looked at the war together, eight years of destruction, a scorched earth military policy that shifted to low-intensity warfare in 1983.

U.S. military strategists, determined to avoid the Vietnam quagmire, changed the nature of U.S. intervention in Central America to the less controversial "low-intensity" conflict. But the U.S. strategy is of low intensity only in its commitment of U.S. troops. Low-intensity conflict is unconventional, undeclared, and virtually hidden. Its destructive capacity is intense and massively dispersed into every aspect of Salvadoran life: political, economic, psychological, and military. It is, according to Pentagon Colonel John Wahglestein, "total war at the grassroots level."[32] Control is a linchpin in low-intensity conflict.

In October 1987 after almost a year of negotiations with the governments of Honduras and El Salvador and with the United Nations High Commission on Refugees, forty-five hundred refugees of Mesa Grande camp collectively decided they were going home. Their resettlement movement is of such spiritual and political audacity that it has been called the Salvadorans' Salt March, after Gandhi's march to the Indian Ocean.

When officials of El Salvador as well as of the UNHCR continued to stall, the Mesa Grande repatriates set the departure date for October 10, 1987, informing the UNHCR that if buses were not provided they would walk back to El Salvador. Their only protection would be a small delegation of North American religious leaders on the Honduran side and an accompaniment team of seventy on the Salvadoran side. The North Americans began the journey with the people but were never able to cross the border with them. This is a description of the event by one of the accompanying international volunteers, Mary Ann Corley, director of the American Friends Service Committee's Chicago office and board member of the National Sanctuary Defense Fund:

The day before the move, President Duarte sent representatives to say that El Salvador could not receive them. It was incredible how they organized themselves. They called forty-five hundred people together in groups talking until midnight. Their decision was still firm. When we woke at 3:00 A.M. there was hardly a sound in the camp, but the people had themselves lined up in the dark, placing their belongings in a long line where the seventy buses would arrive. Everyone knew their community's bus members. Each family carried a wooden box that the carpentry collective had made for their journey — a kind of farewell gift. No one was sure if the buses would arrive.

Just at daybreak we saw the buses come over the hills, and a Canadian volunteer group that had recorded the refugees' song "Pedimos Paz" (We Want Peace) blared the tape over loudspeakers. Then the remaining three thousand began to say goodbye to those who would go ahead — having no idea if they'd ever see each other again. Everyone was crying.

We boarded the buses and traveled up to the first military roadblock. The Honduran military wouldn't let anyone disembark while we waited on the Honduran side of the border. It would be twelve hours before the refugees crossed that border. They sat in the sun baking, and when they had to defecate, the UNHCR representatives gave them garbage bags and refused to permit their leaving the buses in any numbers and only for several minutes at a time. I watched little children sit without moving, holding their one chicken in a rickety cage for hours. The only time the children became animated was when they saw wildflowers and wanted to pick them for their mothers. Most of the children under seven had never seen flowers in that abundance before.

They squealed when they saw a flock of birds close by. In Mesa Grande they saw birds only in high flight because there were no trees.

At the border, the Salvadoran military refused to let international volunteers pass into the country. They also refused the refugees' request to go to San Salvador for a Mass of thanksgiving at Archbishop Romero's tomb at the cathedral before returning to the designated resettlement areas in the departments of Chalatenango, Cabañas, and Cuscatlán.

When the buses were permitted to leave Honduras and cross into El Salvador community *responsables* pulled us out of sight of the commanders to thank us for our accompaniment and solidarity. You never saw the same *responsables* twice — they learned to hide their leaders so that no one could be identified in a leadership role. What irony that they should thank us — we who had received an experience of such impact that it would mark our lives forever. We just wept.

A missionary friend who met the repatriating refugees entering the deserted village of Guarjila described scenes of undistilled joy and sorrow when the refugees took children to the graves of their fallen fathers, sisters, aunts. "This is your land," they repeated, weeping and laughing, "the land of our people." One woman dug up a grinding stone for tortillas she had buried years before. They all sang "Dále, Salvadoreño!" ("Go for it, Salvadorans!"). Then the pastoral team led the people in a liturgy of thanksgiving to a "God who brought us to our promised land, a God who has never forsaken us." In spite of the military patrols skirting their village and the sound of bombardment in surrounding areas, they were home.

Resettlement is sustained primarily by women, children, and the elderly. As Mary Ann's testimony reveals, the decision to resist enslavement is a decision to risk personal annihilation so that a people may live. The people construct the future, which is never simply given but is fashioned as they act, as they risk. Paulo Freire, the Brazilian popular educator, has said: "Existence is not despair, but risk. If I don't live dangerously, I cannot be. But if my existence is historical . . . that means to exist is first and foremost to risk oneself."[33]

Resettlement represents a *campesino* decision to walk, not simply into a wilderness, but into a war. They journey with children and seed in hand into patrolled areas, ringing with sounds that still jolt their dreams — the crack of M16s. They go back defenseless, in order to plant and harvest a corn or watermelon field, to demand peace with their lives, to intercept a war in order to sow *milpa* (cornfields) once again. Resettlement disrupts LIC's strategy of driving *campesinos* from the land into government-controlled camps or the urban resettlement areas of San Salvador to cut off support for the FMLN. The tactics used to drive the people out included indiscriminate bombing, which has helped create thousands of displaced Salvadoran *campesinos*. The intensity of the air war led Alexander Cockburn in 1985 to write in the *Nation:* "The U.S. has been organizing, supplying, overseeing, and in many cases actually executing the heaviest bombing and most ferocious aerial war ever seen in the Americas, and not one coherent report of the extent, viciousness or consequences of this campaign has appeared in any major U.S. newspaper or magazine."[34] The voices in this book break that silence, testifying to the human cost of air wars in an advanced technological era.

U.S. media silence was an objective that low-intensity conflict accomplished. According to a report, "American Military Policy and the Lessons Learned from El Salvador," dated March 1988 written by four lieutenant colonels at the John F. Kennedy School of Government:

> Rather than ignoring the media . . . Senior officers . . . embarked on a campaign designed to educate journalists. . . . Improved reporting has taken the edge off domestic opposition to the American presence in El Salvador and has even contributed to the creation of a modest consensus. . . . (63–64)

In spite of this achievement the lieutenant colonels indict low-intensity conflict as a failure because of U.S. militarists' inability successfully to conduct "the other war," the part of counterinsurgency that uses psychological operations, and civil defense, civil patrols to pacify the civilian population. "The other war," say the lieutenant colonels, "illustrates the cumulative effect of the flawed American policy in El Salvador."

In spite of the lieutenant colonels' indictment, another high-level strategic policy statement regarding the efficacy of low-intensity conflict, titled "Discriminate Deterrence," was drawn up in 1988 by distinguished bi-partisan policy analysts, including Henry Kissinger, General John Vessey, Zbigniew Brzezinski, William Clark, and former Secretary of War Fred Ikle. "Discriminate Deterrence" projects the necessity of low-intensity conflict as the preferred form of warfare in Third World nations for the next thirty years. Deployment of U.S. troops is discarded and support given to a permanent state of military control over civilian governments, which still preserves formal democracy. And this long-range plan was proposed in spite of the lieutenant colonels' indictments.

> Our failure in Vietnam still casts a shadow over U.S. intervention anywhere. . . . [This] and other setbacks . . . have had . . . an adverse

cumulative effect on U.S. access to critical regions, on American credibility among allies and friends. . . . If this cannot be checked . . . it will undermine America's ability to defend its interest.[35]

President Bush's "victory" in the Middle East did much to roll back the loss of U.S. popular support for the military following the Vietnam war. The international "collateral damage," however, suggests that a return to covert military dominance through low-intensity conflict is likely. Low-intensity conflict will become increasingly hidden, allowing the "U.S. government to maintain official silence."

What the Kennedy fellows and the prestigious Washington strategic planners cannot account for as a strategic counterforce to low-intensity conflict is a people's will for liberation. This dimension of national liberation struggles escapes them.

Nothing has removed the peasants from the land. Not A-37 Dragon-fly bombers, which can deliver 750-pound bombs; not AC-47 gunships mounted with .50 caliber machine guns; not Bell "mike" helicopters, which can put a bullet in every square inch of a football field within minutes; not "total war," the military system's preferred form of warfare used in the slaughters of the early 1980s; not low-intensity conflict, the sophisticated form of U.S. counterinsurgency; not the rise of ARENA and the cutting off of access to the countryside for all international delegations. Despite forced removal, government camps, the demoralization of seeing so many driven to exodus, and the hunger and harassment suffered by those in the resettlement areas, the peasants are on the land, struggling for another harvest.

The *campesinos'* identity is tied to the land. The nation's own sense of itself is tied to the peasants; they, by their faithfulness to the land and to each other, preserve national identity. They carry in memory the symbols of the land — corn, the ceiba and ocote trees. And the peasants themselves have become symbol. The burning ocote signifies the flame for freedom that consumes the peasants. In spite of technologically destructive firepower directed against them, they have burned brighter than the furnace of war. The *campesinos* preeminently fulfill Jose Marti's prophetic admonition at the turn of the century, "Now is the hour of the furnaces, only light should be seen."

Lupe

We are the blood of the earth
the seed that fell into the furrow.
Chan, "Love Poem II"

Lupe's story is the story of her family's escape from the purges in the Aguilares area following Father Rutilio Grande's assassination. But it is a story of danger that seems without end. When I took this interview, Lupe spoke of her town as the town of her deliverance. Yet, three months after this interview her town was bombarded by the Salvadoran Air Force in an attempt to dislodge FMLN guerrillas who held the town during the November 1989 offensive.

Amid chickens and children, Lupe had explained to me that she would have to continue making atol (a liquid corn drink) with her daughter during our interview. When the taping session began her husband left the room but listened in a side room. When he saw that Lupe was distracted by squeezing the thick maize through cloth, he quietly took over her task and worked with his daughter making atol for the next two hours.

In the past fifteen years, during the death purges, Lupe has seen her brother, a delegate of the word, murdered; her husband and brothers fled to the hills where they slept every night for five years; her sister was captured; her home was surrounded by soldiers; she was interrogated by a member of ORDEN; her daughter's godmother was assassinated; her husband's cousin was killed with machetes — by "chopping off parts of her body, starting with her nose." Yet Lupe remained in the village with her husband, five children, her mother, and her sister-in-law, refusing to quit her clandestine Bible study meetings with the base community.

I was born in Tres Ceibas near Suchitoto. That's where I grew up. My husband lived in a valley very far from me. For the feast of Flores de Mayo [a May celebration of the rosary] I went to the home of my husband's grandmother. I was fourteen, very young. I saw him and he saw me. My aunt said to me, "I think he likes you," but as I was young, I gave it no importance. But I felt something in my heart that set very well with me.

He didn't speak to me directly, nor I to him. But when I was fifteen, he began to speak to me. He was older and had other girlfriends. But I was afraid to accept him as my *novio* [boyfriend] because I was young. My parents said, "Maybe he won't marry you but just leave you pregnant. He may not respect you!"

But when I was eighteen we married, and we've been married twenty-one years. My husband had one and a half *colones* [$.30] in his pocket when we married.

We were married at the time we began to work for the base Christian communities in the mid-1970s. We formed these communities with Father Rutilio Grande. All of us, mother, father, brother, and sisters, worked in the base communities. My brother was killed. My brother worked as a delegate of the word. After they killed Rutilio they came after my brother. September 22 is the anniversary of my brother's death.

My mother still feels his death, and we try to encourage her so she doesn't feel so sad. My mother's brother was a delegate of the word. He was killed when he went to the burial of a friend. They killed him in a cemetery in Guazapa.

The National Guard attacked many of us. I was pregnant with my youngest child when we had to flee. The men took the body of my uncle amid flying bullets back to Tres Ceibas. My grandmother, who is eighty-four years old, was seventy-two then. We were afraid she'd have a heart attack seeing her son carried away. She saw this tragedy, but had great faith in God and was able to live through it. The reason she survived this well was that people told her that her son had served the community generously. He had never made excuses not to serve.

But the situation became more and more terrible. It got to a point where our young people would be taken by the military. So our people began to say to our youths, "They're coming, they're coming! Flee to the hills!" My brothers, sisters, and husband did not sleep in our house but in the hills instead. For five years they slept in the hills. All of our people began to flee but I stayed behind because I had five children.

One of my sisters was captured in 1979 and I couldn't leave. I participated in the base Christian communities and I also worked in Aguilares with three-day Bible study conferences. Once I was a participant in a conference where a man arrived along with some religious women. He was an informer for the death squads. During this time of persecution he knew me and I knew him. He followed me to my house and said,

"Listen, give me your husband's weapons."

"He doesn't have any," I said.

"Yes, he does. Where is he now?"

"He's taking our sick child to the hospital right now." But I only said this as an excuse. Actually he was in the house all the time playing with a top with the children. He'd just arrived back from two months in the hills. Some people came by and warned my husband to get out.

Then a group arrived at my house and said, "Hand over the weapons. Hand over your *cédula* [an identification card]."

"There it is on the table," I said.

We had been warned that they would send the women into houses and surround them. That's when I told them to go into the house and get the *cédula*.

"So you're the one who meets with your uncle who has taken courses in medicine," they said.

"It's true my uncle can give injections and deliver babies. He is at the service of the whole community."

"So you're going to be meeting," they said. They meant our Bible meetings. I said no, that I had no time for such involvement because of my small children. I denied this involvement. We had to bury our songbooks and Bibles because if they found them it meant death for you.

They killed many people. They killed my husband's cousin, who had a small child. My husband's cousin thought she would not be taken because of her child. But they took her and left her child at a house. Then they killed her with a machete by chopping off parts of her body, starting with her nose.

Our houses were made of grass and clay tiles. They set fire to our house. Everything was burned. We had put our clothes on the clay roof to dry and they were all burned also. Seeing our houses burning, we gave thanks to God that we were not burned ourselves.

Then we heard reports of friends who had been killed. They came to kill my daughter's godmother. The death squads came and demanded to be fed and my daughter's godmother was fixing them dinner. Then they took her away to kill her, leaving her little daughter crying and crying in the house.

I haven't told you about threats to me yet. I don't know how I felt when they insisted I was meeting with subversive groups. I denied it, but inside I prayed, "God help me to defend my children." I felt my body didn't exist, that I didn't exist. I felt great pain in my stomach.

They kept demanding and I denied everything, especially when the informer accused me. He had a toupee and a special sport coat and a cowboy string tie. He had some wool things on his arms. The people knew he was an informer.

I denied I was involved in these meetings. I kept asking God to free me, to free me. Nearby I heard shooting; perhaps it was those soldiers. When the informer heard shots he left. I felt great anxiousness. The same day they put a rifle in my mother's stomach. They accused my brothers of also being involved in these meetings. My mother denied this saying, "My children aren't involved in anything." Then they said, "The next time we come through, if you don't hand over your children we will kill you."

Just three of us, my mother, my sister-in-law, and I, stayed in the house that night. The others were in the hills. I didn't have courage to go to the hills, to leave my children. I said if they kill me at least it will be in the house. My mother said, "Isn't it better to go to another town?" She knew a neighbor called Trinidad, who had a brother who lived here as a catechist, a good person who would not refuse us.

So we left with my children, my mother, and my sister-in-law, but my husband wouldn't come. He said, "No, I won't be a coward. I won't leave my people." My brothers and father and husband stayed behind. So we came here but always with the thought of them up there. While living here I went back two or three times to bring them things, sugar, food, knowing they couldn't go into town to buy food or they'd be captured and killed. When we went the first time there was no problem. We left at night. But the second time people told us not to return to the city because an army battalion was active. All night long we heard the shooting. I decided not to go back.

Finally in 1983 my mother-in-law and others left. They were the ones we were bringing food to. My family members, brothers, father-in-law, and sisters left one by one until all returned here. My father-in-law died here as an old man.

To walk through the hills, especially with children, is impossible. But when we came here we felt sad because we didn't know anyone. We thought people would say, "Those people are from up there," and they would kill us.

And so I was afraid. I don't know how to express this. I had participated in the church and now I could not. I felt...I don't know what.

In the year we came, we saw a group of helicopters shooting close to here. We felt isolated, without our normal surroundings. But little by little we met people and began to form communities here. That's how we came to participate in the Christian communities. They asked me if I wanted to become a missionary. At first I felt like saying no, but then I said yes. I kept wondering, Will the same thing happen here that happened there? With a bit of fear we began little by little. Now I feel strengthened. I feel that all this community is mine. We know all the communities. I feel very, well, happy. The profound fear I'd felt is gone. The Gospel of St. Matthew says to us, "Happy are those who are persecuted, who are spoken evil against, happy are those who are killed because of my cause. They will be given the kingdom."

St. Matthew gives us great strength. If we die for this cause I feel at peace. This fear I felt before has left me now. We have so many people we know right now. Everyone in the community is my family, like my own, as if all of us were a family without fear.

I want my children to stay involved with church, not to follow another ideology. We have a daughter twenty years old. We advised her not to continue her relationship with someone involved with the army. This boyfriend didn't ask about her family. He came here and I asked about his family and he said they were involved with the National Police. This young man had been in a military operation in Chalatenango where many were killed. He said they took three young men who denied they were involved. He said the *muchachos* [guerrillas] died with their fists raised. That doesn't surprise me because the *muchachos* have their own promise to keep just as the soldiers have their promise to keep. They didn't die by selling out.

I told this young man if they die because of their commitment, it is the same commitment that you make. He said he saw all those demonstrations of UNTS [a coalition of the popular organizations]. I told him they were demanding justice, even though people told not to speak so frankly because it's dangerous. I told him that UNTS was demanding good prices for grains for basic living. But he said "These people always have weapons." My daughter was listening, sitting there, and she shook her head. After he left she called him a *pendejo* [son of a bitch]. I said to her, "Think this over carefully, daughter. Remember what we suffered. Don't you remember how we trembled up there? How your father, brothers, and aunts were not at peace?"

"That's right, mother. I hadn't thought of all that and also he had not told me all this." My daughter stopped her relationship with him. Later she had another boyfriend. His father worked for the police.

I told her, "Look, his father works for the police." She said, "Yes, but that's his father, not him."

It could be true; the son doesn't necessarily follow the path of the father. But I keep praying to God that she finds a man not involved in the military, or whose family is not involved with the police.

She broke up with this man. Now she is with a man whose parents were both killed. They were in the teachers' union called ANDES. They lived in Chalatenango and then they transferred to Apopa, where the father taught classes. Informers accused him and he was killed. I told her to marry when she's ready to, but to someone who has suffered as we have suffered. This boy is very conscientious.

What worries me the most right now is the forced recruitment, because I have two sons and a brother. They recruited my brother, but a nurse in the parish with connections with the air force was able to get him out. I'm always worried when my boys don't come home. I go out looking for them.

When I know they are recruiting I'm afraid. With the new government, ARENA, there's no way to bribe them. I don't want my children to kill our own people. If they go to kill, what are they defending? This is what is affecting me the most right now.

My family was Catholic. My grandmother was a *rezadora*, one of the official prayer persons. Six of us grandchildren would go travel with her all day. I felt a great desire to follow her example. During the two-week missions, we'd reflect on the gospel and I felt my faith being formed. But when they killed Rutilio, that's when I felt a desire to go out and do this work even more. One time when we went to meetings in Aguilares,

I thought, Why do they kill people for going to meetings to struggle for justice? The struggle inspired me, and now I hope to continue. My job in the mission now is to go visit communities. We go to neighborhoods where there is no base Christian community to help people form one.

The faith I feel is that through our communication the people will become conscious of the situation in our country. Many people don't understand the sin and injustice we live in, and we hope to help them become aware.

To coordinate the mission we meet every Wednesday to discuss the Saturday meeting. We discuss questions of the gospel and our objectives in the communities we will visit. We consider whether a community is losing its spirit. If it is, we want to go to give it life.

We haven't yet reached a point where we can discuss women's issues. But in the meetings we always show that women's roles are as important as men's. Women were stepped on, marginated the most. If women saw their value they would be involved in the work of the church rather than with advertising, which does not respect their dignity but uses their bodies to sell more. I think all us women should get together and refuse to buy products from companies that use women.

Venancia

If in the face of the empire
you surrender hope and truth
who will proclaim the mystery
of utter freedom?
—Bishop Pedro Casaldáliga,
"Questions for Climbing and
Descending Mt. Carmel"

This is the story of a mother and catechist's sojourn in charred and stinking villages; her involvement in the conversion of a Salvadoran commander sent to annihilate peasants; her exile, then return to pastoral work in a war zone and her involvement with the Congregation of Mothers. The significance of the Congregation of Mothers is not that they stood up to the army and the archdiocese — two bastions of male power. The Mothers' historical significance is their invention of themselves as the crucible of communal survival. They constituted themselves materially to feed and heal the community and spiritually to reinvent hope and resistance.

Since the time I was very small, I have wanted to be involved in pastoral work. Maybe when I was thirteen or fourteen, since my grandfather was the *mayordomo* of the church, I had a chance to be very close to the temple of my people. Through the rosaries, the celebrations of the word, and the Masses with my grandparents and other family members, my desire to teach catechism grew. At fourteen I began to give catechism classes, without any real instruction, but just from what I had heard or had read in a few books about catechism. I had learned the rosary and I liked praying it very much, being in church and sharing the holy rosary with the community. I was also involved with home visits. Although I wasn't clear about what pastoral work meant, I've discovered that, without realizing it, perhaps since I was quite young, I've been doing it. I always felt drawn to it and in my heart I always felt close especially to the poorest people. I spent a lot of my time visiting the sick.

As I grew up, at about sixteen or seventeen years old, I became more interested in the Bible. For me reading the Bible was to discover new things, although without any pastoral orientation since the only pastoral care we received was from a priest responsible for visiting our village who had a very traditional mentality. Some of the songs with liberation themes began to appear at this time — in 1975 or thereabouts. The songs were not too explicit, not as strong as they were later, but they were a change from the very old songs like "Forgive Me, O Lord," and "Praise to the Most Holy," which didn't have a liberating message. But when the new songs began to appear, this traditionalist priest got upset because often we wanted to sing the new songs at Mass. We felt restricted when he was present, but when we were alone, just with the community, we could sing these songs. This was when we began to read some Bible verses and even to celebrate the word. In my village it was only when the priest arrived every six months or once a year to celebrate *la fiesta* of our patron saint that the community all gathered. But little by little we began taking the initiative to develop the celebrations of the word and a more formal catechetical program, which included teenagers. We reflected on a text, people made some comments, and that was it. These weren't really reflection groups like the ones formed later on. I think that my pastoral work as such began in this period.

In the mid-1970s a new priest came into our area. This change was very fruitful because the ideas of this new priest had a very positive effect in all the communities, not just in my village but especially in the smallest villages of this part of Morazán. More serious pastoral attention was given to reflection groups, to home visiting, to catechesis — not just of children, but of adults as well. That was how the people began developing a Christian consciousness and what could be called a political consciousness. From about 1975 on, people were working in an organized way. When the government and the armed forces became aware of the existence of this movement, when they realized what was being born in the countryside, they responded with fierce repression to try to stop this movement for liberation.

Large-scale military operations began, attacks against Morazán. One of the largest military operations we experienced took place on October 5, 1980. More than five thousand troops with powerful weapons and air support were involved in order to stop what was being born. They had a scorched-earth policy. The army arrived in a community and killed every living thing, including the elderly, the children, and the animals. This was really terrible and many communities were massacred in this way. When other communities saw what the army had done, they began to flee. They left their houses, their animals, and their few belongings. The only thing they were able to save was their children.

My village, Via Rosario, was the only one of the local villages that had never had an army post. So the people, seeing that this village was free of soldiers, that the enemy wasn't here, chose this place as their refuge. More than six thousand people came here. It's a very small village but we were able to put the people up in schools, in the corridors, in some big houses, and also in the churches and chapels; there was an evangelical sect called the Assembly of God in the village. All these places were full of people. The army was advancing through the villages, killing people, and its destination was Via Rosario. When they got here, the troops began to mortar and bomb the surrounding area. Everybody thought that this village was going to be destroyed by all the air power that was used against it. The ground and the houses shook because of all the explosions. Almost everyone was crying because we didn't know what was going to happen but we knew that in other communities all the people had been massacred.

When the troops arrived, they killed about ten people. But when they saw the large number of people they were surprised because they saw that there weren't any weapons. There were people, people who were refugees, people from other villages. We got everybody together, the refugees and the people from the village, and we all gathered for an assembly in the town plaza. The number of people was enormous, more than six thousand. So we met and there was a problem. The people in the church didn't want to leave. So the soldiers surrounded the church because they thought that that was where the weapons and the guerrillas were. The troops aimed at the door and told the people to open it. The people opened the door and a procession of people began to leave the church. The children were crying and when they saw the soldiers they clung to their mothers' skirts. All in all it was a terrible sight. When the soldiers saw so many people, they calmed down because they realized that the people weren't guerrillas.

The Conversion of a Commander

The person who had called the assembly in the plaza was a captain named Francisco Emilio Mena Sandoval, who is now a commander in the revolutionary forces with the nom de guerre "Manolo." At that time he was commanding a battalion. He told me later that when he saw this terrible sight he felt very badly and that that day the Lord opened his eyes and made him realize that the poor people were right to organize and that the troops were giving them only bullets. They weren't really listening to the people. We were all gathered in the plaza, and Mena Sandoval said right away that it was late and that all the women and children could go home. Only the men had to stay. There was a long list with notes and the soldiers kept the men so that they could check whether they were on the list. It was late by then but the soldiers checked all the men's names to see if they were on the list. Some were, and they and others who didn't have identification were separated from the rest along with still others who were simply refugees.

Some of the young people from my village had formed a group so we could serve all these refugees in some way. We went every day from house to house to ask for corn or other food to try to get enough to give all the refugees at least a little to eat. Mena Sandoval found out about this group and came looking for us. He came to my house and asked about the people in the village. We told him that the people were starving. They had come looking for refuge in our village because this military operation was devastating them, it was killing every living thing, and the people had the right to save their lives. That is why we had given them shelter and were trying to find ways to feed them.

This man proved to be very compassionate and told us that he felt the suffering of the people and that he was criticized by others in the armed forces who said that he, too, was a guerrilla because he had "advanced" thoughts. He told me that he wasn't a guerrilla, but that he felt the suffering of the people. "The people are asking us for bread and what we're giving them is bullets." Then he said to me, "I'm going to order that food be sent here, and tomorrow."

There was also another captain who was called Juan Cruz Cruz, who felt the same as Mena Sandoval. When he saw so many people, he began to give anti-dehydration fluids to the children. I think he knew a lot about medicine. A lot of people were sick from hunger and many children had even died of hunger. This then was the sad situation when the food that the captains had requested for the people arrived. We began to coordinate how the food should be distributed.

While there was a sector within the armed forces that understood the hardships of the people, there was another sector that was very cruel. All they wanted to do was to kill the people. So there was an intense conflict within the armed forces. They even came and had meetings at my house several times. They had big arguments, very heated disputes. Many times we even began to think that they were going to kill each other because one side was defending the people and the others said no, that all these people were guerrillas and it was necessary to kill them. So even within the army itself there were these two ways of thinking.

We were working with the sector that was sympathetic to the people and the next day they again called us to receive the food supplies. But when we went to get the food we discovered that there were several dozen men who had been tortured and that this torture was being committed by soldiers who were against the people. They had been there all night torturing the men. The soldiers had put boxes and furniture on top of the men and soldiers kicked and jumped on top of them. When we saw this scene, when we saw the men's bloody faces and their tied hands, I didn't have any enthusiasm discussing what we were going to do with the food supplies. My house was close to this place and I ran to my house and began to cry. I said to myself, "How is it possible that they bring food, but at the same time they're killing the people?"

Mena Sandoval was very worried and asked what had happened and if we were distributing the food. I was very upset but also angry and I made up my mind that if they were going to cut off my head, then let them cut it off. I said that I wanted an explanation. "If with one hand you're giving a little bread to the people while with the other hand you're killing them, I won't be an accomplice and I don't want to get involved in this food distribution." He got red in the face because he knew what we had seen, all those people who had been tortured. So he told me, "I want you to understand that I don't approve of this killing. I'm against it and all night I argued with the others. It's not necessary to beat them. But you have to understand that within our army right now there are savage beasts who don't care about killing other human beings." So there was a lot of arguing and the army stayed for about two weeks in our village.

The soldiers who wanted to kill the people always went around insulting and yelling and threatening everybody. And the people came to us, the young people's group, to see what we could do. One day one of the officers told the people to get out of the village immediately, that they had no reason to be there. The people came straight to us to report this. It was about six in the evening and there was a big rainstorm and the people were crying. So we went to look for the officer who had told the people this and began to protest. We told him that he had no reason to expel the people, that we who were from the village had given them refuge and that the army didn't have any reason to expel the people.

Furthermore, I told him, "If you expel them, if they go back to their houses, what houses are they going to find since all the houses have been burned?"

He was furious. He took a good look at us and turned around and left. He went to complain to Mena Sandoval that there were people who were scolding him and protesting and that those people were us. So Mena Sandoval came and told us to be careful. It was military men like this that he had spoken about before. They were the savage beasts.

So it was very tense until the army left the town. The people stayed, but little by little as the days passed the people left and began to rebuild their little farms and their huts since all their houses had been burned.

But this wasn't the end of the repression. The Red Cross managed to come to the town and distribute food every month. But the soldiers from the security posts took away the little that the people were given. The soldiers threw it in ravines. They trampled on the rice and they threw the milk and the oil into wells because they said that all this food was for the guerrillas.

In spite of all this repression, life in the communities went on. But later, when the popular organizations of the FMLN began to appear in the area and to establish war fronts, all these communities joined the FMLN. Those who were able to become combatants joined the guerrillas and those who couldn't began to flee to other countries since there were always military operations in this area. So all these communities joined the FMLN and the elderly and the children went to Honduras and other countries for refuge.

The repression against the people of the villages didn't end. The military operations were constant. With all this repression they wanted to make the people leave. So all of us from the village decided to leave when we saw the massacres that were being committed by air strikes. And not just by planes. In addition the security forces from the surrounding villages came with people we call "ears" [stool pigeons] to take people out of their houses at night and kill them. There were even times when they came at five in the morning and would take eighteen or nineteen people and kill them right in the patios of their houses. People who really weren't involved, even some people who weren't sympathetic to the guerrillas were massacred.

A whole family was murdered just because one son was married to a woman who had a sister who was part of the revolution. The army came one morning when the woman, who had five children, was preparing bread. The soldiers asked her where her guerrilla children were. And the woman said, "Excuse me, but I don't have children who are guerrillas. My children are working and right now are bringing firewood to bake the bread." While the soldiers were talking to the mother, four of the children arrived, each with a load of wood. The children laid the wood on the ground and the bursts of gunfire hit them. The kids didn't even know why they died. They just fell over on the wood. And the soldiers said to the woman, "Because you denied that your children are guerrillas and because you gave birth to them, we are also going to give you the death penalty." They began to cut off her fingers, her breasts, her ears, her hair. They did whatever they wanted to. I know this because we went to recover the bodies. At five o'clock we buried the woman and her four children in one grave. Only an eight-year-old child survived, and the soldiers even told this eight-year-old, "If you become a guerrilla, the same thing is going to happen to you as happened to your brothers." This child ran away and became insane. Today they say that he's still around but is out of his mind.

When all this repression took place we were forced to leave the village and we went to a city. From there I went to another country and there I continued to be involved in pastoral work. But I began to see the people's struggle more clearly and I couldn't feel at peace. It's true that I was working with Christian communities, doing pastoral work, but I wasn't content there. I remembered everything the people in Morazán had experienced. I especially remembered the time in 1980 when all the refugees arrived in my village. It was a profound experience because I saw each person's courage and commitment and conviction. Perhaps some people didn't have a clear vision of a new society but they did see clearly that it was possible to construct a new society. I admired above all the Christian conviction with which the people understood the process. This helped me a lot. Being away I was able to see everything more clearly. I had a broader view of the whole situation in my country and as a result I couldn't be at peace where I was. It was this consciousness that made me return because I couldn't imagine being so far away and knowing that my people, the communities, the Christians, were continuing on the path toward something new. So I returned to my country to try to make my small contribution.

I returned to Morazán in March 1983. Father Rogelio was in the war zones of Morazán and also Father Miguel and some catechists who had remained in the communities. Some of the other catechists had joined the revolution. We began to work in some of the communities, having celebrations of the word and doing catechetical work, but the work was quite unstable since there was always a lot of persecution, a lot of repression, and this destabilized the Christian communities, which had to move from one place to another. There wasn't enough stability to do pastoral work. But as the years passed, after '83, '84, '85, the situation began to be more stable and people began to work in their communities. This was when we began to think in terms of planning a pastoral program.

Some catechists joined to form a pastoral team. Before, the catechists had been isolated in their different parishes. The priests had gone to visit them, but they had still been quite isolated. When we began to visit them and to show that even in a war zone it is possible to have pastoral care and that this pastoral care is necessary, all these catechists were encouraged. They joined to form a pastoral team to provide pastoral care to the communities of northern Morazán. The evangelization went in stages. We began with celebrations of the word and with catechesis for the children. Also very important were home visits since now the objective of these visits was to develop confidence in the people and to make them feel that they weren't alone, that the church was present in this time of pain and suffering but also of hope. The people found this helpful. It was a consolation and a source of hope to know that the church was present and was helping to explain what was happening at the national level.

The Women Organize

From 1983 to 1985 we organized celebrations of the word, catechesis, reflection groups, home visits, and presacramental talks. But later on we talked about how important working with women was since the majority of those who attended these activities were women. We felt that it was possible to develop a pastoral program oriented toward women. That's how the idea was born for what we now call Congregations of Christian Mothers for Peace and Life. We began to form small groups made up entirely of women. This was very interesting because it was also a result of the great problems that the communities had. There was no education, no health care. The basic cause of this situation was the repression, including the bombing, illiteracy, and hunger. We met to reflect on the word of God and to see what it was saying to us and what we could do in our communities. The women were enthusiastic and said, yes, it's important that we meet and get motivated to act. Another source of inspiration was Matthew 25 where the Lord says, "I was hungry and you gave me food, I was thirsty and you gave me something to drink, I was a stranger and you gave me shelter, I was sick and in prison and you came to visit me." This is how the congregations were born.

When the women began to struggle to do something for the community, for example, to start a school, to organize a community supply of medicines, to begin a small baking or sewing workshop, all of this was dangerous. But when the women started doing these things, by their actions they spoke to the men, telling them that united it was possible to overcome the repression. Then over a period of months, as the women were working and even confronting the armed forces and demanding their rights, the men also began to discover that they too could do something in their communities. That is how the community *directivas* [councils] were born, as well as what we now call PADECOMSM

[Coalitions for the Development of the Communities of Morazán and San Miguel].

These congregations have to some degree defeated the government's policy of repression against the zones controlled by the FMLN. For example, the government decided to put a military cordon around the war zones to prevent the passage of all kinds of goods and food supplies. In response, the women took the initiative of going to the archbishop's office and asking him for food supplies. And if the small amount of food that they bought wasn't permitted into the area, then they saw the need to find appropriate ways to see that this food reached their communities. They went to the archbishop and, in spite of neglect on the part of certain bishops who didn't want to give them food, after twenty-two days they succeeded in obtaining food supplies. Of course, they knew in advance that to try to bring in food was to provoke an intense struggle with the armed forces. However, this didn't deter them and they began the task.

On their first trip, they returned with four truckloads of food, but they had to wait because they were stopped in Gotera. Gotera is the capital of Morazán, and there is an army barracks there with a commander. They met with him and requested permission to bring the food into the zone. The commander, Colonel Vargas, began to insult the women. Furthermore, he said, it wasn't the archbishop who decided whether the food could enter the zone; he was the one who gave the orders. Then the women began to tell him that they, too, had the right to struggle for the lives of their children and that they weren't going to go and beg on the streets or die of hunger. They would rather die than see their children die. As a result of all this discussion, they succeeded in getting Vargas to say okay, they could bring in the food. But he didn't say it willingly; he gave them the permission angrily. When the women arrived at the army checkpoint, the last checkpoint before entering the zone controlled by the FMLN, the soldiers were surprised that Colonel Vargas had given permission for the trucks to pass. Their instructions were not to let more than a very limited amount of supplies through and, so it didn't make sense to let four trucks pass. Vargas had written a note to the soldiers at the checkpoint telling them to please search all the supplies box by box. But the soldiers got very angry and began to insult the colonel. They said that they weren't going to search any boxes and that the trucks could proceed. So the women happily got back into the trucks and were able to pass the checkpoint.

Every month they had the same argument, but the women always succeeded in carrying out their plan. Each of their successes was a cause for reflection, and sometimes we had celebrations for their victories over the repressive policies of the enemy. The women, on the basis of their faith, were making this struggle for life and peace their own.

In regard to what has motivated me and encouraged me at difficult times during all these years in this war zone, well, as a result of this experience, I've discovered the gospel more. Not perhaps in the Bible so much, but in each *compañero,* in each brother and sister that is here struggling day and night for life. Each of them testifies to the gospel that Christ speaks about in the Bible. And this is what fills us with conviction and faith and hope that we are going to achieve this new society, which is a path toward what Christians desire most, the Reign of God. At many difficult times, like when the repression is at its worst in the war zone, during bombings or combat or when the enemy is near, you find strength in seeing the other *compañeros'* courage and generosity. You find the strength that inspires you, too, to be one of them.

I think that the church of the poor in Latin America and specifically here in El Salvador began to be born many years ago. It began in those little reflection groups, and if we look back to the 1970s, or perhaps a little earlier, the late 1960s, we can see how that seed has been growing. That's why I now have much more hope in spite of the difficulties that, as a church of the poor, we are encountering at the institutional level of the church. Those in the hierarchy see these small groups as a parallel church. However, I think that it is they who are separating themselves from this new experience of church, from this recovering of the gospel values that Jesus brought us. I think, as I mentioned earlier, that this is the hour of God, this is the hour of the poor.

It's also the hour of the rebirth of that church that Jesus came to found, of the true church. And it is our responsibility and a great challenge to all the poor, to all the Christians of El Salvador. It is a challenge to the institutional church, which often obstructs our progress. During all these years we have felt how the institutional church acted as a brake and has been an obstacle to our development and our progress and our accompaniment of the liberation process. I believe that we have a responsibility as the church of the poor and as Christians to be immersed in the revolution; this is a way of getting closer to what all Christians deeply desire, the Reign of God. I think that a Christian who is not part of this revolutionary process is also not part of the search for the Reign of God. I believe that the way we can be a church of the poor, the way we can be Christians, the way we work for the Reign of God is only through being part of this history, part of the revolutionary process. In short, it's the people who make this history.

We must admire the many *compañeros,* those Christians communities who joined the political struggle. They continue to cultivate these gospel values. For example, in the war zones, you can see that this kind of community exists, that this kind of generosity exists. In the people who struggle for a new society you find the values that Jesus brought us. And at the same time they are doing what Jesus asked of us.

Women are rising up in our communities. They are waking up and they are recognizing that as human beings and as women they are capable of making a contribution equal to that of men. As women and Christians or pastoral workers, we have a very big role to play since many communities need this motivation, this increased awareness, to go forward in the liberation process. And also in politics we, as women, have a very important role, since over the years our ability has been increasing as we have gained experience. For example in the war zones many women have told us that the majority of the women who are there are *campesinas* who sometimes don't know how to read or write but who nevertheless over the years have attained an impressive level of development.

Looking at it from a Christian point of view gives us the strength and hope to continue this pilgrimage. In the exodus the people of Israel increasingly demanded their liberation from the pharaoh. The pharaoh became more and more brutal. He treated the people worse and so did the overseers who punished the people more and gave them more work to do. As the people increasingly demand their rights, as the people are organizing both in the countryside and in the city, because that's what's happening, this ARENA government is getting more brutal. They can't discover that the solution is to give the people what they need; rather they think that beating them more is going to destroy their combative spirit of struggle. I'm hopeful because we have seen over the years that neither massacres, nor abductions, nor torture, nor prison have stopped the people. There have been almost ten years of war. And these ten years speak to us. In these ten years God has been present in all those brothers and sisters who are in the mountains, who are in the cities, who are in the prisons. Even those who are in graves continue speaking to us, telling us that, yes, it's possible. Because they can't silence this voice of justice.

If we are in the hour of God, the hour of the poor, perhaps this isn't only for the Salvadorans but is also for the whole world. Our situation in El Salvador isn't speaking just to the Salvadoran people but to the whole world. Through this situation God is speaking to the people of the whole world and is calling them to conversion. I think that the strong voice of God has been heard during these ten years and my call as a Christian is that you North Americans reflect very deeply on the Gospel of St. Luke, the tenth chapter, the story of the Good Samaritan. I think that this is what El Salvador needs and also what you as Christians need: to become brothers and sisters, to make ourselves brothers and sisters so that we can rise up and walk on the path toward the Reign of God.

Hortensia

Besides coffee
they plant angels
in my country.
—Claribel Alegría,
"Documentary"

The farm cooperative named Buen Pastor (The Good Shepherd), where Hort-
ensia lives, lies behind a clump of ceiba trees. The land is open and verdant,
burning with stillness, broken periodically by a sweep of sonsonate birds
across the milpa. Rising in corners of the blue distance are the Guazapa and
Salvador volcanoes. The land is Aguilares, where farmworkers began organ-
izing and dying fourteen years earlier. It is where Hortensia began a struggle
in 1978 that carried her from San Vicente through years of flight, to settle-
ment camps, to another farm cooperative attacked by the army, and finally
back to where it all began in Aguilares. The community at Buen Pastor is a
remnant of women, children, and the elderly. There are only six men. But
they have returned to the land to harvest, to remember, and to resist.

I guess I'll start by telling of our suffering. I feel my earlier history is not
interesting. I don't remember very much. What I do remember a lot of
is when I was an adult woman and we began to suffer. I'd rather start
right there.

I have five children. I had my first in 1970. You know the situation
here has forced us to leave our children in order to serve the people. My
sixteen- and eighteen-year-olds are not with me. When I had those girls
I had a home, poor but peaceful. It wasn't like now. We were always
poor but we didn't know why we were poor. Later I discovered that, as
women, we had to give so much for a minimum wage. When I had these
two girls I had to leave them alone to go out and pick coffee to support
them. This was in San Vicente.

After a long time of working like this, about the time my oldest was
eight years old, we discovered it was necessary to struggle. We realized
the poor worked very hard while the few became rich. We saw a need to
protest. The protest began on the coffee farms. When we saw that things
were unjust, we workers organized to say the salaries weren't just. The
first *campesino* protest was in 1978.

Because of this struggle some plantation owners paid a little more.
We were a lot of women with similar experiences and when we achieved
a small success the movement grew. At the same time, these men, these
owners of all the capital, realized that our workers couldn't be exploited

anymore. So they sent out civilians; we called them vigilantes. They were also workers. After them they sent the army in. Then it all began.

After that they wouldn't let us work. There were huge offensives, invasions. At first in these army operations they only looked for men. When we saw this we sent the men away and we women stayed in our houses with the children. At that time the soldiers still had respect for us, they left us alone. There was no sexual violation. But when they realized they couldn't find the men, they were filled with rage and they would rape the women and then leave them. After that we were very afraid.

I was worried when I heard that the army was coming and we were there alone as women. We wore old clothes so they would leave us alone. We even uncombed our hair. Some young girls were killed because they resisted rape. At that time we gathered to discuss what could be done. We agreed that the next time they came we would all flee to the mountains.

On June 4, 1981, we fled when a military operation came into San Vicente. Airplanes, and on land — it was so awful. I don't even want to remember. We gathered the children and the old people and headed like ants up the volcano. That operation caused a horrendous massacre at a farm where we stopped as we fled. We were up on a hillside above the farm when the soldiers started to fire. Out of desperation some people threw themselves down the ravines.

We had to flee under a rain of fire, knowing others were being massacred. We began a long walk that, because it was our first experience, was awful. People were carrying sick people in hammocks. I remember an old fat woman we were carrying. But when the army closed in we had to leave her because there was no alternative. Those women who took a change of clothes for the children couldn't bring it. We had little food and even what we had, had to be left.

From that day on we began walking hours and hours, sometimes entire nights, often under mortar fire. It was so difficult when the children cried from hunger. The children didn't care about the army's presence. Some women, because of their care for their children, had to be left behind.

This was from 1981 to 1984. The flight. We lived under plastic in the open. Our lack of experience in where to find refuge made us more afraid, and we were afraid to come down from the mountains. We had no rest from flight from one operation to another.

During those years I tried to work for others. I worked three years with young children in that suffering. I worked for the army that our people had formed. I made clothes for the *muchachos*. It's difficult work physically. I'd often work for hours without rest, then walk for hours. I began to develop an infection. I became so sick they told me it was better that I leave. Reluctantly I left and went to a refugee camp in San Salvador with my youngest children. I was there eleven months.

101

In the refugee camp there were many young people who could work. So we selected those who could leave to make spaces for the sick, old, and newly arriving refugees. Several families got together to move to Tres Ceibas near Apopa to establish a settlement.

There were sixteen families. Most of us were women. Almost all were widows. We had decided ahead of time that we would work collectively. It was the only way to get the work done. Because women's capacity is not like men's, it was better to work collectively. It was one more experience of suffering together and living together.

As women we've suffered much repression. Women have been captured. We're always waiting for this to happen. For example, in September 1986, just a year after arriving at Tres Ceibas, seven people were captured. Some were kept in Mariona prison, some were released. The amnesty of 1987 and pressure from our people gained the release of some. In July 1987 others were captured, including Sister Ana. Thank God they were released because they captured a French nurse and Spanish women with the others. I was the last person captured, on June 13, 1988. They took me from my house and held me for three days at the army barracks in San Carlos and three days in the National Guard. In those three days I was tortured but I was released because of the people's protest. Many mobilized for my release.

This is what women suffer and will continue to suffer while this war continues. The only peace we have is the peace of the cemeteries. I feel happy to share this small testimony. We have suffered because we demanded our rights — simply for thinking it was unjust to leave our children and to work for a minimum wage from sunup to sundown. That's the origin of our rebellion — simply that. The poor majority simply asked that we share in what the minority has gained through our labor and sweat.

During the interrogation I was accused. Everyone who is captured is accused of collaboration or belonging to the guerrillas. I was blindfolded, stood day and night, stripped naked. This is humiliation for women. I wasn't beaten. But psychologically I was tortured. They took me in and made me watch them torture the men. They took off my blindfold and I watched them crush the men's fingers. Then they took a metal wire that they shoved up into a man's nose as far as they could. They tried to terrorize me into speaking to them.

They kept the air conditioning on day and night, so that we were freezing. Interrogation is constant all night, all day. They told me they made seventeen pages of my testimony. At the end they brought in a declaration and said I would be released.

"What's your position in the archdiocese?" they asked. "Why is the archdiocese so supportive?"

I told them I didn't work for the archdiocese. So they told me they would take off my blindfold so I could sign the declaration. Nothing in the declaration was prejudicial so I signed it. But then they told me to put the blindfold back on. Then I could feel the presence of many in the room. They tried to convince me to collaborate, wanting assurances. They promised to care for my children and to pay me. They said I could pass them information when the guerrillas came past our place.

But I told them I couldn't do that. I said I might suffer from the other side if I did that; at least, that's what I told them. So then they released me to the government human rights commission, where there was a lawyer who quickly took me away.

My hope is that even if those of us here don't see a new society, our children will. Perhaps we women have the same rights as all, the same dignity as a man, a child. The poor, the rich, all are human beings with some dignity. This includes our worst enemy. In terms of dignity we're all equal. The call I would put forward to all women is to *own their dignity*.

My sister was captured with her two children. They tried to take her away but the boys wouldn't let her go. They were thirteen and fourteen and so they took them also.

My sister and her whole family were killed in 1981 in a bombing. My youngest brother was killed in 1976 in San Salvador. My other brother was captured and later his body was found on the road. This was May 1976.

[*Hortensia's mother listened to the whole testimony while standing behind her.*]

I'm thirty-nine. My mother's seventy-five. I think our energy comes from God. My mama is stronger than I am. She has a lot of strength. She's had real suffering yet she keeps going. She makes her own decisions and sticks to them. When they captured me she took my kids. I think she has the stronger faith.

[*Hortensia's mother spoke: "One time they put all the women in a school during an offensive. We were still sitting there at five o'clock. I got up on a bench and looked out and I said, 'I'm going.' They said, 'No, no.'*

But they took heart from me and that night we were in our houses eating. Then the muchachos let one bomb go and that scared the soldiers good.

Those soldiers always did that — put us in a room. Then they went and took our animals and crops. That's what they were doing — taking our things.

3

THE HOUR OF WOMEN: WOMEN'S ORGANIZATIONS

Photo by Jim Harney

Who clamor for
a more kindly world
a world with less hunger
and more hope
—Claribel Alegría,
"From the Bridge"

Hunger is the other war, a bomb exploding amid children, heaving up
broken bodies and the ragdoll living. The women live this war, rock the
starving babies too weak to howl, carry the tiny white coffins out to
the fields. Almost 60 percent of Salvadoran children die before reaching
the age of five; 73 percent of children under five are malnourished; Salvadorans have the lowest caloric per capita intake in Latin America.[36]
In El Salvador, where health conditions rank "with such countries as
Bangladesh and Haiti,"[37] the mothers are fighting for a "world with less
hunger." Every "glass of milk" campaign in the resettlement zones, every
crop planted in Usulután or Morazán, every collective kitchen formed,
is an act of war in a nation where counterinsurgency objectives attempt
to seal off the countryside by starving out resettling communities.

And these statistics predate ARENA's rise to power or the November 1989 insurrection that left San Salvador's infrastructure ruptured,
the meager public social and health services exhausted. Church social
service programs, like clinics and food distribution centers, limp along
without personnel, many of whom were forced underground or, in the
case of foreign missionaries, deported.

A 1988 women's study claimed that two million Salvadorans (out
of a population of 5.5 million) live in extreme poverty.[38] For mothers,
extreme poverty, as opposed to "normal" poverty, means that they will
bury one-quarter of the children they bear. The cycle of infant deaths
runs this course: because of the mother's anemia (this condition affects
one-third of the population), the weakened mother cannot breast feed
and the parasitic water-and-maize mix that she gives her baby will cause
diarrhea that she cannot control because she cannot afford to purchase
antibiotics. For women, extreme poverty means working as market vendors, selling vegetables or Chiclets to feed their children who play in the
streets nearby from dawn to dusk.

Extreme poverty for the eight hundred thousand desplazados (persons
displaced by the war) means living in a plastic-and-wood hut along the

106

railroad tracks and sewage ravines skirting San Salvador. Extreme poverty means giving your twelve-year-old over for domestic servitude in the city, knowing she may be sexually abused by the father or sons of the household and fired once she becomes pregnant. In the countryside extreme poverty means working on the large plantations for a few months a year, toiling ten hours a day in the pesticide-drenched fields while laying the babies in hammocks if there are trees near the fields.

In conditions of such radical poverty, pregnancy becomes a terror rather than joy. The death rate at childbirth is five times higher than for U.S. women. There is one maternity hospital in the country, and in 1977, *before* the war, there was one doctor for every 3,700 people and one nurse for every 4,000.[39]

Those who "clamor for a more kindly world" have made their own hope. Women have independently formed, or joined, popular organizations that could address these fundamental problems of survival. The popular organizations trace their genesis to the mid-1960s when farmers' collectives began to form in the countryside. But it was a teachers' union, formed in 1965 and led by women, that galvanized a national strike and burgeoning resistance in 1968.

ANDES, the national teachers' union, which is 90 percent women, went on strike on behalf of the nation's school children as well as the women teachers' need to feed their own children. The strikers shut down the schools and the Ministry of Education, which they occupied for fifty-eight days. Unable to break the strikers' solidarity, the government turned to its enforcer, the military, who opened machine-gun fire on the strikers, killing two and wounding many. Thousands were arrested.[40]

Mothers of the Disappeared

By 1977 the Committees of Mothers of the Disappeared entered Salvadoran history. These organizations, formed to protest the disappearance or imprisonment of children and husbands abducted by the security forces, walk in the international footsteps of organized widows, with the stubborn Mothers of the Plaza de Mayo in Argentina and the Grupo de Apoyo Mutuo (Mutual Assistance Group) in Guatemala. These mothers step into streets of terror without hesitation. Even after 1981, when military violence matching Nazi brutality cleared the streets of popular movement protest, one group remained walking and protesting in the blood-stained squares and plaza of the capital. It was the Mothers in their black dresses, white kerchiefs, and plastic sandals. Widows and mothers who have nothing left to lose are a front of the war difficult, if not impossible, to break. The U.S.-Salvadoran counterinsurgency experts were never able to outmaneuver the presence and international appeal of the Mothers of the Disappeared. When the Mothers were awarded the Robert F. Kennedy International Human Rights Award in 1984, their representatives traveling to Washington to receive the award were refused visas by the U.S. embassy in El Salvador because the Mothers had allegedly committed "subversive acts."

This "subversive" organization began at the instigation of Archbishop Romero, who advised a group of mothers who sought his help to organize to demand information about their disappeared relatives. Few of these women are educated, most can't read or write, but they — along with the nongovernmental Human Rights Commission, Socorro Jurídico, and the Archdiocesan Legal Rights Commission — have been a beacon drawing terrified peasants and workers who have lost relatives to testify. Their courage, in spite of the security forces' Jeep Cherokee parked outside their offices, has remained a constant light in the darkness of the past decade. For ten years they have documented torture, rape, and mutilation, matching pictures of once comely teenagers with the bruised and smashed bodies dug from shallow graves. They have held sobbing survivors and offered the solace that can be provided only by those who have lived with the unimaginable loss and desecration of one's child.

The Mothers rescue passion for life from the engulfing state passion for *thanatos* — the god of death. It is the Mothers who construct an ethic of life, not in words, but deeds. Here is an ethos that defeats the ethos of state terrorism. And this ideological struggle for power takes place within crucial public space. As Michael Taussig has shown, "the space of death (which is the space also of immortality, communal memory, a connection between generations) is particularly important as a site of struggle in the colonized areas of the world, and this struggle is of necessity ethical."[41]

The Mothers engage the military and paramilitary in a struggle over meaning. By refusing to accept death as an end to life, to history, they refuse to allow the triumph of the national security state and reject the state's authority to interpret death's significance. The Mothers determine not only the meaning of the loss suffered by the people but they do so as the immediate recipients of such finality. They insist on naming the dead and disappeared. It is a contest the state cannot win. The bearers of life confront the destroyers, refusing to let the dead be anonymous, refusing to allow the mutilated thousands to remain "subversives" and "terrorists." The mothers carry pictures of their disappeared relatives to attest to a particular violation of the body, a beloved humanity, their child or husband. In a "nation of graveyards" the dead do not remain statistics or terrorists or anonymous — a psychological objective of counterinsurgency. The Mothers, according to Jean Franco, "were able to interrupt the dominant discourse and resacralize the body."[42]

The Mothers have countered another military objective — the creation of powerlessness in the face of massive, institutionalized terror. Relatives of the mutilated, the disappeared, no longer dependent on the state for verification, have organized representatives to investigate murders and abductions and to comfort relatives. The Mothers' social presence maintains historical continuity and moral transcendence. The Mothers have opened and held the space for survival and life's continuance through a refusal to remain private in their grief, or to be driven into insignificance and invisibility that is the traditional role for women.

Remaining public has been costly. In 1989 alone, Co-Madres, one of the three groupings of Mothers, had their office attacked and eleven Co-Madres and two international volunteers working with them were arrested, beaten with rifle butts, and subsequently tortured. Their offices were also bombed, and medicines and all their office equipment were destroyed. By December of 1989, only a month after the November offensive, the Co-Madres reopened their offices, the first of the Salvadoran human rights groups to reclaim public space. In January of 1990 a Co-Madres representative presented a legal document to the director of the Treasury Police that requested that they return all confiscated property taken during the November 15, 1990, seizure. First Brigade Commander Colonel Francisco Elena Fuentes told the press that they had confiscated explosives used to carry out terrorist actions.

No longer simply the "mothers of terrorists," the Co-Madres are accused of being terrorists themselves. The "loco" women are taken seriously, are targeted as "fronts" for the enemy, as the enemy itself. And this is because they refused invisibility, challenging the notion that women belong to the private sphere and thus demythologizing "natural" masculine and feminine roles.

The Mothers' tenaciousness is legendary. One Co-Madre's story typifies their audacity. María Teresa Tula was picked up by security agents twice. She was tortured and the second time gang raped before being sent to Ilopango prison. When international pressure against El Salvador's human rights abuses intensified, President Duarte decided to grant political amnesty to prisoners in Mariona and Ilopango prisons as an act of "compassion." Duarte's amnesty also legally forgave all crimes committed by the military from 1980 onward.

María Teresa Tula was one of the prisoners who, after eighteen months, would be released from Ilopango prison under the amnesty decree. Duarte's advisers had prepared a press conference where prisoners would be publicly granted official amnesty. A bevy of Salvadoran reporters, with *gringo* journalists bored with the predictability of it all, awaited the public formalities. Photographers clicked off a first round of photos when the president declared his intention to express mercy. María Teresa, a tiny mother of six, sat on the stage inattentive to the president's words. When it was her turn to receive amnesty, the press laconically prepared to report "her gratitude to the president, etc." Instead the small, trembling hand grasped the microphone as if to steady herself. Then María Teresa denounced the Salvadoran government for its violation of human rights, for supporting a military that had caused so much death and suffering. She couldn't be stopped. The president and military attachés were helpless watching the press corps combust into motion. Then María Teresa Tula left the stage and went to another woman cradling an infant. She returned with the baby held above her head saying to all present: "Here by the grace of God is my son, Alejandro, born in Ilopango, the seed of violence, named for joy. Proof that good comes from suffering."

AMES: The *Campesinas* Said Yes

By 1978 the Popular Forces of Liberation (FPL), a member organization of the FMLN, founded what would grow to be the largest women's popular organization, the Women's Association of El Salvador (AMES). Focused on the needs of the marginalized such as market women, domestic workers, and shanty dwellers, AMES sought to organize a base among the poorest of urban dwellers and *campesinas*. AMES developed the first social theory about women's specific role in the liberation process. Early documents indicate theoretical differences within AMES and an evolving theory on women's social role. In a document published by AMES in 1980, "Participation of Women in the Revolutionary Process," a social analysis of women's condition never specifically mentions gender oppression, claiming that men's and women's interests are the same:

> Women have joined the struggle because their fundamental and immediate interests are the same as those of men. They are of the same class and therefore their enemies are the same: imperialism and the oligarchy along with their governments and armed forces.[43]

Within a year of that document a representative of AMES delivered a paper in Costa Rica at the First Latin American Research Seminar on Women, identifying men's and women's relationship to production as the same but insisting that the movement's social theory had ignored "reproductive relations, thus minimizing women's concrete oppression and social contribution." The paper concluded: "The parties and movements of the democratic left have not, in general, dealt with the problems of women.... Their pronouncements are limited to the realm of class struggle.... This omission assumes that feminism and socialism are opposed to each other."[44]

The liberation of women, according to the AMES document, had not previously been seen as integral to the national liberation struggle. Thus

110

women's struggle is left separate, individual, and privatized. Without a recognition of men's and women's different gender interests within the liberation process, women's liberation becomes social and collective only *after* "the exploited sectors have their liberation in some distant and unpredictable future." The revolution's goals, according to the document, seek to change the relations of production but not to address the relations of reproduction: "Society is to be overturned economically and ideologically, but nothing is said about changes in the family, which is the sphere not only of consumption but also reproduction of labor power, as well as the strategic locale for the transmission of ideology."[45]

The theoretical challenge of AMES to the revolutionary movement was grounded in practice. Beatriz, an AMES organizer who in the late 1970s worked in the FMLN's central front (Chalatenango, Cabañas, and Cuscatlán), describes revisiting one of the zones a year after she organized women in the area: "I came across one of our *compañeros*, a *campesino* who was there making tortillas. I felt so happy to see how much improvement he had made. He had been one of those who had been reluctant to let his wife participate in AMES."[46]

And where was his wife while he was attending to household tasks? She was with other *campesinas* organizing protest marches by day and stealing chickens to feed the community at night. Some 150 women gathered at the San Vicente volcano, then streamed into surrounding villages shouting for an end to the napalm and white phosphorous bombs that scarred and maimed their children. And this protest took place in the midst of a war! Beatriz tells the story of the women's predawn raid on a large poultry farm. With the help of the local militia, the women "expropriated" seven thousand sleeping chickens to feed their community.

These triumphs occurred because AMES had organized women to refuse an ancillary role in the struggle and because the war itself was opening new space for women. For *campesinas* the embodiment of future freedom is experienced in the midst of war's suffering and demands. The women's solidarity with each other, their ingenuity in raiding farms and marching in contested terrain, rewrites the cultural text. Husbands who feed their families by pounding maize into tortilla patties for two hours each morning bury, like a stinking corpse, a cultural taboo. AMES was opening another front in the war.

Women's freedom in those early years of popular government in the FMLN-controlled zones was enabled by the people's commitment to popular democracy and a construction of daily life that was collectively organized, mostly by women. In spite of the war's losses, women were for the first time gaining a hold on their own authority and power. Children raised in the common houses saw both their parents active in local government as well as household work. While it would be too sanguine

111

to say that women's social role was transformed, the effect of popular government on women's lives has been irreversible.

The Train of History

> That new sectors of women are advancing to join in the work shows that the process is not stuck, that the train of history is moving forward and will not pass us by.
>
> Linda Fuentes — UMS, 1988[47]

In the early 1980s the same force that sought to silence Archbishop Romero was unleashed against those who were "organized," with barbarous force. Just as Romero had predicted, he was resurrected amid those masses, never so palpably as in 1986, when the popular organizations resurfaced more organizationally and politically advanced than in the early 1980s, and more strategically astute.

By the mid-1980s President Duarte's economic austerity programs, international pressure to control military repression and allow some "democratic" space, and the government's inability to respond to the catastrophic social problems following the earthquake gave rise to a rekindling of open popular protest and organizing. The murder of Herbert Anaya, director of the Salvadoran nongovernmental Human Rights Commission, sparked an intensified popular protest. Because of the blood purges of the 1980–83 period, urban resistance lagged behind resistance in the countryside. When workers, united to form the National Unity of Salvadoran Workers (UNTS), the popular movement had resoldered its weakest link.

Aware of the strategic significance of UNTS in uniting popular resistance, the Salvadoran military bombed the FENASTRAS office on October 31, 1989, *during* the peace negotiations between ARENA and the FMLN. The bomb injured thirty-six people and killed ten, including UNTS spokeswoman Febe Velásquez of FENASTRAS. A few months before her death Febe had described the unity that was crystalizing in the popular organizations, as well as the growing militance of the organized:

> We feel the repression increases our ability to organize and to take more combative actions. For example, the last time the military attempted to abduct workers here in front of the office, many of our people, unarmed, rushed the military and physically rescued those who were being taken away.

Even as the popular movement was increasing its willingness to confront ARENA, there was internal pressure to "democratize" the process. "We needed more popular democracy within our movement, to have more meetings with our bases of support. In the past months we have undergone a renovation of the base."

November 1989 was decisive. Popular organizations were a front representing a new militance and unity. The FMLN, according to Commander Villalobos, saw the war as "90 percent political and 10 percent military."[48]

Women's organizations were born in the midst of the popular organizations' resurgence in 1988. The sector that had been all but invisible in the early 1980s when AMES was organizing health clinics and schools in the countryside blossomed in the late 1980s. And this occurred in spite of increased attacks on popular organizations, with specific infiltration and repression of women's groups. Just as the right had consolidated power by 1989, the popular movement had likewise advanced. The popular movement developed internally to the point of recognizing, though not fully embracing, the claims to liberation not only of the poor majority, but also of women.

By 1983 AMES had "disappeared" due to repression. Women who survived, who didn't go into exile or join the armed struggle, reemerged in the work of the popular organizations in 1984. Corina is one of three former AMES organizers who came together to organize women. They formed the National Coordination of Salvadoran Women (CONAMUS) in 1986. CONAMUS promotes and maintains a health clinic and legal aid clinic, both of which treat and assist women who are victims of domestic violence and rape. Additionally they produce a weekly radio program that publicly encourages women who are victims of abuse to seek these support services.

Corina, who is president of CONAMUS, claims that the early organizers were faced with two problems: (1) how to talk about feminism in a way that responds to the needs of war; (2) how to form the organization without creating a division in the popular organizations with men.

Even use of the word "feminism" is unprecedented, given the popular identification of feminism with bourgeois First World women's interests. Although CONAMUS echoed the advanced theoretical challenge put forward by AMES in 1981, the war has so demanded concentrated popular resistance that few women could wrestle with its implications in terms of the sexual division of revolutionary labor.

In spite of the war's urgency, CONAMUS does not hide its feminism. It insists that consciousness-raising groups are aimed not simply at empowering women to struggle for the *pueblo* but also, as Corina put it, to "become aware of the conditions affecting our gender." Indeed some of the strongest criticism of CONAMUS has come from other women's groups that consider the necessities of popular unity in a national liberation struggle an imperative superseding the struggle for women's rights. "Some say we can't divide the popular organizations," says Corina, "but we are clear in this and we must treat gender issues seriously even if men

113

are not supportive. We don't have to wait until the triumph in order to take women seriously."

Still Corina insists that gender cannot take priority over class because such a position would remove women "from our historical conditions right now." As examples of this error Corina spoke of women's groups that put forward radical feminist theories but were unable to gain a mass base and have therefore remained organizationally small and isolated. CONAMUS, which has three thousand members and has committees on mental health, legal rights, and health and family assistance in marginal communities, believes their task is "to expand and unite with the popular organizations." According to Corina, "We must give in a little and if we are to broaden our base and address women's real needs, we must bring in the most marginalized women. We hope that women's participation will lead to social transformation."

The "giving in a little" seems to refer to the way CONAMUS should function in relation to men in the popular organizations, with whom, says Corina, "we try to treat the issues in a friendly manner." But within the women's movement Corina is unflinching in challenging an analysis that gives priority to class oppression as the galvanizing organizational principle. "This is our difference with other women's groups," says Corina. "Some women's groups say *war* is the first priority." Such a position "lacks dialectic because it fails to work on the two conditions shaping women's lives — class and gender." Moreover, such a theory fails to heed the lessons of history, to take account of the assessment of Nicaraguan women. Their lesson, according to Corina, is that women must always struggle for women's freedom within the revolutionary process because there are *no* guarantees that women's liberation will be given after the triumph: "In the case of Sandinistas they have had ten years in which the whole structure has changed politically, consolidating the Sandinistas. But women continue to have limited participation."

CONAMUS has been instrumental in publicly raising issues of sexual violence in a milieu where "since we've been small we've been taught to associate honor with sexuality. Thus sexual violence is a violation of one's honor and cannot be expressed." Other women's groups, such as the Institute for Research Training and Development and the Unity of Women, University of El Salvador (MUES), have also opened legal assistance and health clinics for women and children who have been victims of domestic or sexual abuse.

Since 1986 several new women's organizations were formed. Although not organized under one umbrella group, several have formed a broad coalition. These groups have produced a booklet, *Guía para las organizaciones de mujeres salvadoreñas* (Guide to Salvadoran women's organizations, September 1989), which lists the following women's or-

114

ganizations: the Association of Salvadoran Women (AMS) with five thousand members, the Association of Salvadoran Women (AMIS) with thirteen hundred members, the Movement of Salvadoran Women (MSM), the Association of Salvadoran Women (ADEMUSA), the Women's Committee of the National Federation of Salvadoran Workers (COFENASTRAS), the Organization of Salvadoran Women for Peace (ORMUSA), Unity of Women, University of El Salvador (MUES), and the Institute for Research Training and Development of Women (IMU).

While women garner scarce resources to open legal assistance and social service clinics for abused and raped women, they — like the other popular organizations — have become targets of security forces because of their opposition to state repression. Both the CONAMUS and AMS offices were watched by security forces while we interviewed women organizers. Isabel Ramírez of CONAMUS was followed by a Jeep Cherokee and then detained after the murder of Cristina Gómez. "We don't know when another *compañera* will fall," she says apprehensively. It is within such a context that the First Women's Encounter acknowledged that the war was both transforming women's lives and thwarting further advancement.

Women's Demands: The Other Front

The crisis and the war are in practice transforming the traditional role of women. . . . [The war] has focused the energy of the various organizations on dealing with the conflict, postponing . . . resolution of the problem of social disequality.[49]

The First Encounter of Salvadoran Women drew together six hundred women in September 1988. Five women's organizations, including one not already described, Committee for the Unification of Salvadoran Women (COPROMUSA), produced a document at the end of the three days that advocated a negotiated settlement to the war and called upon the Salvadoran government to control food prices, grant lines of credit, provide schools, housing, and dispensaries, and establish unemployment insurance. The gathered women committed themselves to work for specific reforms, such as a revised family code, protective rights laws for women and children, equal pay for equal work, regulation of domestic work, child care centers, and cooperatives for women market vendors.

Isabel Ramírez of CONAMUS offers a brief summary of the economic roots of women's poverty and apparent productive marginalization:

Ten years ago a pound of beans cost thirty centavos but now it costs six *colones*. Before the war, about fifteen years ago, the whole eastern part of the country, the departments of Usulután and San

115

Miguel, produced grain. But as a result of the famous Alliance for Progress and the oligarchy's decision to produce export crops for profit, the textile industry was established. So now we have the largest textile factories in Central America. This opened new horizons for the oligarchy.... This was the origin of the increase in the cost of living.

Both cotton and coffee crops displaced the staple grain that sustained *campesinos*. Women, forced to work on the plantations, are paid lower wages than men and must support their output with their children's labor. The owner gives the women one meal, "tortillas with beans to give to five children." Desperate, the mothers emigrate to San Salvador, but because they traditionally are the ones with the least education the women end up marginalized and driven to the streets to sell produce or, the most frantic, to sell themselves. "So here they walk for miles and miles with baskets on their heads in order to earn even 5 colones for a pound of beans."[50]

The women's labor force in Latin America, concentrated in the informal sector, has rarely been recognized as an essential productive contribution. Women constitute up to 70 percent of the informal sector of the economy. Economist Kathryn Ward argues that women's participation in the informal economy demonstrates "women's essential contribution to the operation of the capitalist world economy at several different levels."[51] In addition to reproducing the labor force, "women are further contributing to capital accumulation through their informal sector participation that has enabled the capitalist class to pay lower wages to family members employed outside the home."[52]

With El Salvador's economy in its greatest crisis in a hundred years, with unemployment at 50 percent, with a massive flight of capital that has left the economic infrastructure in tatters, the fact that the economy has not totally collapsed seems miraculous. But the economic saviors are hidden. Two primary sources of capital influx have been exiled refugees and women in the informal economy. Refugees — particularly in the U.S., where there are approximately one million Salvadorans, living clandestinely, and working in the U.S. informal sector — send money back to relatives in El Salvador. An unofficial estimate speculates that a total of about a million dollars per month enters the Salvadoran economy.

Women workers in the informal sector, those market vendors considered unproductive, are a stabilizing prop that has bolstered a nearly collapsed economy. "Unpaid female labor ... subsidizes the capital accumulation process through (1) unpaid domestic labor in the home and (2) the informal labor market."[53]

116

Without women's work in the informal sector, starvation, homelessness, and high mortality rates would propel social collapse in the form of demoralization and chaos. Women's productive as well as reproductive work is structurally essential to the economy.

Although this insight is not shared by government economists, the emergence of an organized informal sector is a threat to Salvadoran elites. Just as UNTS and other popular organizations have been targeted by the military, so have the newly formed organizations of marginalized women. On August 14, 1988, the First Assembly of Marginalized Women met in San Salvador. Their demands were for fundamental rights taken for granted in the First World. To say they demanded better housing, employment, health care, food, and a cessation of forced military recruitment is too abstract. Here are the demands in their own words:

We do not have proper housing. Our houses are shacks made of tin, cardboard, plastic, or other junk. Some of us live in *bajareque* [houses of mud and sticks]. We have to wrap our children in plastic so they will not get wet. The land where our shacks are located is next to the rivers filled with sewage. We live with fear that the rains will carry our homes and children away.

The health of our families worsens every day. We cannot pay private doctors because we only have enough money to survive. We almost never have steady work.

Nutrition is always deteriorating because our low wages do not permit us to buy enough food....Many of our families survive by picking through the garbage for food, or simply by resigning themselves to waking up and going to bed hungry. The government, instead of searching for a solution to these problems, creates other problems for us, such as forcing our children into military service. Our sons...do not even know why they are fighting or why they die.[54]

These marginal women, the "nobodies" of history, possess the hour. The voice of marginalized, peasant women rings from the shantytowns of San Salvador to the cane fields of the *campo*. No longer silent or compliant, women are another front of the war. Mothers have reproduced not only the new revolutionaries but new men and women — young women with an emerging self-possession that neither crushing poverty nor ten years of mass state murder has destroyed. The new women are their mother's gift to the revolution.

América Sosa

Rachel has found you out, Herod,
and you will have to answer for her desolation.
—Bishop Pedro Casaldáliga,
"Ode to Reagan"

I interviewed América Sosa, a mother of seven, on May 10, which is Mothers'
Day for Salvadorans.

América went to the U.S. in 1985 to open a Co-Madres office in Washing-
ton. She was offered sanctuary by the Dumbarton United Methodist Church.
On March 28, 1989, U.S. INS agents entered the First Congregational Church,
where the Co-Madres office is housed, and arrested América for "illegal en-
try." On January 30, 1990, former U.S. Ambassador to El Salvador Robert
White appeared as a witness on behalf of América's request for political asy-
lum. When INS agent Bingham testified that Co-Madres could be a front
for the FMLN (the exact charges made by the Salvador government) Robert
White countered, "They are a front for civilization."

I was born to a single mother. I didn't know my father. It is part of the
culture of poverty that young women are taken advantage of by men and
become pregnant. When she was sixteen years old my mother became
pregnant by a married man, but she believed in him, not knowing he
was married. She decided not to stay with him because she felt betrayed.
She then worked with single mothers.

My mother is an orphan. She was working with these single women
in a bakery. I lived with her and ate with these women in San Miguel.
The women wanted to adopt me because my mother was young and
an orphan and couldn't provide for me. Also, my father wanted to have
custody. But my mother didn't want those women to adopt me because
she said "only criminals give away their children."

So my mother fled when I was three months old. We went to the
countryside. My mother found a man who would support her and I grew
up with this man until I was nine years old. I studied until second grade.
My mother then returned to the city of San Miguel, where she found
relatives and through them obtained work in San Salvador. We suffered
a lot. She worked cleaning homes and they didn't want children. So she
had to leave me with strangers. She earned about $10 a month. The cost
of living was cheap, so it wasn't so difficult. The woman she worked
for got an interview with a presidential aide to ask for a scholarship
so that I could study. I received a scholarship to study in a Catholic
elementary school until sixth grade. When my mother took me out of

school, I studied at night and worked in a medical laboratory. When I was sixteen years old, I met the father of my children. That year, at seventeen, I married.

The tradition in Latin America is that when someone has a boyfriend, people think they're having sex. People were criticizing me, and my mother was concerned that I'd become pregnant. So she made us get married because she didn't want to hear criticism. But the criticisms were just not true. After our marriage my first daughter was born. I felt the marriage was forced, because we weren't ready for marriage although we loved each other. Living with him I learned to love him. These social prejudices still exist but they're changing. People want you to get married as a social protection.

I lived for twelve years in San Salvador. I had nine children; two died after birth. Then our family moved to San Antonio Abad, an area on the outskirts of San Salvador. During the 1970s I began to gain political awareness because my children's teachers began a strike.

I began to participate in the base Christian community in 1973. We reflected on our national life from a Christian perspective — looking at social injustice in light of the papal encyclicals. What happened at Medellín was very important. The church that identifies with the poor was born; it was the birth of liberation theology. Within that context we began to understand the historical significance of our struggle. We began to support the struggles of workers and students.

In 1976 persecution against the base communities began. The community named me a leader of the pastoral team. We prepared talks for Christian initiation together with Padre Guillermo Deneux from Belgium. There was a group of forty adults and the youth groups. Guillermo took eight of the youths and youth leaders to study more in depth. I learned about the social context and the differences between rich and poor. The rich had private clinics while the public hospitals lack fundamental health needs. The houses of the rich are different from the houses of the poor. There are differences in education between the rich and poor. In work we couldn't even approach the owners of the company, only the manager, because the rich owners were far removed, vacationing in Europe and the U.S. while the workers couldn't afford even a radio. We were always in debt, with our children suffering from malnutrition.

Our awareness came about through our readings of the gospels. In 1977 Father Guillermo was captured with a young catechist. The Treasury Police beat Guillermo and exiled him. The catechist was tortured for seventy-two hours.

Then we felt the persecution against our communities of faith. We began to take security measures; we thought there were spies in our community. But we went forward in our work, continuing a clinic and a

119

cooperative store. Sometimes Archbishop Romero came to offer Mass. We gained confidence from his encouragement to maintain our faith in spite of persecution.

In 1979 Archbishop Romero named a priest for our community. Octavio Ortiz came to San Antonio Abad. Because we had already organized the base communities, the priest did not have to start from scratch but simply be the coordinator.

In 1979 we planned for the first retreat of our youth. It began on a Friday and finished on Saturday. During this retreat, Father Ortiz was assassinated with four youths. These four youths were outside cleaning up and the women were in the kitchen preparing food when the army fired bullets killing the boys. Then they burst into the retreat house with a tank. The priest tried to stop the tank but it just ran right over him.

The nuns, sister, youths — everyone was captured. When two youths tried to hide in the water pipes they were badly beaten. They didn't want us to see them killed so they rounded us up and captured us. Meanwhile they took the boys up to the roof and put guns in their hands to make it look like they were guerrillas. Then they called the media, who took pictures of the boys and called them terrorist communists to blame the church for fostering subversion.

This began a fierce persecution against the leaders because the police took the files that named all the base Christian community participants and leaders. They assumed anyone with pastoral responsibilities was a communist leader.

When I returned from work at a sewing factory, on the day of the killings my children met me at the bus stop to tell me not to return because the police had asked for me three times. The next day I looked for a room to take my children to because they would have captured me.

My sister, who was a volunteer in the clinic, was on the death list. The soldiers destroyed the clinic and it remained closed for two months. The army was placing notes under the door of the clinic warning the doctors and workers that they would capture them. My husband was not political. He was scared. He warned me to stay out of trouble.

My children, husband, mother, and younger brother didn't participate fully in the base Christian community. The participation of women is an individual decision.

Even though it was against the will of my husband I still participated. When we had to flee the community, that's when problems began with my husband. "This is what happens when you get involved in this shit," he said.

Before my fourteen-year-old son, Juan, was captured, my husband and I separated. Juan was in the eighth grade and a volunteer for the

Green Cross. He was tortured and held for ten months. The younger children stayed with my mother and husband. The oldest children stayed with me. I took Marina and Joaquín with me. Beatriz was already married.

When Joaquín was captured, his father went to visit him in Mariona prison in November 1980. When my son was sent to Mariona I went to see him twice with false papers because I was on a National Police list.

My husband's capture was related to the capture of my son. After Joaquín had been in prison for ten months, he was released and went into exile in Mexico. [Joaquín was a member of the nongovernmental Human Rights Commission.]

My husband never participated in anything, but he was captured in 1981. My husband was tortured. [Her husband died two weeks after his release; the security forces admitted he was the wrong man.] That was when I joined Co-Madres. I knew of the mother's committees from base Christian community work. When both my son and husband were captured, Co-Madres assisted me.

We were taught how to resist torture, how not to give into the torturers' demands, to act like we didn't know anything. The members of the Christian communities told us what we would face and how to hold out.

They taught us that when we were blindfolded and all our strength and identity were gone, we should think of beauty. We had mental exercises to think not of family or children but of beauty.

I joined Co-Madres in 1981. In the first few years I was part-time with Co-Madres because of working to support my children. As the situation became more violent the clothing factory where I worked closed. I was older, and it's difficult to find work if you're over thirty-five years old. The owners were trying to keep out unions, and since I was a union member, it was hard to find work. In 1984 I was offered full-time work with the mothers. I worked with the refugee communities, visiting mothers and families in refugee settlements: Domus Maria, San José de la Montaña, the archdiocesan refugee camp, the Basilica, San Roque, San Jacinto. In these camps are people whose families were persecuted or killed in bombings.

In November 1984, we received an invitation to receive the Robert Kennedy Human Rights Award, but we couldn't get visas. Only the Co-Madre who was in Canada could go to receive the award.

Before women weren't involved in popular organizations. It has been the repression that has taken us outside our homes. Women have claimed the right to work and to organize. Women are part of the *directivas* and have taken leadership even among men. Women have begun claiming their most fundamental rights.

121

The Hour of Women: Women's Organizations

A woman I admired was Marianela García Villas, who was a friend. She was an attorney, middle class, a Christian Democrat, a member of the legislative assembly. When she realized the Christian Democrats were not protecting the poor, she renounced her legislative position and joined the popular organization of the Social Christian Democrats with Rubén Zamora's party. She worked with the nongovernmental Human Rights Commission in 1979. Despite increasing repression she continued to show that the Salvadoran army was using chemical weapons and napalm. She went to Guazapa in 1983 to obtain proof of the use of chemicals to present to the United Nations. When she was leaving Guazapa with photos and other evidence, the army attacked her jeep and then tortured and killed her.

A mother fears her children will be taken away. We can suffer poverty and sickness but we cannot bear the taking away of our loved ones. Separation of family is our fear. Seventy percent of single women are solely responsible for their families. They must care for and protect their children. Mothers must provide shelter, food, clothes, education. They have to defend their children like female lions. It is a struggle simply for a child to reach the sixth grade. Women struggle in trade unions, risking their lives to be organizers.

The most inspiring part of my commitment is the community. The *campesinas* have been a source of inspiration for me. I was a child of the *campo*, but we had food and clothing, even if we had to exchange chickens for clothes. I worked with *campesinas* in our cooperative and realized that some Salvadorans suffered even more than we did in the city. When I learned about their lives I knew the conditions of my people had to be changed. That's why I am now considered a subversive, because I wanted things to change for the poor.

I wouldn't talk about revolutionary hope but about the liberation process with all its limitations and logistical deficiencies. To be able to continue seeking freedom is the hope that sustains us, to confront oppression and obstacles. I believe an individual who has hope and faith can triumph. In this struggle of the Salvadoran people, those who initiated the struggle and have fallen are the ones who have triumphed. They may not be here physically, but spiritually they live among us. Those who join the struggle now take their place.

Rebecca

At the end of the road they will ask me
Have you lived? Have you loved?
And not saying a word I
will open my heart full of names.
    —*Bishop Pedro Casaldáliga,*
        "Heart Full of Names"

What does it mean to be an organizer on behalf of peasant women in El Salvador? Rebecca's life is one answer. What she doesn't reveal in her life story I learned from others.

Rebecca has been a target of the army and security forces because she organized a farm collective of women. The women took over abandoned land, wrote proposals for seed money, and planted corn fields. She lives in an all-women household with her four daughters and mother. Her husband was killed, one daughter was captured, and she was captured three times herself. The last time she was captured it was because she had a party for one hundred children to celebrate the Year of the Child. The party aroused the army's attention. They arrested her, assuming that because of her history she was up to some kind of organizing.

⚔

My name is Rebecca. I'm the secretary of the Association of Salvadoran Women (AMS). I am thirty-eight years old. I was born in a small village of a very poor *campesina* family. Due to the poverty when I was a little girl, I began to work in the countryside. Because I was female I wasn't educated, nor expected to read or write. I was a maid in a home where I was treated badly. This was my youth. When I was sixteen I had my first child. I was abandoned by the father and I had to raise her alone. Now I have four daughters. I had a son, but he died stillborn because there was no prenatal care or vitamins. When I was pregnant I couldn't get a job and couldn't buy the necessary vitamins. My poor children had to work as farmworkers. My daughter wanted to study. I wanted her to learn to read because I couldn't read.

In 1985 I started to work organizing communities in Usulután, and I experienced a lot of repression. We organized six women's committees in Moropazo, Usulután. Now we have 108 committees nationally, taking in the eastern part of the country. There are six thousand people in our organization (AMS).

In 1983 the *hacienda* where I was working was bombed. When the bombs fell from the plane nine of our people were killed, but the news

123

said it was guerrillas. The people killed were my friends from the base Christian community. One of the children was four years old.

After that we went to live on the shore of the Río Grande of San Miguel as refugees. The Atlacatl Battalion arrived and they surrounded my shelter. I was crying and they said, "Why are you crying?" I said "Because of your rifles." We were living in *champas* [lean-to's] by the river. They took me and my children — one newborn child in my arms — and two others. I was alone except for my children. They accused me of being a guerrilla but finally let me go.

In 1986, between August and December, I was captured three times by the Marines. They brought me to the hills to walk for three hours with my three children. The third time they took me in a helicopter to the Sixth Brigade barracks. My youngest child was five years old. The children and I were blindfolded then separated and interrogated for five days, then released. They used psychological methods to get the names of others. In October 1988 we were celebrating the International Year of the Child, when at 7 P.M. soldiers from the Sixth Brigade de Lempa Corps captured me again. They brought me to a hill to sleep where they said the next day a helicopter would take me someplace else. During this time a hurricane destroyed my house and we had nothing, and my mother and children were without help. But actually it was because of hurricane Juana that I was not put in that helicopter because they couldn't get through. They held me under a bridge until a pickup truck with five men dressed in civilian clothes came. I knew they were torturers from the Sixth Brigade who are in charge of capturing people.

They took me out in the storm blindfolded, to the Sixth Brigade. They told my family I was not there. But there was a paid ad placed in the newspapers and Amnesty International sent telegrams demanding my release. I was tortured for four days. They put me in a room where they said I was no better than a dog. They insisted I was in charge of things I had nothing to do with. On the fourth day of being blindfolded, they took me out to the National Police. For twenty-four hours I had to sit without moving. When one group of interrogators was tired they would send in another group and question me again. They threatened to rape me, to attack my children. They threatened to take a picture of me with a guerrilla who was in prison at the time and then I would be killed because I was a terrorist. My back hurt from the blows; they sprayed something on my back.

Two days later I went to Chinamaca, San Miguel, where they threw me in a city jail with drunk men. I wasn't fed because I had no bribe money. My family finally found me after two days. I appeared before the judge where I was accused of killing two national guardsmen, and they said soldiers would give testimony. They intended to jail me for years because of the sentence such an offense brings. The judge, however, found there was no reason for me to be held and I was released.

December 23, last Christmas, my seventeen-year-old daughter was captured and held by the Sixth Brigade with her twelve-year-old cousin. That is where my child spent Christmas. I went looking for them at the Red Cross and Office of Human Rights. But a detective was following me. If it had not been for my friend who picked me up, I'd have been captured.

When I went to the National Police, they said my daughter was not there. When I left they picked me up with guns and the detective was there. It was a plan they had devised to use my daughter to capture me. I was held for only three hours because a friend had seen this event and intervened with phone calls. My daughter was tortured to the point that they brought in a psychologist to work on my daughter.

On May 27, 1989, I was captured in my house in San Miguel. The first group of soldiers came and demanded I give them food and I did. Then minutes later another group of soldiers came to my house and captured me. It was part of a military operation where they surrounded the town. The rest of my family stayed away from my house when they saw the soldiers. "We're going to kill you and your children," they insisted.

After that I fled San Miguel. I was being arrested because I was trying to help others get a little bit of help. With thirty-five others we were trying to work on a farm project to use herbs for medicines. It is the only way for people to have employment. The majority of us are farmworkers and so many women are alone. Because we're women, the bank won't give us loans, and we have no titles to anything. So we decided to join together and buy a plot of land for the community, another plot of land for women.

The men were surprised because the women got funds and the men were trying to get a loan for a tractor. The men felt a little left out. Sometimes women have eight or ten children. You can't imagine their desperation. I thought of leaving the country, but I don't have money to leave. Also I want to stay with my people. I cannot go back to San Miguel but I still work with others from San Miguel who come here to the AMS office in the city. But we work in La Paz where a hundred women are organized. Members of their governing board have been arrested.

We have projects in Morazán, San Miguel, and Usulután. There are women's agriculture cooperatives as well as chicken-raising cooperatives, and we have health workers who work in the communities.

My hope is that if they kill me my daughters will see a free country. I have never been a true believer, true Catholic. But what I do know is God is among the poor.

María Ester Chamorro

That soon the day
with its childish beauty
will come.
—Marcelino H.,
"Early in the Morning"

María Ester Chamorro left Nicaragua to marry Rubén Zamora, who was to become secretary general of the Popular Social Christian Movement (MPSC) and the vice-presidential candidate of the Convergencia Democratíca (Democratic Convergence), the political opposition party coalition. Her family has had to leave El Salvador three times, beginning with the death-squad assassination of Rubén's brother Mario in the house next door.

In 1989, three months after this interview, María Ester's house was bombed, and two of Rubén's bodyguards were seriously injured. During the November 1989 offensive, the family took refuge in the Venezuelan embassy, and then left the country. By 1990 the family had once again returned.

I was born in Managua, Nicaragua, in 1942. My father was a working man who worked for Texaco. My mother was a seamstress. They worried and wanted us to receive a better education than they had. We went to the United States in 1944, where my father worked in a mattress factory. He worked very hard. It was really hard for my father. He was even getting sick working day and night. He had little rest and it was affecting his health. My mother wanted to help. But he said she should be at home with her children — women shouldn't go out to work. He was very *macho*. He had to work double or triple so that my mother didn't have to go out, even though my mother always worked at home with her sewing. She gave money to the family out of her sewing.

We spent six years in the United States. I think I made third grade at Epiphany school in San Francisco. Then we came back to Nicaragua. We were a peaceful family, no problems, four children. My father never got into politics because, you see, he had the problem of being a Chamorro. The Chamorro family in Nicaragua are of the opposition. So in Nicaragua during the presidency of Somoza, just being Chamorro was a problem. My father was a poor man, and having the Chamorro name was just another problem for him. So he never allowed us to get into politics. None of his children.

So that was my life, a normal life. I went to the university. I received a scholarship to the U.S. in 1960. I went to Connecticut College for women for one year. I was granted a scholarship by, I think, the International

Education Exchange. It was a fancy school. I was part of the exchange program, so I received everything. The trip, room and board, everything. My parents didn't have to pay anything. I really studied that year.

When I came back to Nicaragua I went to the university. I graduated as a language teacher. Then I studied for my licentiate degree for one more year, but I never completed the thesis, because at the end of that year I married Rubén.

We were cousins. He was in the seminary — San José de la Montaña here in San Salvador. He almost graduated as a philosophy major. He studied there for eight years. After that he went to the university.

When he left the seminary in 1964 he went to Nicaragua to spend a vacation with my parents. That's how we got to know each other and how everything got started. We dated for four years. He came four times a year to visit his grandparents in Nicaragua. Then we'd see each other.

During the time we were dating we had to see how we'd cope with marriage. The problem was that he was completely involved in politics and I had no political interest. I had no position. I'd lived a simple life, without confronting big questions about justice and injustice. This was our big discussion — would we be able to have a good marriage, to have a life together?

I came here to El Salvador to become involved in his life. I became involved in the "Jornadas de Vidas Cristianas" retreat program. Young people who wanted to live Christianity deeper would go off for three days to reflect on what God wanted of us. It was like the retreats of charismatics but different because the bonds were deeper.

All this got me involved in Rubén's life, in understanding his life, taking part in it. We still wrote each other every week, talking about politics, philosophy. I have a big box of his letters. When we married I was really involved in Salvadoran politics. However, when I came here it was a shock. It was very different from Nicaragua. In Nicaragua even though I wasn't involved in politics, the political life was very — how can I say it — strange. It was not something that involved people like my family, working people, during the Somoza time. It's different here in El Salvador. Here people get involved in politics, you feel it. For example, the elections here in El Salvador were shocking at first. We never had an election in Somoza's time.

So we didn't have problems over politics. It was my development, I think, in learning, in knowledge, in participating. That's what happened to me during these twenty years. We'll be married twenty years in December. Now I'm very involved politically.

I want to start the process of becoming a Salvadoran national. I wanted to do this before I became involved politically because they could throw me out if I'm not a national. By nationality I am Nicaraguan; by commitment I am Salvadoran. I feel Salvadoran even though I don't want to stop being Nicaraguan because you never forget your country or your family. But politically I am involved here in El Salvador; at the same time I want to keep my own interest in my profession. I remember I discussed this with Rubén, that I should maintain my own interests. He encouraged that. Even though I feel my life has revolved around what he does, there has been a little space for my own interest. I've tried at least.

We came to this house in 1972. In 1973 Rubén was working at UCA [the University of Central America]. I taught at Asunción School. We had three children at the time. One night at 10 P.M. I went to the university to pick him up. But at an army checkpoint they stopped us and all of us were picked up. I never thought they'd pick me up.

We were with two friends. We were taken to the police station. I spent two or three days blindfolded, handcuffed to a chair, with nightly interrogations, sleeping on the floor. This is what happens to everyone who goes to jail.

My parents happened to be coming to visit the very next day after they arrested us. But when they arrived no one knew where we were. We had just disappeared. When my mother saw we had disappeared, she called my brothers in Nicaragua and the Nicaraguan embassy. My mother is incredible, dynamic. She managed to get me out of jail in three days. It was through action by the Nicaraguan embassy in El Salvador.

They kept Rubén and his friend in jail for a month. When I got out, the first thing I had to do was get Rubén out. Finally we managed. They would let him out on the condition that we leave the country.

The first time we left the country was in 1971. The National University of El Salvador gave Rubén a scholarship to study in England for a master's degree in government and politics of Latin America. The scholarship was for us as a family.

This second time we went to England again. That was when he studied for his Ph.D. in political science. But he didn't get the degree. He still had to present a book or I don't know what it is — perhaps a thesis.

I went to the university both times we were in England. The first time I studied at the London Institute of Education. I worked for a diploma in audiovisual aids. I went to London to study, traveling from where we lived in Essex in the town of Colchester. The second time we were in England I received my M.A. in applied linguistics; we were there for two years. Rubén Camile was born in Colchester in 1972.

We also lived in Guatemala in 1979 because we still couldn't come home to El Salvador. We were in Guatemala eight months.

On October 15, 1979, the military coup took place here. That's when they called Rubén to take part in the new government. So in 1979 we came back in a truck from Guatemala with all our furniture.

We've been in this house since the birth of my third child in 1975. We had been in El Salvador for four months when Rubén's brother, Mario, was murdered next door by the death squads, and we had to leave again for exile.

It was a period of terror. That's when I went back to Nicaragua. For me it was great to be with my parents and brothers. My father had been in a wheelchair for five years. He was helpless, couldn't even feed himself. It was a big support for my mother that I could assist my father. I was my father's favorite, so it was wonderful to be with him. I was there for his death three years ago.

Then Rubén came back here to El Salvador and he settled in November 1987. He settled here in the house with his political party. After a year I had to decide, was I going to come back or break up? I had to decide. Also we weren't sure if it was safe enough to come back with the family. I knew he needed us. It wasn't easy. It took a lot of talking, discussing. Twice I came alone to see. Once you are here something attracts you to come back. Even my family said I was crazy, but I was sure and most of the children were sure as well.

So in November 1988 we came back. We began to build our family again in this house. It took some arranging because when we left we were five; now we're seven. We are still settling in but now we feel part of El Salvador. This is where we have to be, to do our work, to support Rubén's work. I have always valued his work, had confidence in what he does. I can't openly take part but I can do his secretarial work. I go with him to diplomatic receptions, to meet new people.

I have to say I don't have a life of my own. I know you are interested in women's lives. I haven't done what I want to do. I have involved myself, our family, in this nation. I have supported Rubén's work. But I think in the future I have to develop myself as a woman in terms of my interest. I was telling you in the beginning that I love children. I think that I could do important work in this area.

But I think I have to be patient, to wait for the moment. I have to become a Salvadoran first, because if I get involved in this kind of project, I would like to get involved as a Salvadoran, not as a foreigner. That's what I am considered right now because I'm a Nicaraguan. So I want first to get my Salvadoran nationality and support Rubén's work for a time. If better times come I would be happy to become involved in a project with children and women. That's where I'd really feel happy and feel that I'm doing something I want for Salvadoran society. The children in this society suffer a lot, more than in Nicaragua. Their parents don't have food to give them. They have so much poverty but also psychological stress. They need to be given a lot of love.

I think that here in El Salvador women are dominated by men. They feel themselves incapable of being equal to men. In El Salvador there's been terrible *machismo*. The new family code says that marriage is woman's inspiration, that marriage is good, and that's the starting point of the law. But then when you start to talk to the women you learn that in this country there is a lot of *concubinato* [a man having mistresses], so the woman is sad. She has to depend on the father coming, on what he decides to give for the children. This is how I look at it. Maybe I'm not analyzing it exactly as I should. Maybe this gives the woman an advantage because she has to work, to be the head of the society. When you say it's women who make society I think it's because they have responsibility. Women here feel responsible. It happens to me. Imagine, it happens to me. I feel responsible for my children because I know Rubén is very busy. He has many political things to do. He's an important man. You cannot bother him so much with the children's problems. The real responsibility is on the woman. You have to assume that responsibility. If that happens to me — I have a loving husband, a conscientious husband, and I'm legally married — what do you think happens to a woman who has to share a man with maybe five families?

So women are forced to take a more active part in the society. On the other hand they are not happy and they don't progress because sadness keeps them back. You make the effort and you struggle but you are sad. Whenever I think about Salvadoran women I think about a sad part of society. They've been very badly treated, a group of people who haven't been able to break the barriers, to hold their heads up. For example, in the news, on the TV, there are hardly any women speaking. Maybe in the base communities the women have a more important voice. But as far as I see women are not an important part of society. That's one thing that worries me as well.

My hope is in the children. This new generation won't accept what the older generation accepted; they'll do things different. This generation will break the barriers. They'll be different from us. We fight with each other, don't understand each other. I find that children don't feel like that. They feel like making friends, talking to the other people, building with each other. I don't think the children are acting like we did. I think they have already felt the consequences of what we have lived and how it has affected them. My children feel affected by our situation. They even resent it. Sometimes they'll say, "Why am I the daughter of Rubén Zamora? I wish I was somebody else's daughter." Not because they don't love their father but because of the political tension, the political burden.

If we could achieve some kind of peace, maybe not the ideal peace but to start living together in society, I think the children would do the rest. We're going to prepare a way, but the real peace is not going to be in us. We adults have no solution, but the children do. Perhaps this sounds utopian but it's the only way I can see hope in this country.

We felt that coming here was our mission. We feel we are instruments of God, of God's plan for this country. Sometimes I think Rubén is an instrument of God even when I don't agree with him. This is part of our marriage. When the children were born I offered them as God's instrument without a fixed idea of what they should be. You can't tell this to children but you tell it to God.

That's our spirit toward our children, that they are God's presence in our family. People don't believe this, thinking, "Oh, they are Marxists, they don't believe in God." But we are a very Christian family in this process of liberation, doing our part. This is difficult to talk about. We don't always go to Mass on Sunday but inside our hearts we are religious.

Last week my seventeen-year-old asked us, "Are you going to impose religion on me?" He wanted to know why we made him go to Mass on Sunday. Sometimes the children resent it because we insist that we all go to Mass together on Sunday.

"We have a commitment," we answered, "a responsibility to make you a Christian, to take part in the religious beliefs of the family. While you are with us, you have to participate because you are part of the family. When you leave home and have a life of your own, then it's up to you if you want to continue or not. But for now you have to go because it's part of the family, of what we believe, of what we want of you." Then he was quiet.

4

THE HOUR OF THE FURNACES: THE MARTYRS

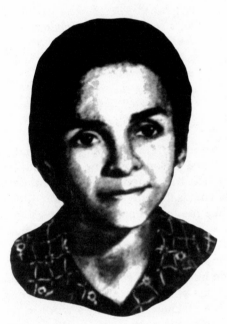

"Ante una sociedad que vive los ideales del poder, tener y placer, quiero ser signo:

• de lo que significa realmente amar
• de que Cristo Jesús es el único Señor de la historia y está presente en medio de nosotros y es capaz de engendrar un amor más fuerte que los instintos y que la muerte, y que todos los poderes económicos y políticos.

Deseo llevar una vida de búsqueda y seguimiento de Cristo Pobre, casto y obediente a la voluntad del Padre para vivir sólo para El y su obra salvífica.

Prometo al Señor serle fiel:

• en la salud y en la enfermedad
• en la juventud y en la vejez
• en la tranquilidad y en la persecución
• en las alegrías y en las tristezas
• en su encarnación entre los más pobres
• siendo pobre y solidaria con ellos, en su lucha por su liberación
• participando de su misión evangelizadora entre los hombres
• concentrando toda mi capacidad afectiva en El y en todos los hermanos
• viviendo en una continua búsqueda de la voluntad del Padre a través de su Palabra, de la Iglesia, de los signos de los tiempos, de los pobres.

SILVIA M. ARRIOLA
1951–1981

When they tell you
that I am
completely, absolutely, definitely
dead
don't believe them
don't believe them
don't believe them.

            —*Ariel Dorfman*
         "Last Will and Testament"

Tonight in a clandestine jail of the Treasury Police or the National Guard, in Ilopango or Mariona prison, someone is holding out, bleeding, pain pumping every muscle, frightened and losing confidence, yet still refusing to give names. That is the only concentration, the one discipline that remains, even while moving in and out of consciousness. This silence has a voice: it answers pain and betrayal in a human body. The body says no.

The martyr's final act of simplicity is steadfast faith. It is a faith that begins with simple intention: to serve the people. Today, before dawn breaks, a woman lights a fire for tortillas, a man moves in the dark readying his one tool, the machete, for a day's work in the fields, a young woman carries letters in the plum light. Each will decide to keep an appointment that evening, at a cooperative, popular organization, or base Christian community meeting. On that human choice, the liberation process rises or falls. That is the fragility of revolution, the meaning of the people's will.

Martyrs tip the scales of choice. Their deaths are a weight pulling toward fidelity, a memory heavier than competing weights of personal safety or advantage. Martyrs are a danger to the national security state. Yet that state *always* cooperates in their proliferation. As the death squads dig the open graves of the assassinated, they dig their own graves as well. As if compelled by destiny, the state pulls the trigger, drops the bombs, tortures the very people whose memory will subvert their dominion.

Memory resides in heart, that nexus of mind and spirit. To say the martyrs live in the people's memory is to say they have become the peoples' heart. Communal memory is dangerous because it carries into the future the defiant lives of those who symbolically represent freedom.

134

As If They Were God

"I'm sick of martyrs," the young woman said, "sick of the Homeland, too."

It was blasphemy and the other women recoiled. Not the old woman. She said, "Look, my son, his lovely body, the flesh I labored to birth, was thrown like a mangled dog down a dump with buzzards. I, too, am sick of death."

"This is what I mean, Abuelita, this death," the woman said.

"But you blame the dead, child."

"I blame the war."

"Our martyrs were every much as sick of war as you, and they loved life as well, too."

Laura López, Silvia Maribel Arriola, and María Cristina Gómez are martyrs who loved life as well, but loved the people more. Enough to lay down their lives for them, to enter the grave of Cuscatlán [the native word for El Salvador]. That soaked killing floor is sacred. The martyrs it holds redeem history by keeping history a promise rather than a rendering judgment. Until Salvadorans embrace cynicism they will embrace hope, keeping a vow to the dead. Each Salvadoran chooses resignation or resurrection. There is no defensible middle ground. An often repeated phrase of family or community members of a slain friend is that "their death will not be in vain." These are not sentimental words but words of an oath. As if they were God or the last revolutionaries of the century, the Salvadorans won't let the dead die.

Laura López

It is time to go forward, Carmelo.
There are moments when the courage
of men and women must become the feelings
Jesus had knowing he was going to die for the people.
—Laura López

The people called Laura López their bishop because she was all they had. No priest had baptized a baby, blessed a wedding, or said the words of Eucharist for years on the Guazapa volcano. No priest would dare. The Salvadoran military considered Guazapa a haven for guerrillas, where the people fed them, so the people were targets. Laura went to Guazapa in 1979 to live as a pastoral worker.

Laura was one of the first casualties of low-intensity conflict. She was "cut down by flying bullets" on April 24, 1985.[55] Her journey from the relative safety of San Jerónimo plunged her deeper and deeper into a life stripped of protection. That path toward the war zones began in 1977 when Laura met Sister Ana, who was part of a pastoral team in Laura's *cantón*.

Ana is slight, olive brown, her black eyes guileless. She speaks softly, with an aura so calming that you forget she is a revolutionary. If liberation theologians are writing about a new church, Ana and the peasants are living it, constructing with their lives a new definition of a revolutionary, a definition far more complex, more communal, than a mustached militant in bandana and beret. Ana doesn't speak of a new definition, but she lives it, ten years in war zones, ten years of furious hope. "My hope is that one day the people will be liberated. My hope is a commitment to go forward in work with the poor. In the people one discovers the God of life."

Like the ceiba tree seeding itself, asking nothing but the wind's breath, Ana and Laura rooted themselves among the people. Nothing, not even the axe, has cut away that bond. Laura was one of the first to work with Ana's pastoral team. She emerged as a leader elected by her community to be a *delegada de la palabra* (delegate of the word). The delegates perform the sacramental function of a priest except that they cannot officially "celebrate" a Mass or preside at a wedding.

Laura asked Ana how to measure the claims of the people. "Up to what point must we give ourselves?" she asked Ana. Ana says she was startled by Laura's question, which was an admission, really, that there are no limits.

In 1979 Laura pledged to go into war zones to accompany the people. Ana assessed the cost of Laura's decision as she watched her leave that day, her small children lugging their possessions up the side of a mountain. "She took her three daughters and two sons. They were so little. She left her house, animals, her basic grains. She took only what she could carry up eighteen miles. She carried her infant in her arms on a terrain that was narrow and dangerous." That's all Ana says, as if history explained the rest, how Laura would travel from village to village on Guazapa, meeting with the base Christian communities encouraging them as Paul would the early church, reminding them that if they were persecuted for the sake of the people they should count themselves highly for such love, such courage. Laura, the "bishop" of Guazapa. The only symbol of her authority was a knapsack she carried on her back. In it she packed alcohol for wounds, communion bread for the soul, and money for the breadless.

Laura's husband had preceded her to Guazapa. It isn't clear why — if he was a catechist or a guerrilla — only that some mission compelled him to leave his family. Ana doesn't explain except to say he died in 1981, three years after the family's arrival. He stepped on one of the hidden land mines that wait like snakes to strike.

Laura's loneliness after her husband's death was the loneliness of the lack of intimacy with a *"compa"* who understands one's commitment. She was well loved. The people turned to her whenever they needed help, even the children. After her death, the children of Laura's friend, María, asked, "And now that they killed our Laura, who is going to bring us candy?"

Though beloved, she felt alone, misunderstood by those who considered her pastoral decision ineffectual. What was the point anyway? her critics asked. What did she offer the people? She wasn't a priest, she wasn't a guerrilla. "There was suffering," says Ana. "She was alone very much. Her Christianity wasn't understood by some *compañeros*. One of the things that hurt her is that her own brothers said if they saw her they would kill her." Two of her brothers were members of death squads.

But her children understood. Her children never questioned her, even when she walked them into a war, saying only, "If we love we must live it." After his father's death, her oldest boy made a commitment he thought would separate him from his family. Aware of his mother's old promise to return to San Jerónimo after three years, he announced gravely, "Mama, I'm going to stay to defend the poor." In 1989 her son, who had joined the FMLN, was killed. It was April, the month of his mother's death.

Her son's decision was not the crucial factor in Laura's decision to stay; the people were. But the boy's compassion must have touched her deeply. This was the point when Laura "made a total commitment, dedicating her life to pastoral work in the zone." Everything was cast. Nothing of San Jerónimo held her anymore, not the memory of their fields sprouting bellflowers and dandelions, the mango and maquilishaut trees that shaded the children's play. Everything moved forward now, pulling to completion.

When the air war began in 1985, Laura met the bombardment with innocent fury, determined to document the bombing of civilians. Each time planes droned overhead, she rushed for a camera and tape recorder to capture the invasion. She sent communiqués to the International Red Cross and letters to the Christian churches and the international press, noting carefully the number of bombs and mortars and rockets launched, exactly how many fields of sorghum, corn, and beans were destroyed, how many acres of sugarcane burned, which families suffered losses, the number of *compañeros* captured or disappeared. On March 8, 1985, she wrote communiqués from a *tatu* (underground shelter) as two A-37 bombers flew above Mirandia and El Zopote dropping ten bombs. The next day she wrote:

All of us are hidden in a bomb shelter because we are well aware that their bullets are waiting for us. . . . At this moment one A-37 . . . is in our vicinity. We are on the shore of the lake. The other A-37 is heading toward Cinquera to continue bombing there. Two bombs have been dropped over the community of El Zopote, leaving behind a giant cloud of smoke. They continue to spew machine-gun fire. . . . Meanwhile another plane is bombing Cinquera. We are trying to defend our lives, although we can no longer defend our huts or belongings.

She closes the communiqué with characteristic simplicity, followed by the fierce confidence the peasants of Guazapa depended on. "God doesn't want it to be that way. They want to terrorize us but we will not be swayed."

She never was. God knows what her flock felt, scampering from village to village, no longer with homes, even safe houses, a community living under the trees, this *pueblo* of poor farmers, children hiding from a military determined to "sanitize" Guazapa, holed up underground for days, thirsty, terrified to surface, watching their children's wounds fill up with worms because they lacked antiseptic.

A member of Laura's pastoral team reflected on her leadership, her ability to calm the people in the midst of crisis:

During our Good Friday celebration, the planes were circling overhead and she said to us: "Don't run, brothers and sisters. We're here celebrating the word of God. Don't be afraid."

Her words had a calming effect on us; all the people became very quiet. She said, "We'll wait for the Devil to go away so we can resume our celebration." Everyone did what she said.

I used to give her a hard time when she wouldn't eat anything. Her excuse was that she had too much work to do, or she had something new to learn. She really loved her people. She always told us to struggle for unity. She would say, "Let's not be indifferent to our neighbors' needs. We must learn to share what we have."

Between December and March the bombing took place daily. Laura's desperation drove her to risk travel to the archdiocesan office in San Salvador. Her delegation walked all night and all day. She told a journalist in San Salvador, "We were barely able to cover the bus fare to the archdiocesan office." The total bus fare must have been $1.50. She expressed fear that people would die of hunger because General Blandón had said the offensive would last three months. "We can hardly bear two weeks," she said. "How will we bear three months?"

The people's suffering was tearing at her. Her own children were so sick she left them in San Salvador. It didn't occur to her to pull back.

Laura López

María Cristina Gómez

Her pastoral co-worker Samuel said, "She never failed us, nor did she ever turn back from the struggle." Logic suggests that Laura felt failure. The community of Guazapa was being pulverized. The army could starve them out. Their homes, crops, and animals had been devastated in "search and destroy" missions. Yet Laura's reflections, taped during liturgies, carry an impression that she felt another dimension to the struggle, a realm of the spirit that transformed the brutality, the impossible grief. Although they were entering a crucifixion, Laura saw it as a process that only the people could embrace:

> The martyr's cross has been placed on our shoulders. . . . Our people are tormented by our enemies . . . but it has to be done. The word of God has to be made a reality. . . . Our people have decided to end this way of the cross but the final triumph is still down the line. . . . We will not wait for people from other countries to show us what has to be done. We are Christians and we know what we have to do. But first we must sacrifice and make a serious decision to do so.

Whatever Laura believed such truth meant for her life, she was clear about those who would be the first casualties. "The first to die," she said, "are those with faith."

On Palm Sunday, Laura led a celebration in the village of Las Delicias. She stood amid toothless mothers holding gaunt children with bellies swollen from malnutrition; the few men held dusty straw hats in leathery hands. Las Delicias was only one of the many small village communities. Laura counted 979 people on the volcano in the grand *comunidad* of Guazapa. "We had twelve communities before," she wrote. "Since then, government troops destroyed six, among them Palo Grande, El Rable, Corozal, and El Espino." But six more, including Delicias, held. The *comunidad* of Guazapa was wounded and scorched like their volcano's open fields. The Guazapa *comunidad* knew and documented the scope of the terror to be faced: four A-37s, a "Push and Pull" aircraft, twenty-eight helicopters with rocket and machine-gun mounts.

On Palm Sunday, in the midst of hell, the peasants of Las Delicias spoke of hope, reflecting on Jesus' triumphal entrance to Jerusalem. The peasants of Guazapa believe they will, in Archbishop Romero's words, "Be resurrected." That intransigence is why the army had dropped thirty thousand pounds of bombs on Guazapa and still the people have gone back to the volcano, back to their lands.

This is the fire that burns brighter than white phosphorous bombs, the fire that counterinsurgency cannot put out. As Laura put it:

> We have gotten used to hating, to being afraid. We have to put an end to that. We have to confront ourselves, to kill the false pride

within our soul, so that a new person may arise, so that a new civilization may come into being — one composed of love.

In the same Palm Sunday reflection Laura spoke about violence and nonviolence. With a depth lifetimes removed from an often abstract First World debate, Laura addressed this theme: "We should not place our faith strictly in weapons, thinking that the gun is God and that the gun will give us liberty and justice." Then, echoing Romero's words that "when all peaceful means are exhausted, it is the people's right to defend themselves," Laura adds, "If it weren't for the *compañeros* in arms we would all be killed even though we have faith. . . . We can't remain passive in the face of this situation."

On April 16, 1985, Laura met with all the pastoral workers in Guazapa, and they reflected on Matthew 25. They were exhausted. Her communiqué says: "Despite the fatigue, after making an escape from an invading army, we give thanks to God for protecting us. The work of the base communities must continue, because if it were otherwise what would become of us?" They were on the run almost constantly now. On April 22, the army invaded again. A catechist testified: "Laura was very worried, and she said to us, 'We can't take off and leave the people here. We have already offered up our lives for them.'" The last line has the sound of mythmaking. Yet it seems characteristic of Laura to talk that way in the face of rising panic, to remind everyone including herself of the reason for their commitment.

The shelling continued relentlessly. One of the targets was the village of Consolación, Laura's base village. When bombardment was close, Laura fled with others into a *tatu*. When a family with children couldn't enter the overcrowded hideout, Laura and her thirteen-year-old daughter gave up their space. Above ground they ran into the canefields of Valle Verde, trying to outrun the ground patrols. By 3:00 P.M. they were surrounded. The scorched canefields of Valle Verde were the end of Laura's journey. This is her daughter's account:

> I was running along just about at my mother's side when she was hit by a bullet in the back. I said, "Mama, they've hit you!" Perhaps she hadn't felt it just yet, because she just kept running. Then another bullet hit her. . . . Now she couldn't run anymore. . . . She gave me the knapsack and told me to go forward [¡Adelante!] . . . By that time she had fallen to the ground.

This moment symbolizes the church of the poor in which the only promise is that if you fall someone else will take your place; a knapsack is handed over, a symbol of that church, bloodstained, useful, holding a pastor's contraband. Laura's fire would burn on.

Laura's daughter was fifteen when I interviewed her. She was so shy you didn't sense teenage energy. More like a wise older child, she sat stiffly with her two younger sisters in the convent's straightback chair. Sister Ana brought them, traveling on two buses to reach San Salvador for the interview. They wore blue and yellow dresses, their best.

Laura's daughter began awkwardly, repeating a testimony she had told over and over, but not to an *anglo*. As if avoiding the most painful part, she focused on her journey after her mother's death. Perhaps, like her mother, she wished to lift from that powerless moment an example of a small victory. It's the story of children outwitting military patrols.

Still carrying the knapsack on her back, she ran into tall pasture grass to hide. Crouched there she saw soldiers shoot a six-year-old from her village. He was hit in the testicles and left for dead. With a pair of socks, she made a bandage to stop the bleeding, then used alcohol for the wound. "But the boy was so thirsty he drank it all — for pain and thirst!" She carried him through canefields under cover of nightfall. But the fields were half stubble from the military's torch policy, so she carried him along a ravine, stopping at 2:00 A.M. to eat mangos. For three days she carried Carlos until they were able to break through the military encirclement and find villagers to attend to the boy's wound.

> They went out to search for my mother's body on Saturday, April 27. They found her with her skull caved in, and it was barely connected to her body. She had been tied up like an animal for the slaughter. They found two other bodies near her, people who couldn't run fast enough to escape and they shot them down. I remember how the soldiers shouted, "Don't run! We won't hurt you!" Then they shot them down.
>
> At about 9:00 A.M. we buried my mother along with the two other people.

Laura's Legacy

Dying, Laura pointed forward. Viewed from the sides of Guazapa, from Chalatenango, Morazán, or Cuscatlán, the war is stark in its simplicity. It is a war between the forces of death and the forces of life, a war waged by elite forces, as well as unarmed mothers and children who refuse to "depopulate."

A year and a half after Laura's death, the army launched another offensive against Guazapa, this time to take Guazapa "inch by inch if necessary." Peasants "rescued" by the army were sent to refugee camps, one of which was Calle Real. Sister Margaret Kling of New Jersey was a nurse at Calle Real who remembered the night the cattle trucks arrived in February 1986. One hundred bombed-out refugees stood crowded like pigs or cows on the trucks, children with parasites, half-starved, numb with exhaustion, pregnant women who had been held by the military for twelve days and barely fed. "They were so sick," she said. "I'll never forget it as long as I live." But more followed. Five hundred were brought in during the next six weeks.

Riding on these trucks, after being "rescued" by the army following twenty-two days in caves without food or water, were villagers from what was to be named El Barrillo, a resettlement community of Guazapa. It took months for them to heal, to knit up the unravelled weave of *comunidad*, the broken limbs, the broken hearts. Several months later the El Barrillo community made a historic decision. Like Laura walking up the volcano to accompany her people, the *comunidad* of El Barrillo decided to return to their land, to reclaim the foothills of Guazapa in spite of the military's presence.

Under the protective accompaniment of North American religious delegations, they were able to enter their village unmolested and begin the physical and spiritual process of reconstruction. In seven months, one hundred families had harvested their first crops, built a school, a clinic, and shelter for each family, dug a 12 x 18 foot water reservoir connected to individual pumps, and constructed a baby chicken coop for two hundred chicks.

I traveled to El Barrillo in May 1988. When the Salvadoran High Command denied a safe conduct pass to the area, I decided to go with Salvadorans who could take me and two other North Americans around military checkpoints.

We boarded a bus in the predawn darkness and headed for Aguilares. In the town square I heard the church bells ring and remembered that the bells rang for days after Rutilio Grande's murder, inconsolable bells, telling what no *campesino* would dare.

That morning the Aguilares market was awake, howling and hawking. Soldiers swaggered past baskets of mangos, limes, onions, plantains, and beans. Half-starved dogs trotted in motley packs, scattering flapping chickens. Tethered baby pigs pulled their ropes, squealing. We watched slouched, bored soldiers, then edged casually toward a road out of town. We walked through corn and cane fields.

At a fork, Teresita, our guide, signaled us left, toward Suchitoto, the "back way." Teresita began humming. The land, her people, surrounded her like a river, or more vast, like a sea. Exactly like a sea.

Teresita knew Laura, traveled with her, when Guazapa communities fled pursuing soldiers. Displaced from the countryside like eight hundred thousand other refugees, Teresita now lives in San Salvador but travels back to her people when she can. Currently she is living with thirty thousand squatters on the outskirts of the city on land that straddles the railroad tracks and the city garbage dump. The *campesinos* "took" the land in 1972. But her "home," which borders a sewage river, was behind

143

her now. On this day she beamed, taking the hands of *campesinos* who pulled her and the *gringos* into the truck.

As we rode through the green lowlands, amate trees, gnarled and burly, spread lush shadows on the road. In only twenty kilometers our truck unloaded all, farmers carrying cumas and machetes for the day's hacking, as well as Teresita's *gringo* friends with backpacks. It was scorching. The fields hissed with drought.

After two hours we stopped to rest and drink. Teresita, who is a grandmother, seemed reluctant. But she took a duffel bag full of supplies and food from her head and rested. She had balanced her load over rugged terrain, in a blistering heat, walking erect, easy, at a clipped *campesino* pace that left us breathless.

Before Valle Verde I wandered from the trail to pick mangos, and Teresita was uncharacteristically harsh. *"Nunca"* (Never), she scolded. One never leaves a tested trail in the countryside for fear of mines. Valle Verde was pathetic, a few huts stood forlorn in the deserted fields. Valle Verde is now a government-supported refugee camp, but it is barely populated and the *campesinos* we spoke with said they receive nothing from the government. The toll is evident: children with fat bellies, swollen with worms, mothers silent, withdrawn, sit indolently in the shade, waiting, waiting for something. I looked across the field to where Laura was overtaken by the army, but I feared that asking about her grave would jeopardize Teresita.

Across the empty fields two *compas* waved from a ridge ahead, welcoming. They took us down to El Barrillo, one of the first resettlements, in a tractor paid for by a Baltimore sister-city project. The scorched earth rejoices, transformed to a land of milk and honey where each family receives milk from community cows and the beehive project sweetens their meals.

Teresita pulled us into her friend's *casita*, a one-room dirt-floor construction of mud, straw, and bamboo. We ate *pupusas*, the typical Salvadoran food of tortillas filled with cheese, beans, or pork, in candlelight and watched the sun fall through the purple sky to the valley's ink bottom. It was peaceful, deceptive.

In the candlelight Teresita's expressive face sobered, her fifty years marked deeply. She looked old. She became reflective as if the flood of darkness washed memory awake. "We all suffered together back then," she began. "When the bombs drove us out we traveled in *guindas*, moving every night from area to area for eight days at a time. The children were terrified." She spoke of Laura's courage and of Padre Cáceres, a Guazapa boy ordained only a month when the army assassinated him in 1981. "We had faith," Teresita said summarily. "Laura López and Padre Cáceres were ours. They are martyrs of this people. They gave us their lives."

144

We attended a liturgy that evening amid candle flames, wildflowers, and the murmur of cicadas. A large picture of Laura López was tacked on the wall of the open shed chapel. Sitting beneath Laura's smile, the pastoral team, all of whom appeared to be under the age of twenty-five, gathered to speak with me. When I asked about Operation Phoenix, they clammed up, reluctant to talk to a *gringa*, even one accompanied by Teresita. Finally, one of their older members, a man in his forties who was a member of Laura López's pastoral team, reflected on her life. He ended by explaining Laura's title of "bishop":

> Laura was the bishop of Guazapa because she refused to abandon the people even when the bombing had driven many away. She once told us the Good Shepherd never deserted the sheep and she would stay on Guazapa preaching the gospel if only one person remained.

The *compañero* repeated Laura's now legendary last charge: "¡Adelante!" His voice dropped to a whisper and the young people stared at their hands. He gestured to the youthful pastoral team: "Here her work continues." The team shifted uneasily, embarrassed but very serious. Still, they said little, cautious and solemn.

The peasants of El Barrillo keep vigilant for army harassment. Among them Laura still lives. Her presence is felt when the caroa tree bears fruit. A catechist who worked with Laura remembered a Good Friday when Laura prepared their place of worship by staking a cross at the foot of the caroa tree. "Several days after the death of Laura, that tree stopped sprouting leaves in order to give fruit. For us it was somewhat mysterious. I said to the people that it was Laura's fruit and we had to continue in her footsteps."

María Cristina Gómez

> *...when a woman says*
> *that gender is a political category*
> *she can begin to stop being woman in herself*
> *to become woman for herself.*
> —Roque Dalton

In El Salvador there are only hard choices. To choose to risk oneself for others calls forth moral and revolutionary blessings — sometimes annihilation. For a woman to choose her own freedom within the *proceso* calls forth curse and questioning.

Cristina Gómez was a mother who chose the revolution and who chose her own freedom. Both were lonely choices. In the heart of each option she discovered freedom and loss. Cristina walked away from choices considered irrevocable by Salvadoran standards. Once an exemplary wife and mother, a Baptist deacon, an international representative of the Baptist Women's Committee, she spent the last seven years before her death separated from her family, living alone, outside the church. Retracing that geography, Cristina found a way back to her church and her children in the year and a half before she was killed.

On April 5, 1988, Cristina Gómez stepped out of the John F. Kennedy elementary school in the Santa Lucía area of Ilopango. She stood amid a swirl of jumping, bobbing children, bursting with the stored energy of a day in school. Suddenly a group of heavily armed men in civilian clothes pushed into the wiggling chaos and pulled Cristina into a Jeep Cherokee with polarized dark windows. It was the last the stunned first graders saw of their teacher.

Within an hour her body was found in a cemetery in Nuevo Cuscatlán on the outskirts of San Salvador. She had been burned with acid on her back, her face was swollen from blows, and they had pulled back the skin from her arms. She had been shot four times.

Her son Salvador knew about his mother's childhood but could not understand her later choices. What had felt like abandonment to him as a child took on new, more complex meaning as he grew to know his mother before her death, the time of Cristina Gómez's finest hour.

María Cristina Gómez was born into a poor family in Santiago de María in Usulután. Baptist missionaries recognized her potential and gave her a scholarship to their school in the village. But even a bright girl child had a small destiny — a destiny Cristina never learned to accept. Her son Salvador spoke of his mother's early wounds and early rebellion at the Baptist school:

> The basic philosophy of the school was not to help girls get ahead. María Cristina was a girl they really tried to hold down. I realize now the contradiction. The school talked about helping people grow but they did the opposite. Most of the girls of that class who were being prepared for the world — their lives are a mess. They've all suffered under the rigidity of the church. People think because it was a Baptist Mission School it would not be like that.
>
> My mother's friend [who told this story] wanted me to understand how much my mother had to overcome because the school taught her insecurity. Cristina did complete a teacher's certificate at the Baptist school but her stormy relationship with the Baptist

Church had just begun. She taught in Santiago de María's local school but soon left for San Salvador where she became director of a kindergarten school run by the Baptists. There she contended with the school director over the philosophy of education. Unwilling to instruct children only in skills, she believed the school's obligation was to teach them "to serve others." To serve others in El Salvador implies a commitment to social change — an ethical-political agenda Cristina's superiors wouldn't touch. My mother didn't want just to teach children, but to form them to serve others. This is when she had differences."[56]

Marriage, the Church, and Contradictions

Salvador links these philosophical "differences" to problems within her marriage. Although he understands the differences to be political in nature, that is, about social change and the role of women, he cannot articulate a broader framework for his mother's decisions, any more, perhaps, than his mother could have at the time:

The same changes that caused her to have difficulties in the school caused her to have differences within our family, and my parents divorced. She left the house and we had no contact with her for a long time. I was only twelve. For two years we had no contact except regarding papers for the divorce. I assume my mother tried to visit us but there were so many problems; it was very painful. At one point she couldn't come to the house. My father didn't want to see my mother. There was no struggle between my mother and us children. It was between my mother and father. My father was in pain because my mother pushed for the separation. The children decided to stay with my father.

One can only imagine the sense of betrayal the children felt when Cristina was cut off from them for two years. Salvador's comment hints at his anguish and confusion:

I think it's natural that there was a time when I wasn't close to my mother. I feel I'm getting to know her in a new way that helps me not to judge her based on childhood memories. . . . I think I was deeply affected by her leaving when I was a child. . . . I told my friend that maybe it's too late to know my mother, but perhaps it's never too late.

It seems clear that she wasn't able to see her children because of her former husband's wishes. Her loss of the children was an emptiness that nothing would ever fill up, according to her friends. What propelled her decision is not fully clear. The separation was on her initiative and

147

apparently linked to political differences she had with the Baptist church as well as her husband. Her husband was a devout Baptist who didn't understand her quest.

Since her death my father shared that after her trip to Latin America for one of the women's meetings of the World Council of Churches, she came back full of feelings, ideas, as if she was awakened to new contradictions. The main contradiction was that she had grown up in a faith that was only evangelistic, preaching, but she wanted to serve others.

Salvador explained that a person "who truly wants to serve others in our country is seen badly by the government. People could assassinate a person like her." Cristina's desire to "serve others," then, was a political choice that could have implicated others.

Was Cristina's isolation from her family an effort to protect them, or was it the inevitable "price" to be paid for her innovative spirit? A Salvadoran woman seeking a divorce from a respectable Christian elder had little power or comprehensible argument to seek custody of the children. Furthermore, life with one who "served the people" could have meant danger for her children. In any case, the children chose their father.

Cristina's determination seems to have been quiet and her decision, therefore, was all the more shocking to the children:

It was a surprise when the divorce took place because usually kids hear fights. But in this case there was none of that. We wanted to know why they were separating but they didn't tell us. They only said they were separating but the next day she packed and left the house.

From that day on the children didn't see her. Salvador still doesn't understand why. He feels it had to do with the pain involved in the separation, but he also says Cristina wasn't allowed to see the children.

Years later we regained contact. With time passing the pain got less and there could be contact. She'd call and ask to see us. Sometimes she could, sometimes she couldn't. I'm not saying my father prohibited this. There was pain on both sides. We began seeing her again but always outside the house.

Why she didn't insist on seeing the children the first few years isn't clear. Salvador's characterization of the pain of the divorce was emphasized by Edna, Cristina's best friend, who described the separation as bitter. Whatever the combination of reasons for Cristina's isolation from her children, she was in anguish about it for years. Edna said there was a sadness and emptiness Cristina carried as a result:

Her husband got custody of the kids because as a Baptist father and head of the household, it was expected that he should have them. She was the bad one, the one breaking up the sacred entity. The kids also wanted to go with the father. This was part of her emptiness, a big hole in her life.

Edna Flores grew up with Cristina and went to Baptist school with her. She saw Cristina's divorce as a final step away from both her marriage and Baptists "who didn't allow her to develop as a woman and as one committed to the people." Cristina's separation from the church was almost inevitable because a divorced woman could not remain a deacon. Moreover, her divorce was a blow to the congregation. "Her marriage was considered the model Christian marriage," said Corina, president of CONAMUS.

Cristina's problem with the church appeared to be focused on the church leaders' inability to recognize women's lives and authority. The church itself was undergoing a transformation during the 1970s that propelled the most progressive elements to take a prophetic stand in relation to the national liberation process. Cristina helped begin Emmanuel Baptist Church, according to Edna. Emmanuel Baptist Church has followed that prophetic path with such faithfulness that members have been placed on a death list by the far right. Abductions, tortures, and killings dogged the congregation during the 1980s. Cristina took up the church's prophetic mission with characteristic enthusiasm and dedication. "When she preached in church," Edna recalls, "her sermons were beautiful. She had a concept of the justice of the Reign of God. She combined spiritual life with human life. Her sermon had a content of deep spirituality — about our humanness."

It was during the 1980s that Cristina began work with refugees who were pouring into the camp set up in San José de La Montaña Catholic seminary. Edna identifies Cristina's joining ANDES (the teacher's union) as the point when "her life entered into a time of crisis and contradiction between her Christian practice and the national reality, as well as her own identity as a woman." Although recognized as an ideal wife and mother, a church deacon, she was still searching, according to her friend, "to find out who she was."

It was clear she was looking for something more from life. She was always saying, "I want to be myself, make my own decisions. I don't want to carry everybody else's problems." She made radical changes. She broke with her husband and the Baptist Church.

Cristina joined ANDES on October 10, 1986, the day of the earthquake. The earthquake devastated the fragile infrastructure of the shantytowns. The families of Cristina's students were left homeless and desperate for food. She joined ANDES that day as a way to respond to the chaos and suffering in an organized way. Cristina was extending her pastoral skills into a new organizational form.

She became immersed in teachers' struggles, in the struggles of the popular organizations. In ANDES she worked in the Legal Rights for Teachers commission. According to her ANDES *compañera* Alicia, "She was distinguished by her activism, by her willingness to do all the tasks required of teachers as organizers." Each of Cristina's friends and co-workers emphasized her willingness to do the numerous thankless tasks that attend organizing efforts. "I never knew her to say no to an activity," Alicia said. "When I couldn't attend a meeting she took my place." But Cristina's generosity was not just the intensity of a dedicated activism. It was the generosity of a teacher also. Alicia explains that Cristina was an "exemplary teacher who gave everything to students." Cristina was also Alicia's mentor:

> I had responsibility for day care centers and she was so generous she gave me materials she had developed. She would develop these materials right on the spot as I needed them.
>
> The last thing I asked her was what kind of mural I could put up in my kindergarten. She made it for me before she was killed. We lost it during the confusion of her death. But what couldn't be taken away from me was my ability to do it myself — an ability Cristina had taught me.

Cristina's generosity was personally supportive. Even when she was followed by a car with dark windows, she reassured others by her calm manner of continuing the work. To Alicia, "she seemed serene; she never seemed scared." Her sensitivity toward others must have grown out of her own loneliness. Alicia recalls an expression of her kindness:

> One day when I had personal problems Cristina came and stroked my head. [Alicia began to cry at this point and struggled to continue]. She said, "You're not alone. We're all with you here!" I felt great affection for her because of that. Cristina was a very helpful, very human co-worker.

Cristina's friend Edna attributed her compassion to her pastoral sensibility. "She never lost a sense of her own spiritual life. Her liberation occurred when she was thirty-nine. By then her religion was a visceral part of her."

Finding a Home with Women

It isn't fully clear how Edna identifies Cristina's "liberation." She describes Cristina as moving toward a life of commitment and risk implied in her political decision to join a popular organization. Cristina was also constructing a new self as a woman, free of the constraints of church and marriage. After joining ANDES, her own transformation accelerated. She joined her friend Edna in work with CONAMUS. CONAMUS became her community, a circle of women supporters provided the affection she had lacked over the years. "When she came to us she was very depressed," Edna remembered. "I told her she would meet other women with the same problems." According to Corina, "Cristina had to deal with so much social pressure, but among us she felt understood."

The social stigma of separation from one's children left Cristina without any support except from other women who had questioned assigned gender roles. CONAMUS more than most of the Salvadoran women's organizations understood the complexity of her problems. Initially she sought the solace of support, especially from Edna, but once involved she took up the cause of women with fury. Edna explains:

> She was my closest friend. We talked for hours. Like all women who are alone, we discussed our emptiness, an emptiness impossible to fill. I think she tried to fill her emptiness in her commitment to the popular struggle. She came straight from school to work here. She never said no to a task.

Cristina was part of the committee that inaugurated the CONAMUS radio program "Abriendo Camino" (Opening the Way). In fact she named the program. "We saw it as her description of the way women could open new paths for their own freedoms," says Edna. Cristina wrote the first script around the issue of elections and the CONAMUS position regarding the elections. Her children still have cassettes of their mother's broadcasts. With the leadership role she was assuming, they felt increasing pride but also fear for her. "When she joined CONAMUS," said Salvador, "we knew clearly the implications of working with CONAMUS. It seemed a natural move for her to help other women, especially women at the bottom of society." At church the children were teased about Cristina's broadcasts: "Sounds like your mother is raising a ruckus again." But the congregation at Emmanuel Baptist was proud of Cristina also. She had returned to services occasionally but she told Salvador, "The church is not in a building but in the streets." According to Salvador:

> I knew she didn't leave her faith. She always had a Bible with her. She was an evangelist who nurtured and encouraged others in a spiritual sense. I think the energy she had for her work came from her faith. She was never one who could say, "God bless you," and see you were hungry, and go on. First, she fed the hungry, then gave a blessing. She was an example for us that Christian faith is not passive.

Cristina became a representative of CONAMUS at public events. Her energy was indefatigable. "She was going everywhere," Edna said. "She was seen everywhere; she was a great animator and speaker." A woman, a teacher who had spent her life speaking to an audience of kindergartners, had become charismatic. Perhaps it was the Baptist preacher in her or a long strangled word. She wasn't afraid to speak even when the risk was possible capture.

Identification as a leader in a popular organization was a danger all too evident to organizers. To publicly denounce authorities was risked only by organizers who had enough international support to have some (though slim) immunity from disappearance or assassination. Cristina was well aware of the risks she was taking. "Sometimes she was afraid," Edna said. "She would sleep here at the CONAMUS office; other times, she'd appear at my house and say I just want to sleep here."

Cristina seems to have been an anomaly. Her children never quite understood the journey that led her away from them. She left the church but never fully. She was a feminist and a revolutionary but she surprised her co-workers by functioning not only as an organizer but as a minister. Her church had truly become the streets, where she found the dispossessed, especially women, society's lepers. Even Edna couldn't anticipate what Cristina would do:

> Here's what surprised me about her. She would gather up clothes and bring them to "The Door," a place for alcoholic women. I always admired that. It was like she was a little ant dedicated to helping these women. She would pick them up from the streets, bathe them.
>
> She took me to a party once, and she told me, "I don't know if you'll like this because you're a Baptist and these women are alcoholics."
>
> I gave her a dress, but she wasn't grateful at all. She gave it away to someone who needed it more.

Of all her protest activities the most publicly dangerous was her role as "MC" and speaker at the National Debate rally. There were thousands who had come to hear presentations from the church-sponsored National Debate Assembly. All the church and popular organizations, representing the majority of Salvadorans, put forth platforms in support of peace negotiations between the government and the FMLN. "Cristina was a powerful speaker," said Dan Dale, a church worker with the Lutherans, "but I remember thinking she's taking an enormous risk speaking so directly, so truthfully."

Her children were in the crowd, fascinated with the *compañera* and leader their mother had become. Salvador recalls that day:

We went to march in support of the National Debate a month before her death. At the rally she was the MC in front of the National Palace. We saw her from a distance. We'd try to catch her eye and smile at her and she at us. We saw her as one of the leading women. She was in a different role. She was like a *compañera*. But then when we'd get together she'd be simply our mother.

Cristina's activism was a bridge that connected her to her children. Ironically, the path that had taken her from them was now leading her to them. In the liberation process, a catechist once told me, "all paths lead to the suffering people, no matter where you start." Cristina's youngest son, Eli, said, "Even though I was the youngest when she left I always loved her and felt close to her. Even when she became involved, I guess I would say, I felt proud of her."

The pride was not simply the prejudice of one's children. Corina called Cristina "dynamic," and then, as if apologizing, said, "I'm not trying to idealize her but she had a great capacity for relationships."

Whatever struggles Cristina had waged to become her own person, before she died she made conscious choices about her life and possible death. Choosing to give up one's life for the sake of a greater good — to serve the people — is a freedom few can embrace. Cristina did. Edna says, "She knew the time was coming; she knew they could capture her." Cristina must have recognized her increasing danger. The day before she was captured she spoke with Edna:

She said, "I'm leaving all the radio program cassettes so that if they capture me you can go on." She even joked that a photo we had of her should be used. . . . We talked about the many generations of little girls she had formed as a teacher.

They did use that photo both at Cristina's funeral and later when all the women's organizations came together in a "Chain of Hope" to celebrate Cristina's life. It would have pleased her, that ecumenical gathering, beginning to claim their own women martyrs, beginning to claim themselves. It was an encounter of religious women and activists who imitated Cristina's life, her crossover witness — working in the church, working with the popular organizations, living out the gospel injunction to immerse oneself in the people's liberation not only in Bible study meetings, but in the street.

Venancia, a pastoral leader, describes the significance of that women's encounter:

The encounter began two weeks after the death of Cristina and was held every week for ten weeks through June and July. Now all the churches, with all the members of the different popular organizations of women, made the decision to have a meeting to

153

mark the end of this Chain of Hope. This event was very positive, because first of all this was the first time that the majority of the churches in El Salvador, above all the women of the churches, unified to form an association of women where we could undertake a series of activities and where we could, as women, reflect on what we contribute for peace in El Salvador. This would be one of the most important objectives we achieved, that is, to unite. In the second place we thought it very important that the churches were present with the popular women's groups. We were coordinating this meeting with the popular groups and with the international delegation from Geneva. The planning was fantastic, particularly given the participation of women from all fourteen departments of El Salvador.

It was a shame that the hall was too small. The auditorium could hold only six hundred people and it was completely full — more than six hundred women. The first theme we dealt with was the role of the woman, particularly the Christian woman, in the search for peace. The second was about the family code. We managed to discover a few elements that had been hidden from us, which we as women were not informed about, a series of rights that correspond to women. Also, through the meeting a number of women gave their testimony, women from the churches as well as women from the popular organizations. There were very clear testimonies that women have a historic role, above all in the creation of a new society. We discovered through the testimonies how we as women, and men as well, are capable as human beings of transforming this history.

Cristina's funeral also brought together a unique mix of people whose lives she had touched. A few women from "The Door," the center for alcoholic women, entered the Baptist church to bid farewell, not to a revolutionary or feminist or Baptist, but to a friend with a compassionate heart. School children came also to remember a teacher who taught them "to serve the people." "All the Baptists came," said Edna, "even my church, the First Baptists. At the funeral, the church took her home."

After her death CONAMUS workers were continually "watched." "The same gray microbus followed two of us," said Corina. "It was a form of psychological terror. We even had the license number of the truck that picked her up, but the driver is still driving around in the capital." Corina believes Cristina's assassination was a warning to CONAMUS because of its radio broadcasts and large base among poor women. CONAMUS organizers are convinced that Cristina was killed by death squads as an "example" of what will happen to women activists, because no effort was made to obtain names from her — a process of torture that takes days.

Cristina was assassinated within one hour and her terrible mutilation was meant to terrorize activist women. However, Corina says, "They gave us another martyr, another reason to struggle."

Cristina's legacy to her children was a life that "served the people." However mysterious and painful their mother's journey away from her traditional role was to them, toward the end of her life, she had reached a path they understood. It is a path they hope to follow. This is her son Salvador's summary of his mother's legacy.

> My mother's personal example shows me why it is important to make a commitment to help others. I think I can speak for all her children in saying that we have learned from her what it means to be committed to our people and we all want to be committed also. ...She's our mother but one of our people also. She's one more example of what must be done to bring peace to our people. The most honor I can do to her memory is to follow her example.

Silvia Maribel Arriola

> All of us together have more death than they
> but all of us together
> have more life than they.
> —Roque Dalton, "We All"

On Silvia's fifth anniversary Mass in 1986, the people offered gifts: flaming ocote, a knotty wood cross, doves that fluttered upward following the fall of light from the high windows of the church. Her *comunidad* sang "Silvia, Where Are You Going?" Silvia "answers" the refrain in the language of *mística*. The song marks years of the people asking her destination, years of Silvia answering.

Silvia's base Christian community knew the literal direction of her journey in 1981 to Santa Ana, a war zone. But they didn't know where the final journey would lead. That journey ended in fire. Silvia and ninety-one others ran for three days, their legs pumping with the fury of animals outrunning the hunters, hunters with precise, high powered rifles. Traced by radar, pursued by helicopters and planes, the band of FMLN militants, the wounded, doctors and nurses like Silvia, were surrounded and virtually incinerated. It was January 17, 1981, when Silvia fell with the ninety-one others. For the community who knew her, the sisters she lived with, and the poor among whom she is legend, Silvia continues her journey symbolized in flame, cross, and the flight of doves.

She died at twenty-eight in Santa Ana, the town of her birth. Her family was privileged enough to send Silvia to an exclusive Catholic girl's school, Colegio Guadalupano, in San Salvador. Sylvia's mother, who is a Mormon, now lives in the United States. Only Silvia and her father remained in El Salvador when the family left. Faithfulness to her people would cost Silvia everything. It would cost her life, but not, says Sister Emma, who met Silvia as a youth, her death. Her death cost the authorities because, says Emma, "They couldn't kill her. She'll only die if we let her, if we fail to continue her work."[57]

I met Sr. Emma and Sr. Luisa, who are members of Silvia's religious order, on January 17, 1986, after the Fifth Anniversary Mass commemorating Silvia's death. "Religious order" is not exactly the correct designation. What was remarkable about Silvia's public vows was that they were made to her *comunidad de base*, and as such bound her in fidelity to the people and not to Vatican ecclesiastical authorities. Silvia pronounced these vows in the presence of the base Christian communities and Archbishop Romero:

> In a society whose ideals are power, possession, and pleasure, I pray that I may be a sign of what it really means to love. I will do my best to be a sign that Christ Jesus alone is Lord of history, that he is present here in our midst, and that he is capable of inspiring a love mightier than our own instincts, mightier than all the economic and political forces, mightier than death itself. My one desire is to lead a life in the following of Christ, he who was poor, chaste, and obedient to the will of his Father. I wish to live for him alone and his saving work, as his disciple.
>
> I promise our Lord that I will be faithful — in sickness and in health, in youth and old age, in tranquility and persecution, in joy and sorrow. I promise to do my best to share in his incarnation among the poorest of the poor, and to imitate his poverty and solidarity with them in their liberation struggle. This is my hope and desire: to share in his evangelizing mission among human beings, concentrating all the power of my will and affections on him and on all my sisters and brothers, and living in continual quest of the Father's will: in his word, in the church, in the signs of the times, and in the poor.[58]

My meeting with Luisa and Emma took place in Silvia's community church, where I saw my first picture of Silvia. The faces of Silvia and Padre Octavio Ortiz, a priest killed with four youths of the community, stare down from a wallboard that reaches from floor to ceiling.

Silvia began her journey from a comfortable life not so much as a dramatic conversion — like the young Francis of Assisi putting aside his finery to take up the sackcloth of beggars — but more as an accompaniment, a following of the path of a people.

Silvia's conversion to the side of the poor did not begin when she entered the convent, but when she encountered *los desplazados*, the displaced refugees. She had entered a traditional order whose ministry was teaching and nursing in the Guadalupano area of San Salvador. But she questioned her order's class preference, its dedication to healing the middle class, to educating the privileged.

She first encountered the poor when she took a group of her students to a poor area with Sister Luisa as her guide. Sister Luisa remembered that day:

> I was speaking with a group of women in our base Christian community when Silvia asked to learn about these groups. She returned after that first visit. She wanted to know about our lives, why we did our work, who we were. It seemed she had to respond to the moment; it was her temperament. Even while she was a teaching sister, she was drawn to the movement of Charles de Foucauld and developed a relationship with the Little Sisters of the Poor. When a person with this spirituality and this call to evangelization confronts the poor, a crisis starts.

The crisis was personal, and though it would lead to Silvia's break with her traditional religious order, the leave-taking was amiable. Like a moth to flame Silvia drew closer to life with the base Christian community. She worked with the displaced community and attended the *comunidad*'s meetings, returning to the convent later and later each night. The convent doors closed at seven and she kept extending the time, slipping in at the last minute. When the mother superior insisted that she keep the rules regarding prayer obligations and that she come home at specified hours, Silvia insisted that the religious community become involved in her ministry. But she knew this invitation would likely be refused because the Salvadoran nuns were afraid that attending base Christian community meetings would compromise their work as teaching and nursing sisters. And it was dangerous. Her superior, apparently sensing that it would be pointless to circumvent Silvia's commitment, requested that she at least cease wearing her traditional habit when going into the poor areas.

The situation was growing irreconcilable as Silvia became more and more involved in the work. She had to decide. The decision was precipitated when it came time for Silvia's renewal of vows. Her order decided before Silvia did. She received a letter before her renewal that suggested that she would be happier in another congregation.

I asked Luisa if the situation had become acrimonious. I had started to picture Silvia as the order's token radical. But no, the order's letter was "affectionate, because she was loved; but they didn't really understand her," says Luisa. And so Silvia left her order and its safe, middle-class lifestyle. Says Luisa:

> When the moment came to break off, it was very difficult for her to surrender to another life, to disengage. In the convent she was someone important, a religious, but with us, with no juridical link with the church, now who was she? Also, her family could no longer say with pride, "My daughter is a nun!" Now what would they say: "My daughter belongs to a small community"?

Silvia's decision to leave her order's safety and legitimacy in the midst of burgeoning terror and explosive repression was not the inevitable path that the entire church of Central America trod. The vast majority of the Salvador clergy have not taken such risks. The martyred Archbishop Romero is an anomaly, still criticized by segments of the Salvadoran church who contend that he went too far and insist that he should have attempted reconciliation. Many of the clergy respect Romero but emphasize his more spiritual statements while ignoring or forgetting the statements like the following: "Neutrality is impossible. Either you side with the Salvadoran people or you're accomplices in their death."

Those who stand with the poor have only their embrace with which to face the Goliath of state power. It is the poor majority who have stood up again and again, waiting for the church to enter the arena and engage the forces of death with a willingness to suffer for the possibility of life. That moral claim explains Romero, Silvia, and many of the women in this book, but it does not explain why their numbers are so few. The question is not why was Silvia who she was, but why should she be distinctive? Silvia and the sisters of her community are a surprise, a gift that the poor didn't expect. Each step Silvia took dismantled her identity as a middle-class professional. As she acted to construct a new church, she authored a new self, discovered in the common longing and jeopardy of the poor. Silvia learned to become empty in order to enter into the heart of life. A difficult loss was silence for prayer.

Living in a slum with four other sisters, working half-time to help pay living expenses, ministering to the homeless refugees pouring into the city for the other half of the day, and attending base community meetings at night, left Silvia with little time for contemplative prayer. When she let that longing go, the people became her prayer. And she theirs. "People in the base community were moved by her choice of them," says Luisa. I spoke with a co-worker of Silvia who referred to Silvia as having "surrendered to the people." Magdalena, a Co-Madre, remembered Silvia:

I remembered her patience and her gentleness with the people. What really touched me was that she learned to be poor even though she had never been poor like us. She was rich. I'll never forget this, never. Silvia used to come to where I was living. She had ulcer pains and was doubled almost in half, but she wouldn't stop. I didn't know how she could keep going. Her deep commitment brought her to martyrdom.

Another member of her community explains Silvia's illnesses as due to her being a premature infant and frail. She describes Silvia as under five feet and very thin but her energy was explosive. Both these women, who are themselves *humildes* (humble ones), refer to Silvia as humble. This quality seems to suggest less of the traditional pietistic meaning and has more to do with a deepened class option, a forsaking of privilege, but more even than that, it implies an uncomplaining commitment.

If Silvia started her journey tentatively, once she had begun she fairly ran toward her destiny. According to María Elena, another woman who worked with Silvia in Cuscatancingo:

Of all the sisters who lived in that small apartment, she was the most humble. There wasn't a house she didn't visit. Toward the end before she went into the countryside, she rarely slept in the apartment but she stayed with us in a different apartment every night. She was completely handed over to the people.

At the same time that Silvia was working with the base Christian teams, the mass popular organizations were emerging and this "provoked tensions in the heart of the church," according to Luisa. Previous to this the community had been shaped by the witness of Martin Luther King and Gandhi. "But at that moment," said Luisa, "practice challenged theory. We had to deal with the popular organizations and the military organization of the FMLN. With our people, we had to face the question of where we stood."

As more of their community joined the popular organizations the sisters were challenged. "We had our theory — a Christian attitude that continued to protect us, a paternalistic attitude. People's suffering helped us understand the commitment of others attempting to change things."

It was during this period that Silvia met Emma and her youth group in the poor Mejicanos neighborhood in San Salvador. It was holy week when the sixteen-year-old Emma attended the traditional way of the cross that she had heard was being led, incredibly, by a woman — Silvia:

We had always had a traditional way of the cross but Silvia's reflections were very different and beautiful. It made an impression on me that a woman who was so young was leading the way of the cross. Also I'd never seen a religious who was on the streets with

159

the people and not cloistered within a convent. At that moment I spoke with Silvia and I said: "Who are you? Why have you come?"

That first encounter with Silvia was powerful for a young woman with spiritual ideals, living in a country at war. Meeting the demands of committed youth in El Salvador requires in an adult not ordinary maturity but heroism. Silvia didn't disappoint. She was in fact more than Emma's youth group could keep up with. In life and death Silvia was just a step ahead. But what compelled the youth group of Mejicanos, according to Emma, was not her charisma but her love, her friendship. "Silvia truly identified with us. Besides being a friend, she was a sister we could share with. We could go to confession to her better than with a priest. For me she was someone who fulfilled herself, who was happy in her work."

Emma described Silvia's patience, even devotion, to their youth group, taking them seriously in ways they had not expected, taking them more seriously than they had taken themselves. Emma drifts back to those days recalling the lunch meetings her small group had with Silvia once a week sitting under the trees at Planes de Rendero, where they spoke of their hopes and dreams:

> We were searching for a life in which our spiritual longings could be fulfilled. Silvia was the occasion of awakening my vocation. I was looking for a life of community, working with the poor to give support to the people who in turn would give me life.

Emma's journey would reach beyond Mejicanos, beyond the city and into the countryside, into the war itself. In addition to Mejicanos, Silvia had been working in a poor area at Tutunichapa with a lay minister named Alfredo. As Alfredo explained his pastoral work with Silvia, I pictured the odd couple — this lumbering bear of a man and the tiny Silvia. He explained that their base community's response to the rapidly expanding repression catalyzed the pastoral team's decision to divide into a group of twelve and go into the countryside. They went to three different *cantones*: Zapote, San Roque, and El Amate. Silvia lived at El Amate for one year, immersing herself in the material and spiritual life of the people. After a death threat from one of the right-wing paramilitary groups, ORDEN, Silvia became a pilgrim traveling from one small community or family to the next, never staying too long, lest her presence draw danger for the family she lived with. Silvia, like so many others, had become *quemada* ("burned").

By 1980, according to Alfredo, "the struggle of the masses had become very active and that's when Silvia decided to do pastoral work in other zones of the country, to work in the impossible areas. Silvia, another sister, and three priests split up to go into these difficult areas, with Silvia going to Santa Ana."

On January 3, 1981, Silvia went to Santa Ana accompanying the people. Her little community of sisters affirmed her decision. Sister Luisa explained that Silvia's journey "reached a point where people asked her if she could provide pastoral accompaniment in one of the war fronts. We went through discernment and we decided it would be appropriate for us to be with the people in this way."

While working in Santa Ana, Silvia continued to return to her base Christian community in San Salvador. As the human needs of people under siege grew desperate, she returned to one family in the community in San Salvador weeks before the FMLN offensive would sweep Santa Ana. She asked one of the mothers if she would come out to Santa Ana and bring two of her older children for work.

That mother, Marta, explained her last meeting with Silvia:

It was a few days before she died that she came to the house. She asked that some of us return to the countryside to minister. I remember we were in the kitchen and we told her we'd wait to make the decision. But she returned without our decision. If we'd gone with her we'd be dead now.... My best memory of Silvia was her option for the poor.

Emma explained the circumstances of Silvia's death. Shortly after Silvia began working in and around Santa Ana and just before the 1981 rebel offensive, the Salvadoran soldiers in the Santa Ana garrison mutinied and joined the FMLN. The FMLN then took over the town of Santa Ana. During this period Silvia gave a talk in the town plaza on the theme of Christian commitment. A woman religious thus addressing the assembled people, the mutineers, and the guerrillas was comparable to a twelve-year-old boy standing in the temple to lecture Jewish elders on the meaning of the scriptures. Such revelation evoked amazement in both cases. Emma comments, "Those guys were struck that a religious woman was in a place like that. They were amazed at the strength of a faith that prompted her to such a commitment."

Following the mutiny everyone understood the army would return bent on reprisals. The town prepared to depart or join the guerrillas. Silvia chose to go with the FMLN contingent with the intention of offering her nursing skills in care for the wounded.

A Maryknoll sister who worked in Santa Ana at the time describes the FMLN takeover of the town in January and the events that followed:

The *muchachos* [guerrillas] went house to house advising us to stay in and not be fearful. By 9:00 P.M. the barracks were taken. During the night the Green Cross center was used for the wounded brought in from the outskirts of the city.

That night it was quiet, and the first part of the next day. People went about daily life. The young boys were instructed in the use of

161

guns. There was a fearless, cozy attitude. But later in the morning when I was at the Green Cross a helicopter came in and began firing. But the houses were frail. Then we heard bombs in the city, but we didn't feel them in Lamatapec. But then cannons fired on us. Helicopters came in and people fled into the chapel and convent where we set up mattresses against the bullets. We played a game to calm our fears.

At 3:00 P.M. the army came with tanks and the *muchachos* fled. An office and a clinic were destroyed, and the baby scale, which was difficult to come by, was taken. We saw this from the chapel. At 4:00 P.M. the Salvadoran military set up a transmitter and guided the movement of the helicopters, directing them to follow those who had fled over the hills. We were appalled at this, knowing that it was U.S. technology that would track that group that would otherwise have been free. It was an American voice that I heard across the street. Someone said, "That's all, let's go."

Days later the group of *muchachos*, doctors, and nurses who served with Silvia were caught on the road to Metapan. They were slaughtered, then thrown in an open grave.

When Silvia's base community received word of her death, they were stunned with grief. But in the poor barrio of Mejicanos where Silvia had worked, there arose the deepest response. Two members of the youth group who were especially dear to Silvia responded to her death as an invitation to a more committed life. When Silvia fell, others stood in her place. Sister María and Sister Emma made the decision to enter Silvia's small religious community and publicly vowed themselves to obedience, charity, and poverty, to the God of the poor. Sister Emma remembers:

Given Silvia's commitment and ours, we felt we couldn't sit "with our arms crossed." At the moment we learned Silvia had been killed, the youth group came together to reflect on her life. Sister María and I asked to be accepted into the community. Two boys from the youth group who intended to enter the seminary went to the war front and they're still there. They've never come back. Three more stayed in the city and joined in the base Christian community ministry. The other four became frightened, left the work, and stayed behind. Even now they do nothing.

I asked Emma if there was a marker on Silvia's grave because I wanted to visit it. Now Emma's eyes rimmed with a hint of tear. "No," she said, "the zone is still controlled by the armed forces so we can't find it. But when the revolution triumphs we will make a pilgrimage to that site." She smiled at the thought, blinking away tears. Emma's final reflection about Silvia was concise: "For me Silvia is not dead; she lives on in my ideals. She lives on in the commitment of the Christian community. Silvia could die if we let go of our faith."

Such a faith goes beyond the boundaries of what language can express. It is faith that those who fall do not fall in vain. The proof is in practice, in refusing death's dominion, in resurrecting the dead. Where does the meaning of Silvia's life lie? Feminist biographers would search the "text" of her life. Poststructuralists would point toward the war itself, the postcolonial context of repression and her response to her moment in that history. Social psychologists would point to family relations, her mother's waning influence, Silvia's bonding with her father who wouldn't leave his people. All these interpretations elucidate some meaning in Silvia's life. But the people for whom she lived and died have a less complex criterion for discerning the meaning of Silvia Maribel Arriola's life. The individual subject of their evaluation vanishes in one sense, but in another sense she is never more present. For her *comunidad* the meaning of Silvia's life is discovered in the effect of her life on those for whom and with whom she struggled. It is "Silvia" who shifts the focus from herself. The song her community wrote allows Silvia to speak once more. Addressing the people, she points beyond herself:

> Don't seek me in my tomb
> I am among the people
> I go opening furrows
> of a new history. . . .
>
> —"Silvia, Dónde Vas?"[59]

5

THE HOUR OF WAR:
THE MILITANTS

Photo by Steve Cagan

The people are our mountains.

—FMLN

Melida Anaya Montes had eyes dark as black pine, deep and bright. Her face was moon-shaped without an angle, wrinkled at the brow and the corners of her eyes, but soft, open. Anaya Montes's girlhood figure had vanished years ago, and her waist had grown thick. But she could still walk five days and nights carrying a pack and a rifle and move like a cat through brush. Without her uniform Comandante "Ana María," as she was called, looked matronly, like someone's aunt or mother. She was just another one of the "fish" in the vast sea of her people. It was for such "fish" that General Blandón would "drain the sea," slashing and burning a third of Chalatenango and Cabañas. Melida Anaya Montes was the second highest commander in the Popular Forces of Liberation (FPL), the largest of the FMLN organizations.

Ana Guadalupe Martínez is from the younger generation of daughters that followed Anaya Montes. She is still lean and beautiful. Her mind and hands move like *sonsonate* birds, quick and fluid. Though from the countryside, she joined the Popular Revolutionary Army (ERP) in 1974 as a university student leader, urbane and intelligent. When she walked into the mountains of Morazán north of the Torola River she felt stupid, like a schoolgirl faced with the superlative lesson of endurance, a task that loomed impenetrable as the mountains, a lesson the *campesinos* had long mastered. So they taught each other — the student revolutionaries and the peasants. Martínez was quick. By 1975 she had risen to the position of chief of ERP's armed forces in Morazán. She grew stronger, prepared in the words of the FMLN song, "to be the last one to eat, the last one to sleep, and the first one to die."

Melida Anaya Montes and Ana Guadalupe Martínez occupy the two highest command positions held by women in the FMLN. Anaya Montes began organizing as a teacher and founded the National Association of Educators of El Salvador (ANDES) in 1965, where she continued as secretary general until 1978. It was Anaya Montes who led the ANDES strikes in 1967, 1968, and 1971. The 1971 ANDES strike, held by women, was one of the most massive national strikes ever led against the government.

Ana Guadalupe Martínez was only a high school student during the 1968 ANDES strike. But as a student leader during the 1971 teachers' strike she took note of the strike leader Melida Anaya Montes, the only

166

woman among the nine hunger fasters sitting in front of the presidential palace. Martínez did not forget the vicious beatings of the hunger fasters by palace guards. She also joined in nonviolent student protest initiated to change university admission requirements that favored the middle and upper classes. She joined the general strike of Arcos Comunes in 1969–70. But as repression intensified students joined the newly formed guerrilla organizations.

Neither woman was ideologically driven. Ana Guadalupe says:

> Our participation was a natural process of realizing the injustices around us and then beginning to act. That participation carried us to deeper and deeper commitments, which we naturally accepted because . . . of our decision to struggle. These decisions came because you realize that behind you there is a whole people willing to struggle. In a way, a year passes, then another. We began to struggle when we were young, and now we have been organized for ten to fifteen years, and it feels like no time at all has passed.[60]

This is not to say that the women did not uphold Marxist strategic principles. But their motivation, the source of their commitment, was more the people than ideas or principles. Nor were these women unwilling to engage in ideological conflicts. Melida Anaya Montes was murdered precisely because she would not back off a principled position that directly challenged Cayetano Carpio, the commander-in-chief of the FPL. The principle over which they struggled was whether *guerra prolongada* (prolonged war), Carpio's tactic, or Anaya Montes's position, which sought a political solution to the war, would obtain. Following Anaya Montes's assassination Cayetano Carpio, considered the father of the revolution, committed suicide. The FPL issued a statement denouncing Carpio's moral and political bankruptcy for his part in Anaya Montes's assassination. In the seven years since Anaya Montes's death, the FMLN has increasingly embraced the political strategy for which she argued.

Ana Guadalupe Martínez's role as an FMLN negotiator with the Political-Diplomatic Commission of the FDR/FMLN, involved in the UN-supervised peace negotiations, carries forward this legacy of strategic vision. The path leading to her current diplomatic role involved torture in a clandestine prison of the National Guard in 1976. After she was released from prison in 1978 she wrote a book that sought to publicize the existence of secret prisons in El Salvador. Painfully explicit in her book is the sexual nature of torture that women must endure. Ana Guadalupe does not analyze or interpret this dimension of her suffering except to say that it was this humiliation, even more than electric shock, beatings, and blows, that left her "a worn and crumpled cleaning bag, tossed to the ground."[61] Having endured every other form of psychological and physical torture without breaking, it was rape that brought her closest to despair.

Ana Guadalupe Martínez and Melida Anaya Montes are two of a handful of women among an FMLN high command that is otherwise all male. Are these women tokens? Yes and no. Yes, because they are so few. Yes, because there are no national liberation movements in the world where there is equal power sharing with women. No, because among the emerging national opposition movements the Salvadorans are leaders in advancing women's participation beyond tokenism. Even when they complain forcefully about the seeming endless vestiges of *machismo* that obstruct or minimalize women's participation, Salvadoran women insist on placing their dilemma within a context of historical possibility rather than idealized speculations.

Women's vanguard role in ANDES, as well as their political role in the FMLN, is largely responsible for Salvadoran women's evolving transformation. The war itself, as this book has tried to demonstrate, disrupted the semifeudal socioeconomic patterns shaping *campesino* family life. Historical necessity placed new demands on women. But that is not all. There is another side to the dialectics of historical change, however cataclysmic, and that is the historical subject's response. Salvadoran women in both the city and countryside, as the ANDES strikes showed, *initiated* a response to their nation's suffering. They did not receive history; they made it. From the popular organizations to the FMLN, Salvadoran women have challenged the passivity that held them in the servitude of impoverishment and dependence for centuries. Women's early participation in the FMLN has, in the words of Ana Guadalupe Martínez, "profoundly determined the character of the people in this struggle."[62]

The Farabundo Martí National Liberation Front

The Farabundo Martí National Liberation Front (FMLN), founded in 1980, is a united front composed of five guerrilla armies: the Popular Forces of Liberation (FPL), the Popular Revolutionary Army (ERP), the Armed Forces of National Resistance (FARN), the Salvadoran Communist Party's Armed Forces of Liberation, (FAL) and the Revolutionary Party of Central American Workers (PRTC). But the FMLN is not only a military organization. Each of the five groups has a political organization based in the popular struggles of the poor majority. These groups grew out of the highly politicized working-class and peasant movements of the early 1970s.

Many women, as well as men, who had been urban organizers in the late 1970s and early 1980s felt compelled to join the guerrilla forces when their companions were murdered or had disappeared between 1979 and 1981. In the eastern part of El Salvador or in the mountainous northern areas, young women and men involved with the base Christian communities and peasant cooperative movement responded to the massive bombardments and peasant massacres with a determination to obstruct and transform the spiraling destruction confronting their people. They joined the FMLN, swelling the ranks to twelve thousand combatants in the early 1980s.

Because of its deep base among the peasants, the FMLN was able to join with *campesino* initiative for self-governance as embodied in the cooperative and base Christian movement in the countryside. Wherever the FMLN provided protection in zones under their control in Chalatenango and Morazán provinces in the early 1980s, the people organized popular governing councils. The FMLN assisted by providing, from its own ranks, technical assistance for the creation of the social infrastructure and new social institutions based on principles of participatory democracy. Former teachers and medical personnel in the FMLN assisted the communities in setting up schools and clinics. FMLN women were especially involved in working with these projects, which were an extension of their previous organizing work. In a special way FMLN women shaped the emerging process of self-governance. Their very presence in the zones overcame *campesino* reticence about women's social roles. The newly forming democratic process aimed at transforming gender and class limitations. Although the relationship between the new popular governing structures and the FMLN was close, they were not institutionally linked. As the years passed the *campesino directivas*, especially those currently existing in the resettled zones, have insisted on their own political autonomy.

Nevertheless, the people's sympathy and support for the FMLN remain intact, a factor that confounds U.S. counterinsurgency experts who have poured millions into civic action programs that have never captured the peasants' hearts or minds. Counting on their base among the peasants, the FMLN launched a "final offensive" in 1981. However, lack of unity among the five FMLN organizations resulted, according to the FMLN's self-criticism, in undercutting the offensive. The destructive disunity of the first half of the 1980s has been largely overcome. The FMLN functions as a united army under one five-member general command, the FMLN directorate.

By 1987 the FMLN had established its political or military presence in all fourteen of El Salvador's provinces. In 1989 the FMLN made unprecedented political concessions in its demands for a negotiated settlement to the war. First, it abandoned its demand for transitional power sharing, and, second, it expressed a willingness to participate in the electoral process. Further, the FMLN reiterated its alliance with the Democratic Revolutionary Front (FDR), a political alliance of three center-left political parties — the Popular Social Christian Movement, the National

Revolutionary Movement, and the National Democratic Union. This affirmation sought to quell rumors generated by the U.S. embassy, perhaps wishful thinking, that the FMLN-FDR alliance was ruptured.

There are accusations that the FMLN's transfer of the revolutionary struggle to the electoral arena is opportunism of the moment, a reaction to the events in eastern Europe, the dissident Soviet challenge to communist ideology as anti-democratic, and the defeat of the Sandinistas. Moreover, the massive U.S. assault on Iraq demonstrated to Third World nations U.S. willingness to decimate challenges to its "strategic interests." Such critique, however, fails to take into consideration the FMLN's own documents, written before these historic events, which stated willingness to seek a political solution.

Other fears persist: on the right, that the FMLN's commitment to the electoral struggle is only a posture with the hidden intention of future governance by a "dictatorship of the proletariat"; and, on the left, the FMLN will *not* support the leadership of workers and peasants and that a socialist economic model will be abandoned. The FMLN responds that social reality, not ideology, determines its objectives. Political and economic democracy are its declared goals. FMLN leadership claims that global events have made it clear that a socialist regime is not possible in El Salvador at this moment. This is not the same as abandoning socialism but rather a search for transitional economic forms, a recognition that the process of reconstruction, in a country whose economic infrastructure is shredded, will be long. The lessons of many blocked or failed socialist-based economic models in the front line nations of Africa, as well as the blow of the Sandinista defeat, led the FMLN and FSLN leadership to conclude that a military victory against U.S. imperialism was not possible[63] and that economic modernization is a first and desperate need for the developing nations as a step toward economic democracy and ultimately socialism. The FMLN has stated:

> In today's world, a combination of the public and private sectors can lead to more rapid development of Salvadoran society than a supposedly more radical and closed model.... Our objective is development. An ideological approach is of no use if it does not solve the problem of poverty.[64]

New Lessons

For its part, the FMLN has learned from the electoral defeat of the FSLN in Nicaragua the necessity of immersing itself in the people and promoting participatory democracy over representative democracy. The vertical party system of the FSLN, a seeming necessity to consolidate unity and a strong front against U.S. attack, did not encourage popular consolidation, creativity, or ownership of the revolutionary process when economic conditions grew extreme. In the elections an impoverished people, no longer envisioning themselves as co-creators of history, turned away from FSLN leadership and toward a weary vote for partial relief. Sandinista commander Victor Tirado has argued that the national liberation struggles of underdeveloped nations cannot win prolonged wars in which the U.S. sustains an intense economic war against the base of the society.[65]

The FMLN is ready for a new phase of history, a phase of radical democracy and of people's leadership, not vanguardist leadership. It is a new hour in history, far more the hour of women than ever before.

So the FMLN bends as if it were a woman, or indigenous, or spiritual. And this confounds the U.S. embassy and the CIA, and even the left. Negotiating is considered a weakness rather than an expression of strength and political maturity. It is precisely the presence of a new dialectic in revolutionary history that accounts for such flexibility — the voice and vision of women, the blood of the old people, indigenous blood that flows in Salvadoran veins in spite of the genocidal elimination of native culture in the 1932 massacre, and finally the presence of Christians in the people's army and organizations.

I sought in this final chapter to add another dimension, another expression of revolutionary motivation, if only to change the pattern of the life histories. I had expected the FMLN militants to express a motivation different from those of the other sectors. Yet the stories remain similar, stories of women formed in families steeped in a communal tradition of fidelity to *pueblo*. The success of the base Christian communities was in preserving this ancient indigenous fidelity. Women's unheralded accomplishment has been in nurturing *comunidad* as the cultural form that shapes and carries forward the life of the poor. The FMLN sensed the tactical advantage of appropriating these deep cultural bonds. Father Rogelio Poncelee describes the FMLN militants who work in his zone in Morazán as more humble, more generous than he, who had been spiritually trained for a life of selflessness. The lessons of the poor and the war itself have reshaped the image of the individual self that the Western world upholds as sovereign. Padre Poncelee, after six years at a war front, reflects on the FMLN guerrillas he has come to know:

> I have learned from these *compas* the meaning of humility. We priests are not humble but proud and individualistic. We think we are important because everyone puts us in the center. The *compas* know how to wait. I am impatient, I don't like to wait, I have important things to do, I can't waste time. . . . But for these *compas* it's different. They don't boast either, but have respect for each other.[66]

171

Rebeca Palacios

You will have to toughen your hands to reconstruct the country . . .
you will have to erode the cliffs of terror
reduce the mortality rate . . .
shake dust from the roses.

—*Mirna Martínez*
"For the Youth of the Future"

Comandante Rebeca Palacios is a member of the Political Commission of the Popular Forces of Liberation (FPL) and a member of the Political-Diplomatic Commission of the FMLN.

I grew up in a middle-class family, not wealthy, but comfortable. We had the advantage, however, of being a family with a democratic tradition and a history of political involvement. And, of course, the other advantage was that we were three girls and one boy. This meant that our older brother could not push us around because there were three of us! And besides, all three of us were developing as women, as human beings, and, eventually, as revolutionaries.

One of the things that made me decide to get involved with the struggle was, in the first place, an acute awareness of the injustice in our country, of the oppression that the vast majority of our people suffered, and their tremendous poverty. And this led to my awareness of the need for changes, changes that would benefit the majority, that would create equality and opportunities for our people, and possibilities for their development.

The other thing that contributed to my getting involved was the example of my parents themselves. They never let themselves buckle under or sell out or compromise with what they believed to be right. And they always taught us that when you believe in something, you should commit yourself to it, heart and soul, even if it should cost your life. So, in this way they really put their stamp on us.

Now, in terms of my decision to join the organization, the most important thing was deciding to get involved in the struggle because that implied a change in everything, a change in the way I saw things, a change in my behavior and in the course of my development. I had the opportunity to become a combatant and a candidate to the party, then later to be a member of the party, to work in different areas of the organization, and now I am working in the party's Political Commission.

I can assure you that it's been no easy road, even though the statutes of the organization prohibit discrimination against women. The fact is

172

that the whole culture is sexist, and there is not a single comrade who is not affected by this. If it's true that our organization provides the opportunities for women to develop themselves in daily concrete work, it is also true that the woman herself has to overcome a thousand and one obstacles — with her *compañero*, with her children, with her co-workers, with the organization itself. And above all, she has to overcome the idea that being a party militant requires her to be less of a woman, that if she really maintains her essence as a woman, she cannot fully be a party militant. It's a constant contradiction in the development of all women in the FMLN, especially for those in the leadership.

Perhaps the most difficult moments have had to do with the deaths of my sisters and brother, as well as the death of my father. I have a brother and one sister who died in combat and another sister who was "disappeared," and just recently my father passed away. Those were very hard times. Above all, I think, you're always prepared for the possibility that something could happen to yourself, but you never really think that something might happen to the people you love. And I think this is very painful. Especially in a family like ours, where we were all *compañeros*, people involved in the same struggle with the same goals, with the same beliefs and outlook. We had built such strong bonds that we were more than comrades, we were truly friends, including my papa. These were difficult times for me.

Another very hard period for me was when I was in San Vicente. I was in charge of all the political work in the FMLN-controlled zones during the time of the famous "CONARA Plan." This was the government's three-month plan that brought many troops of the elite "Regional Brigades" into the area to capture civilians. It was extremely difficult moving about in that region, to be responsible for eight thousand persons, without food, trekking through the mountains, with children who were dying, actually dying of hunger along the way, without water, all of this necessary in order to frustrate the enemy's plan. I can tell you that there I saw suffering like I had never seen before. And it hit me very hard.

I think you can overcome this kind of experience, as well as personal tragedies, only if you are genuinely convinced of the real possibility of victory for the Salvadoran people. And I have a tremendous conviction that all this effort is not in vain, that we are able to build a different kind of country, with liberty and democracy, with social justice. And, too, I have a deep confidence that I am not going to let my people down. Maybe if I weren't so sure of my own commitment, I wouldn't be able to stand seeing others suffer so much. But it's really the faith that I have in myself and the faith in our victory that are the key factors that make it possible to overcome all the blows we are dealt. It's your faith, and the great responsibility you carry, that enables you to overcome these blows and give you the will and strength to keep on going. But yes, there have been very difficult times.

Another hard period was when our first- and second-in-command died in 1983. [Here she refers to the assassination of Melida Anaya Montes and the suicide of Cayetano Carpio.] All our members, and especially the leaders, had to make a huge effort to preserve the cohesion and the political direction of the party, to not allow it to break apart. And generally, this requires you to put aside, or make a big effort to put aside, whatever personal problems you may be having in order to give your full attention to the greater demands of the whole process at any given moment.

My happiest moments? The first was when I joined the organization. Believe me, when I first joined, it was like my first love. I had the feeling that I had begun something totally new, totally different, which was what I truly wanted. And it's what gave my life meaning. This was one of the greatest moments of happiness in my life. And even now, seventeen years later, I still celebrate within myself each anniversary. I've never had a moment's regret. It's one of the greatest joys I've ever known.

Something else very positive that I've been a part of has been to see how not only the armed struggle has grown and developed, but also how the people, the Salvadoran people, as my older sister used to say, "in spite of everything, still know how to sing." In other words, to know without a doubt that in the most difficult of times the people have always been there and continue to struggle; they have continued to grow strong. This is something that gives me great joy, that truly delights me. I don't know how to explain it, but it's something that really moves me.

And naturally, the other big joy has been my children. As you know, I have two, as well as a niece who is like a daughter to me. And if I haven't been able to be with them very much because of the war, I can assure you, nevertheless, that it's been one of the greatest experiences, even though it's often been our terrible fate to be separated. But the fact of being separated has never diminished the fulfillment I've found in being able to be a mother and a revolutionary, to be able to do everything required of me. Regardless of all the problems, to know that one can be a revolutionary, a political participant, and a mother, for me this is truly one of the greatest satisfactions in my life.

One important factor is that, at the very least, our organization has no positions that oppose women's participation. In fact, the organization itself, at every level, struggles for women to be involved. This is fundamental. Even if this struggle is not enough to change the so-called natural, everyday attitudes of the majority of the male *compañeros* in the party, at least it is a very good starting point.

The other important thing is your own decision not to be a coward. I mean as a woman. In this kind of *macho* environment, an environment that our organization cannot escape, it's not easy to stick to one's own position, to adhere to one's own standards, to have the necessary time, according to one's own needs, for political work. This all implies, of course, some objective problems, especially in one's personal life. Nevertheless, I've always told myself, look, you can't be a coward in the face of this challenge, and what's more, if we women don't begin to face this challenge, when will the vicious circle ever be broken?

I could give you many examples of how, in any given situation, what you need is determination. If we women don't have this determination, we will never get ahead. There are lots of women who, because of their husbands or their children or because we're told it's not "feminine," never take a step forward. And we, and here I mean the women in the leadership of the FMLN, believe that the FMLN's positions are very positive. But, on the other hand, we've committed ourselves to take it even farther, to use the FMLN's policy as the basis for creating a new model of what it means to be a woman, or at least to live as a new kind of woman. It would be very presumptuous to say what kind of model of a new woman is actually needed, but at least one can be true to what one believes it to be.

You know, before I joined the struggle, I was looked at as a sort of rare bird. At best, people might say I was frivolous, always running around, going out at night, coming in late, you know? That I didn't have "good morals." And given all that, you really have to be determined and also consistent in your conduct. I feel good about the efforts I've made, but you go through a lot. And I want to emphasize that you should not struggle for self-fulfillment, but to make a contribution, especially if you are in any kind of leadership position — to help open the possibilities for other women. In the case of El Salvador, it's not easy because the majority of the militants and combatants of the FMLN are from the countryside. And in the countryside, women are really bound by tradition. They are really held back. So of course the struggle is that much more difficult. It's much harder.

The development of the revolutionary struggle in El Salvador has given birth to a consciousness among many sectors of the population, and women are part of this phenomenon. It's true that within the struggle of the Salvadoran people, of which women are a part, that at first the particular demands and problems put forth by women had a "low profile," as you mentioned, but now people have seen that they have merit. And this is the fundamental thing, that there's a real growth in the consciousness of the people, in their level of rebellion and in the participation of many sectors, including women. And as women have

175

Ana Guadalupe Martínez

Comandante Rebeca Palacios

Gladis Sibrián
Photo by Rick Reinhard

become involved in the struggle, particularly in the cities, we've come to see that we can't simply struggle for overall revolutionary changes in the country, but, just as the workers have their specific demands, and the *campesinos* have theirs, that women, as a special social entity, also have their own particular demands And in this way a consciousness about women's struggles continues to grow within the country. You say that there are nine women's organizations, but, we still need a better organization oriented to the grassroots and a greater variety of instruments for the women's struggle.

Now concerning what you said about women's demands being considered "ultra-feminist," we still have a long way to go. Some years ago I was telling some *compañeros* how, some time ago, a *compañera* was considered "petit-bourgeois" if she didn't want to work in the kitchen. It was as if she were rejecting her historic role. No kidding. To a large extent this argument was used and well received among certain sectors.

But now women are realizing that we cannot be subsumed in other sectors. We are a sector with our own special demands and needs. In the case of El Salvador, this is very concrete: women earn less; the business of prostitution is an unresolved problem; the repression of women, the abuse of women continues. These are facts. And I think that what we've seen so far isn't enough. But I'm absolutely convinced that this movement will continue to grow and become even more authentic, effective, and broad.

You can't subordinate the concrete problems of women to the general class struggle. Just as women can't forget their class position within society. Working-class women naturally have to fight for the demands of the working class. The women of the cooperatives have to struggle within the cooperative movement. But this doesn't deny that working-class women, the women of the cooperatives, the women students have common problems that aren't resolved strictly within the labor movement or the general political struggle. And this is a point that still hasn't been fully accepted. I'm not referring so much to the political positions of the FMLN, because the FMLN has an overall political position toward the organizing of women en masse and within the FMLN. But the ideology of *machismo* weighs heavily. And that's precisely where there's still work to be done, to deepen the awareness of this problem among men and women. It's not just a problem that men haven't accepted; it's also that the great majority of women are still not aware, or are afraid to become aware, of their own situation.

I'd like to make it clear that the FMLN is probably one of the Frentes with the most women in its leadership. In fact *compañeras* who died in combat were in the national leadership. And we have *compañeras* who are currently serving in different leadership positions that are integral to the liberation struggle of our people. I could give you many examples.

There's an enormous number of *compañeras* who have given their lives: Comandante Ruth, Comandante Susana, Ana María, Clara Elizabeth Ramírez, Arlen Siu [the nom de guerre of a Salvadoran woman, not to be confused with Arlen Siu of Nicaragua]. In other words, many *compañeras* have fallen in the course of the struggle. But there also are *compañeras* who are currently developing their capacities within various important forms of work. There is Mercedes del Carmen Letona, Marta Valladares [Nidia Díaz], Ana Guadalupe Martínez, all of whom are members of the Political-Diplomatic Commission. And within our own organization we have women in leadership. In other words, it's not true that my case is so unusual.

Nevertheless, this is still not good enough. And the truth of the matter is that in relation to the numbers in the Frente, we women are a small percentage. I'd estimate that women are about 15 percent in the leadership. And this is a result of all the things I've been talking about, the sexist conditioning of both men and women in Salvadoran society, on the one hand, and on the other, the effect of this conditioning on the political work that is directed at women's participation, specifically within the organization.

Right now we're involved in a campaign to get more women actively involved, to make it easier for them to participate in the struggle. We've been carrying out discussions throughout the guerrilla-controlled zones, in the cities, and even outside the country, about how best to encourage greater participation on the part of women. And we've concluded that the starting point is direct work with the women themselves. The second step is to work with the men to develop an attitude that is not only supportive, but is aggressive and forward-looking with respect to women's participation.

Basically, my confidence, my faith, the convictions that I have, are rooted in the fact that the Salvadoran people have shown that they are no longer willing to be anybody's slave. The people have an immense longing for democracy and the people themselves are mobilizing, with more initiative, with more enthusiasm, to struggle for basic social transformations. So if my people, an illiterate, poor, underdeveloped people, have this kind of spirit to keep on struggling and moving forward, in spite of what has been done to them, in spite of the bombings, in spite of the massacres, in spite of all who have been "disappeared," if seventy-eight thousand victims are not sufficient to make this people quit, then I have absolute confidence that this people has the moral and material strength capable of changing the destiny of our country.

Clelia

Like a rose
you shall multiply.
　　—Cutumay Camones,
　　"Comandante Clelia"

Clelia joined the FMLN because of her mother's involvement. She began her political work at age thirteen.

I had always lived in the city with my mother when I was young. This was in San Salvador. Her job paid very little, but through our efforts I managed to go to school. Our family wasn't originally from the city and so once in a while we would go to visit our relatives in the countryside. We visited my mother's sister, and once when she was very sick, my mother decided not to leave her alone. We stayed until her death, living about a year and half in the countryside. And that was when things were really starting to happen with the organizations in a major way. People began to organize clandestinely.

Well, I really didn't know anything about what was occurring because I was very young. I was thirteen years old and I didn't understand politics, but my mother was involved clandestinely. She began to identify with a particular organization and in 1981 she made the decision to join the guerrilla force and I went along with her. I also had a sister, but she was with her partner and so that just left me, the youngest, with my mother. My mother was very committed and she was actively involved for two years; luckily, I could stay near her. But later that became harder. And sooner or later we had to separate, and we did that in 1983. It was necessary for me to go to another area in the same department, but still far away. Six months went by and I hadn't had the chance to see her.

My first job was in press relations, written communications. But then I became a radio operator (*radista*). I was in the area around Tres Calles in 1983 when I was wounded. The combat was very difficult and the enemy surprised us. There were very few of us, twelve in all and two of us were women. It was too difficult for my companions to get me out and they thought I was dead. They left without me and, practically speaking, I was lost. I stayed alone in that isolated place for almost two days. I was wounded in the back and the bullet had crossed into my lung. It was hard to get out and I stayed there; after two days, luckily, a civilian boy found me and got me out. He wasn't related to our organization although he had a relative who was a combatant,

179

but he came to my assistance when I needed just that. He brought me food and clothing and said, "Let's get you out of here. You can't stay here." Since he seemed to know the area, he took me to where it would be less dangerous. The next day some *compañeros* came by. The *compas* recognized me and saw that I was still alive. So we reestablished contact. The boy stayed with us and later joined the guerrilla forces.

Later I had to go to San Salvador for an operation I needed. I went with the Red Cross. Two months later I went back to the camp and the boy who saved me was still there. When the *compas* had thought that I had been killed, they had tried to keep it from my mother, but she somehow learned that I was wounded and presumed dead. So I wrote a letter to her, but she didn't believe it was really me until she heard my voice by radio and then realized that I was okay.

Later, when I returned to the front, the commanders told me that I would go to Morazán for a time. This was still 1983. I left Usulután for Morazán, always working as a radio operator. So I went to see what it was like there, having always been curious about that part of the country. Luckily, I was able to return to the FMLN-controlled zone where my mother was. I was so happy to see her and spend some time with her, especially after all that had happened. She was working as a cook. Everyone loved her because she was such a friendly person. Because of her age and the situation, she couldn't continue to participate as fully as she once had; she needed to rest a bit more and not run as many risks as she had previously. That is why she left the front as a combatant to carry out other work with the base in 1984. So our toughest separation was when I went to Morazán and she was left to carry out other work. When we said goodbye, we did not know how long it would be before we would see each other again. And I have not seen her since then.

When I went to Morazán, I thought it would be for a short time, but it became six years. You learn a lot there because it is a kind of school in itself. You can really take the time to learn things that will be useful in the future. I worked in the distribution of information as a typist, but really you can learn a little of everything.

A *radista* means a person who is trained to work with the radios used in communication. But we could not simply use the equipment: we needed to have codes to encode and decode messages. We worked closely with the commanders. As radio operators, we never simply made decisions and sent messages that we personally determined. No, everything is done in consultation with the command. The work of the radio operator is to guarantee communication, no matter how difficult. Many *compañeros'* lives depend on our work with the radio. Our *compas* were dependent on us because in an attack or in a confrontation, communication is essential. That is how we transmitted orders. For example, a commander would say, "Do this, do that" or "The enemy is coming in your direction." In other words, we transmitted information that was very important and that helped to make the attack victorious, that helped us all achieve something. An error means the loss of lives of the *compas*. So the radio operator must be clear on how to do the job, with the best attitude, knowing that it is not easy. Her job is to be constantly alert for communications slip-ups. As long as you have the radio, it is your job to be constantly on guard.

The first time we took Usulután — when *compañero* Gonzalo fell in March of 1982 or 1983 — there were at least forty radio operators going to the attack. Each one knew that the priority was to transmit. We had trays of batteries in our backpacks because that is the radio's food. We carried practically no clothing or anything else. The important thing was to carry what would ensure communication — the batteries. We left for Usulután, each of us with a different area to cover. No two radio operators are ever together; rather, you cover the area that the commander has assigned. After seven days we had not taken Usulután completely. Because we had so much work to do and because we hadn't yet achieved our goal, those were sleepless days and nights. We had enough food because we were in the city neighborhoods and people treated us well. So we did not suffer from hunger, but from being tired, from walking, and from the confrontations. Nothing was easy. As radio operators, we were constantly alert. At night the combatants could sleep because there weren't confrontations then, but our duty was to be ready at all times for a surprise attack and to be ready for any orders. So all night we were alert, and that means a lot of sacrifice: you get worn out from sleeplessness.

Our nights were not completely sleepless because it would be too hard to stay completely awake for seven days and nights. We had posts. Two out of twenty-five *compas* would be on vigil each hour. Each hour one would wake another and then switch off. When it was our turn, we would stay by the radio. Each of us had a code name. When I heard the code of an operator being called, let's say I heard a message for "Sol," I would call her to the radio.

The takeover of Usulután occurred in March 1982. When did you join the FMLN?

It was around May 1981.

I am asking this to determine how old you were in May 1981.

I was fourteen, yes, fourteen. It was hard to have real clarity at that age. In my case, I didn't know anything about political matters. It was really because my mother did it that I did too. I was not going to be separated from her. But as I say, it is hard to be conscious of anything at that age. I hadn't had any idea of how life was in a camp or how to share with the other *compas*. But as time went on I learned how to work on certain jobs. I learned why it was necessary to be doing what we were doing. Other *compañeros* joined after they already had a great deal of understanding and clarity about the reasons for their decision to take up arms. For example, they had seen the difficult life in the countryside, what the children there had to go through. When I joined, I hadn't seen that as clearly, but as time went on I saw that it was a just struggle.

Did you have time to read, to attend workshops, or join a group to discuss ideas to help you understand more politically and ideologically?

Yes, of course. We had courses with people who knew things in particular areas; we learned from them in small groups. Some of the topics were political or military. For example, there were military courses, mainly for those who had recently joined. The preparation is nothing like the training in the army, where they punish and insult the soldiers for absolutely no reason. Our preparation is strict because it is military training, but we don't suffer the way that the soldiers in the army do when they are punished for some small error. Our training is different because our combatants are not there because they are earning a salary or out of personal interest. Our combatants are there voluntarily, because of their conscience, and they know that what they are learning will be useful to them and perhaps to many others whom they will teach.

You said that in the camp you learned how to share. Tell me more about that, about your experiences of sharing and how you learned to do that.

Sharing means that individualism does not exist within a person. There were no privileges for the leadership in the camps. Everything was equal. Food and everything else were shared equally among everyone. The leadership did not have special privileges and their example taught the rest of the combatants. The camps were like a school in which we worked to eliminate envy, individualism, and *machismo*. We learned to be disciplined and we tried to be better. We learned from the others and we saw how the recruits would adapt to this life. It really is a different life there because there are children — young people, no, I will say children — mainly male children who join very young, at age twelve. They join because they don't have anywhere else to go.

Gladis Sibrián

Because we want to create a time that is ours...
all suffering must become ours.

—Mirna Martínez,
"Because We Want to Create"

At twenty-seven Gladis Sibrián has a girl's voice, soft and high. But her words are a woman's. She is currently a special representative of the FMLN-FDR to the U.S.

I was born in Potonico in Chalatenango, that is, in a little village outside Potonico in the mountains. It doesn't even have a name. I have eight brothers and sisters. Because of our economic situation we had to leave the countryside and go to the city. There my father abandoned us, leaving my mother completely without means.

My mother never saw her life as valuable. She always asked my brother or my father what to think. But now she's amazing. She disagreed with the FMLN for boycotting the elections. "Look," she said. "Ungo is running, so why boycott?" She has hope now. She works with the base Christian communities. But in the 1970s when I was a teenager my mother had to support us. She made tortillas, *pupusas*, tamales, and we would sell them before and after school.

In a system of violence, such as ours, the system is transmitted into the family. Sure, my father beat my mother. As a result of her cries, we too lived with violence. So far I still haven't been able to survive the fingerprints left on me from this experience. As a poor person, as a woman, as a younger daughter, my opinion didn't count. The only opinions that counted were those of my father, uncles, brothers, or older persons. My level of self-esteem was very low, as was my sisters'.

That's why when I joined a base Christian community in San Salvador my life took on a new dimension. The communities gave me a life, a sense of self. Before I was really questioning why I should even be living if everything is suffering, everything is poverty.

There in the base community we found a reason to struggle and to live. We formed cooperatives. The best example of this was the lives of the women who worked making tortillas in the market. They came to our community and said they didn't have enough money and didn't know if they could continue making tortillas. It was because the middle men had raised the price of corn and the women weren't able to pay for it. We found twelve women to go together and buy corn in common at a cheaper rate. What the women learned was that by working collectively

183

they could survive. We, the poor, all joined together to work and people began to see that everyone had ideas, everyone had talents, and that together we could make changes.

The effect of the system was to fill people with a sense of fear and oppression. The base Christian community helped people confront that fear. An incredible thing was to watch people transformed through those meetings. At first people trembled and cried, they were so afraid. But through the base communities people grew in confidence. They learned not to be ashamed of themselves. The system had taught us that as poor people we are lazy and don't want to work.

One fundamental area we still haven't been able to handle adequately is mental health education, to deal with the effects of twelve or fifteen people living in one room. The consequence is promiscuity, violence, and child abuse. However, the women's organization CONAMUS is addressing this problem. CONAMUS built a clinic, but it was destroyed during the November offensive. Its purpose was to help abused women and children. The CONAMUS project also helps tortured women from prison and jail, as well as women abused in the confines of their own homes.

But to go back to my own case, we couldn't focus on social problems such as these at the time because of the strong repression in the period from 1976 to 1978. In 1977 violence occurred all over. Fathers Alfonso Navarro and Rutilio Grande were killed. Anyone who spoke out for human rights and against violence was marked. In our communities we asked what all this meant to us. We realized the repression would affect us soon. We decided we would not be cooperative through our silence; we would speak out. In this way a priest with whom I worked was killed in 1978. Then our priest, Father Octavio Ortiz, was killed in 1979.

There were direct repercussions: Antonio, a member of our community, was captured, terribly tortured, then released. When Antonio recuperated from his torture he came to my house to recover. He told my mother that I should leave the country. However, I didn't see that I had committed a crime that would necessitate leaving the country. And so we continued working.

One of the decisive moments of my life was when our priests were killed [Ernesto Barrera in 1978 and Octavio Ortiz in 1979]. I had never before had to make a decision about our self-defense, whether to use arms to defend our people. When I saw those two bodies, one run over by a tank, I spent three days reflecting. I thought we can't just give flowers or prayers when we're receiving bullets. Perhaps for me it was even more difficult because I was affiliated with a religious order, the Sisters of Assumption, Oblates of the Sacred Heart. It's traditional but is adopting a new model that is closer to the people. I was planning to enter this religious congregation. However, my internal contradictions were enormous. I felt I wanted to be a sister, that I had a call. But how could I leave for religious training in Guatemala to be cloistered for two years separated from the people?

So through the years I never found out about my vocation. What I have found is that when I am with a religious congregation I feel at peace.

But at that moment I saw a contradiction. How could I be a sister and be part of the FMLN? I would have to be one or the other. I was not ready to go underground at that point but I was not ready for the congregation because it would mean leaving the people.

Having been raised Catholic I couldn't conceive of taking up arms. But at the same time, as a Salvadoran, I realized there was no other option. This had a great deal to do with going to the U.S. I knew armed struggle was the only option for our people but I was not able to join it. When I went to the U.S. I felt guilty because so many of my friends were killed.

In 1980 one of our members, Cecilia, was captured by the death squads. Twenty days later her body was found on a coffee plantation totally disfigured. She was mutilated and her body had been covered with acid. After that I received an anonymous letter saying that the church was communist and whoever stays with the church pays with their life. This letter was put under the door of my mother's little store.

So I avoided my mother's shop. I remember I was in a bus when two men got on. One went by and he shoved against me so he knew I could feel his gun against my back and he said, "This is for you." I thought, "Well, this is as far as I'll go." So I got off the bus and they did too. Just then I hopped back on the bus and lost them. It seemed that the driver realized what was happening, so he drove past the next two stops, pulled alongside a taxi, and told me to get out quick. I could see solidarity in this driver's face and he understood what was happening.

This was a direct experience with the death squads. After that I couldn't sleep and didn't go out. I was continually worried they would come and get me. I went through a period of psychosis and fear. Then one morning I awoke to find the wall on our house had been painted with the words "You Will Die." That day I took the little I had and slipped away.

I went through the back door, through the garden, then into the farmlands. I lived in one house for a week with one family, then another week with another, and another week with another. Then my mother told me to leave the country. We had no contacts in other countries, but finally my mother made contact with an old friend she had in the U.S.

In 1981 I left the country to stay with my mother's friend. I had three options at that point: first, to leave the country, second, to join the military and political struggle, and the third, to die. I decided to leave for the U.S. At the border the man guiding me tried to rape me. Because

I resisted they beat me up. But luckily some neighbors in that area came and helped me escape.

It was very difficult in that first year because I questioned myself a lot. I felt guilty for coming. I felt like I was already dead. I suffered a lot of discrimination.

I worked as a domestic and the people called me stupid because I didn't understand the language, but they would never bother to repeat one thing. All they paid me was $60 or $80 a week, which is very little. I lived that way for two and a half years, until in 1984 I decided to return to El Salvador. As I said, I felt dead, so I returned out of a need, the need to have more contact with the people, the need to feel that I hadn't been completely broken, and last the need to say to those in power that they wouldn't be able to triumph.

I was afraid in the airport, afraid near the security forces. But I also felt like smiling because they hadn't been able to kill me, neither physically nor spiritually. I came in contact with friends who had joined the FMLN. They gave me a new perspective on how the movement had advanced. Most importantly, they understood why many of us had left in 1981. They invited me to join rather than closing doors because I had left. Later I returned to the U.S. to work with legal, health, and assistance programs for Salvadorans. I helped refugees deal with survival issues with the intention of organizing and educating. I had experienced what so many refugees faced.

During 1986 I established closer links with the FMLN. In 1988 we decided I would stay in El Salvador. Now I only returned to the U.S. for short periods of time. In August 1989 the *compañeros* of the FMLN asked me to officially represent the FMLN to the U.S. That wasn't my intention. I went to El Salvador to be involved in all the different levels of struggle, to make a full commitment. The decision was hard for me. However, the *compas* said I had the language and contacts and I understood the U.S. culture.

It's a great challenge to work in the U.S. representing the FMLN because the U.S. has waged a major campaign against the FMLN, calling us "terrorists" who want to implant a communist totalitarian government. The media give the U.S. people a very negative impression. It's been my task to explain our political platform so people will understand we are not just an army, but a political force that counts on our armed wing. We've used our army to show the government the level of power and organization we represent so that without our participation there will be no solution to the war. Basically what we seek are democratic reforms, cessation of repression, and the ability to express our opinion and organize ourselves. This is our understanding of democracy: that people should control their own lives and contribute to the development of the country.

We realize, as a people, the power we do have. But the problem is how to use it. From my personal experience as a woman, as a member of a family where there was a lot of oppression, and as a member of a society that has suffered a whole century of repression as well as sixty years of military dictatorship, I can say that none of this has been enough to suppress this aspiration for power that we the people have.

According to CONAMUS the position advocated by some women's organ-izations that says, "First the war, later women's rights," can you comment on this?

CONAMUS is at the grassroots and works with those women who are not organized, and therefore what CONAMUS states is, I think, the most correct position. CONAMUS is not struggling simply for women's right to an abortion, but for a total liberation. You can't separate the two, women's individual rights and structural change. CONAMUS confronts the government with its own legal framework to demand more parental involvement of fathers, more child care centers, increased salaries for women. At the same time that CONAMUS struggles for these rights, they organize women from all different sectors — the marginalized zones, *campesinas*, workers, etc.

On the other hand, the women's organizations within the FMLN are different. Those struggles are internal. First it's a struggle to be recognized as women in a leadership role, being listened to as *compañeras*, as representing women at that level of struggle.

Within the top military structure there are no women?

There are, but it's not 50–50. There are women in charge of battalions, military sections, platoons — in charge of hundreds of men. At the inter-mediate leadership level women are in the majority. At the *comandante* level 35 percent are women.

My hope is in the Salvadoran people. When I think about hope I don't think about the FMLN, but about the refugees, our people returning from Colomancagua and Mesa Grande, people willing to undergo severe deprivation, people willing to go back into danger to be free.

A source of hope is that in spite of seventy-three thousand deaths we have transformed pain into energy and action. When I see the levels of organization in the cities and especially among the poor, I see people have already taken power. As long as the FMLN exists, the possibility of change exists.

One thing I'd like to say is that we are a peaceful people, not by nature violent. But we aren't passive; we aren't passive in the face of seventy-three thousand killed. We're in the streets, in the *campo*, constructing a new society.

187

Conclusion

Nothing from our impossible past has died.
—Mirna Martínez
"Because We Want to Create"

By 1991 the FMLN and the ARENA government were involved in intensive peace negotiations that an exhausted but unbowed populace pressed for resolution. A stumbling block was the FMLN's demand that the Salvadoran army be purged of human rights violators and the Salvadoran army's refusal to accept such a restructuring. With El Salvador poised at the crossroads between war and peace and with no convictions following the murder of the Jesuits and their women co-workers, which was a reason for withholding $42.5 million in U.S. aid, President Bush nevertheless released the aid. Senator Dodd of Connecticut said the action was "blatantly irresponsible." It sends "the wrong signal at the wrong time to the wrong people."[67] San Salvador Bishop Rosa Chávez said, "Now is not the time for arms to keep arriving here. . . . The military aid question will be a gauge of the extent to which the United States is willing to commit itself to the peace process."[68]

To most North Americans the very existence of a peace negotiation process relegated the El Salvador "problem" to the soon-to-be-closed files. For the Central Americans, however, the "hour" was critical. Death squad activity during 1991 increased dramatically, and the Salvadoran army stepped up attacks and increased bombardment in the countryside in an effort to drive the FMLN from controlled zones for which they might claim political rights in the negotiation process. Additionally, labor and church groups were targeted by the extreme right in an effort to thwart peace talk progress, which they considered a "sell-out."

In the same year the base Christian community of Sister Matilde and Lupe was "marked" by death squads. In spite of their hope for peace, community members were convinced that some of them, especially the sisters, might not live to see the next stage of their struggle. They said this out of a sense not of fatalism but of realism. Shortly after the Jesuits and the Ramos women were murdered, the sisters returned to their small apartment to find a bloody cross slashed on their wall — a signature of the death squads. In July 1991, after a series of phone threats, their house was broken into while the sisters were out doing pastoral work. A neighbor observed men with machine guns in a car near the house. When the people insisted they move from their "convent," they refused because, they said, "We will endanger whoever we stay with because they'll find us. No, it's better to face them here."

It strains credulity to think that the Salvadoran right could repeat an atrocity like the murder of the Jesuits, but this time target religious women. In international terms, what could be more stupid? But the perverse logic was to disrupt the peace process at any cost, to spark an FMLN counter-response or popular insurgence, and, most importantly, to demonstrate that the peace process is irrelevant, that the "real" power in El Salvador can strike at will with impunity.

The right has never understood that death doesn't end anything in El Salvador. Sister Noemi Ortiz, who is a member of Sister Silvia Maribel Arriola's community, addressed the question of death in El Salvador this way:

> Those who thought that by killing 75,000 of our brothers and sisters, they would do away with the yearning for freedom of our people were wrong.... All of our martyrs have brought forth new life in our people and in our church: they killed Rutilio Grande, and they brought about the conversion of Archbishop Romero; they killed Archbishop Romero and the people became a prophet; they killed the four North American Church women and there was born a great solidarity movement between the people of El Salvador and the people of the United States; they killed the six Jesuits and the two women who collaborated with them, and thousands and thousands of voices from all over the world were raised.... They've killed thousands and thousands of our people, and the people get organized and move forward toward their liberation. Martyrdom makes the process towards liberation irreversible.[69]

The fuel that drives courage is hope. What the Salvadorans, especially the women, have taught me is that courage is a social gift of a people. What I would never have felt capable of risking in other circumstances, I have tried amid these communities of risk. Courage is not, as I had thought, an individual characteristic, gender specific, but rather a social/spiritual product of a liberation process.

This hope of the poor is an elusive, underestimated, yet determinant stratum of resistance. The "secret weapon" that defeats counter-insurgency is insurgent hope that, like a phoenix, rises from the ashes of charred villages, pulses in hands that have been shackled and hearts that have been broken. They cannot bomb insurgent hope into oblivion, they cannot torture it to death in Ilopango or Mariona prison, they cannot kill off hope in the resettled battle zones. It rises again and again. After ten years of war and seventy-five thousand deaths, with one million Salvadorans in exile and eight hundred thousand displaced refugees within the country living under the ceiba trees or in plastic lean-tos, Salvadorans still believe that life, not death, will have the last word. Although elusive, insurgent hope is incarnated. Its historical embodiment is *comu-*

nidad. The agents of *comunidad* are women who lift desire for life from the ashes of history.

Women create and maintain social life, and in so doing they subvert the objectives of counterinsurgency. Women's creative social power in maintaining community is strategically essential to national liberation struggles. This responsibility, however, is presumed and, therefore, rendered invisible. Instead, women's role in preserving national identity, communal consciousness, and social initiative is reduced to a gender-assigned "natural" predisposition toward nurturance.

Yet women's capacity to hold together social life throughout low-intensity prolonged war is of greater strategic importance than the incorporation of women (40 percent) into *comandante* positions in the FMLN. Women are the social infrastructure of daily life and communal cohesion. Without their presence, the world falls apart; there is no "home." Women are the ground of social being. Even when the community is displaced and on *guindas,* women become the humanizing agents, constructing "a life" in a hideout, a refugee camp, a shelter made of sticks and plastic. The women's stories illustrate their role as the spiritual and material infrastructure of the liberation process. Gender, then, defines responsibility for social life even though the strategic importance of the role of women in national liberation struggles is socially underestimated.

In Eduardo Galeano's beautiful summary of the tradition of *comunidad* in the Americas, he too ignores gender as a central feature of communal life:

> From Alaska to Tierra del Fuego, there is probably no tradition in America older than the communal tradition.... The persistence of these communal values points to deeper things, true roots — the idea that earthly goods are not private property, but to be shared in common; and finally the idea that the relationship between [people] and nature can be one of love and not necessarily war.[70]

Yet it is women who create the communal tradition by their daily responsibility for its sustenance. It is women whose sustaining presence calls the fragmented poor to community. If the people do not answer with their lives, there is no *comunidad,* no capacity for resistance. The meaning of community is forged in the dynamic process of resistance to death forces and affirmation of life. For men, resistance has meant a willingness to die rather than submit; for women resistance has meant a refusal to let the community die. The struggle to be a people, *pueblo,* is a struggle to preserve the heart of life.

Robin Morgan has observed

> that male-led revolutions have left dramatic accounts of their crises and heroism — of the Long March, the assault on Moncada, the

191

taking of the Bastille, the siege of the Winter Palace. If such revolutions seemed to have been based on the concept of dying for a cause, woman-conceived transformation seems more about daring to live for a cause, a heroism more difficult because it is daily — and ostensibly less dramatic.[71]

Women and Patriotism

"Masculine" and "feminine" are social constructs that mediate the definitions that men and women give to the concept of patriotism. Patriotism, historically defined as defense of the nation until death, has been a male undertaking. Women render another definition of patriotism, a definition less abstract, less symbolically associated with sentimentality and war. For women the patriotic action is the act of preserving life, of guaranteeing the people's survival when state terror is unleashed. Dying for the nation is not an objective; survival is. The needs of patriotic honor, of heroism, so tied to being a man, are subsumed to the daily heroism of keeping the community alive.

Women's patriotism, expressed in the maintenance of social life, has vitiated the effects of "total war." The FMLN'S ability to mount major strategic offensives has *presumed* mass social cohesion, a cohesion daily constructed in ten years of war, maintaining *comunidad*. This is the nexus of the people's hearts and minds, hearts and minds the state cannot pierce.

Campesinas, Co-Madres, and *comandantes* express a commitment that transcends family bonds. They speak of responsibility for public life, of responsibility for creating history. What they cannot "teach" is the meaning of solidarity for us. Too often, we of the First World have reduced solidarity to guilt. Or we have lionized the Central Americans' capacity for heroic acts of solidarity, while fatalistically expecting little from ourselves.

Yet these stories insist that ordinary people, through fidelity to each other, can sustain a protracted struggle against death's dominion. Solidarity between Salvadorans and ourselves must be mutual, both partners having an integrity of their own. Dependency or paternalism results if solidarity is not mutual.

Bread and Word

When I first traveled into the countryside near the Honduran border, I heard this story, which provided my first experience of how narrative, as revolutionary moral tale, presents an ethic divergent from the liberation texts of men. It is modest as Salvadoran stories go, but it holds immodest determination about shared bread and shared lives.

Two friends, María and Marta, were traveling back to their communal lands in Cabañas after years of exile in a Honduran refugee camp. The truck carrying them on the first leg of the journey overturned on a mountainous curve, hurtling the driver and others down a ravine. Alone, the two women sat beneath ceiba trees waiting until night when it would be safe to walk. As the stars grew bright, so did their hunger. María turned to her friend.

"Here," María said, "take my tortillas."

"But you'll be without anything and starve."

"Please," María insisted, "you have the baby and a new life needs a chance."

With that Marta handed María back the tortillas saying: "Look here, my friend, tonight we will share our bread. Later we will share our hunger."

Remembering this story is dangerous, for it captures the wisdom of women who live and die at the edges of history. It is dangerous because it subverts the values of the dominant powers. This dangerous memory is the "other voice" in history, proclaiming as Mary in the Magnificat did, "The poor shall be exalted and the rich shall be sent away empty."

The story expresses the wisdom of women who, in the words of Noemi Ortiz, "poured out their lives the way a candle wears itself out giving light." María and Marta chose. In the face of a possibly irrevocable choice, they did not equivocate. The last choice is not who will die, but how to live. The testimonies of women in this book attest to that question of existence: How shall we live? If the war determines that many will die, the lives of Salvadoran women insist on deciding, until their last breath, how to live.

María's generosity in this story is shaped by three cultural values: social rather than personal survival, ingenuity born of necessity, and *mística*. A dialectic of persecution and ingenuity has marked the Salvadoran masses with a social consciousness that transforms individualism. This dialectic has produced in the people a new definition of future. If the future is no longer to be waited for, it must be made by those who dare. Therefore, the future is to be created, yielding whatever possibility the people construct from moment to moment. When death lives so close to bone and flesh, fatalism or organized ingenuity are the only choices.

International volunteers who have accompanied refugees back to their lands in war zones recognize the Salvadorans' ingenious style. Confronted with an impossible situation, they shrug and begin circumvention. Bereft of technology, weapons, elaborate communication systems, adequate food, water, or transportation, with only a sliver of power (their trust in each other), they pierce impenetrable military encirclements. I have seen this happen again and again. Stopped at an army checkpoint, our guides scrap plans and invent a new route along back roads.

The ingenious style is not passive but imaginative, a stance made possible by organization. Confronted with impasse or confusion, Salvadorans act, figuring out the next step as they move. Ana María Castillo Rivas, known as *compañera* Eugenia, exemplified this disposition even in military planning. Just before the 1981 FMLN offensive, Eugenia, a guerrilla leader, wrote her final letter to her husband, Javier, expressing doubt and a typical Salvadoran response, which offers us guidance in our own "confusions":

> We'll see if we can pull it off. I'm constantly worried but at least I feel better knowing that I'm not the only one. It's confusing here but, like they say, let's get going and we'll sort things out on the road.[72]

Acronyms and Special Terms

ADEMUSA: Association of Salvadoran Women

AMES: Women's Association of El Salvador

AMIS: Association of Salvadoran Women

AMPES: Association of Progressive Women of El Salvador

AMS: Association of Salvadoran Women

ANDES: National Association of Educators of El Salvador

ANSESAL: Salvadoran National Security Agency

ARENA: Alianza Republicana Nacionalista, Nationalist Republican Alliance; the ruling party in El Salvador

atol: a corn drink made by squeezing liquid maize through porous cloth

barrio: neighborhood

BPR: People's Revolutionary Bloc, called the Bloque

campesino(a): inhabitant of the *campo,* or countryside; peasant; farmworker

campo: countryside

cantón, cantones: village(s)

catequista: catechist, lay pastoral minister

COFENASTRAS: Women's Committee of the National Federation of Salvadoran Workers

Co-Madres: one of three groups of Committees of Mothers of the Disappeared

compañero(a): companion; comrade in arms

compa(s): short form of *compañero,* political militant(s); comrade in arms

comunidad: community; created by the *base,* those most marginalized and ignored — the illiterate, the homeless, the destitute, the hungry, the dirty, the women

comunidades de base: base communities

CNR: Committee for National Resettlement

CONAMUS: National Coordination of Salvadoran Women

COPROMUSA: Committee for the Unification of Salvadoran Women

CRIPDES: Christian Committee of the Displaced of El Salvador

delegado(a) de la palabra: delegate of the word; lay leader of Scripture services in base Christian communities

desplazados: those displaced by the war

directivas: local community governing councils

entregado(a): literally, handed over; completely given over to the people; totally committed

ERP: Popular Revolutionary Army

FAL: Armed Forces of Liberation (Salvadoran Communist Party)

FARN: Armed Forces of National Resistance

FDR: Democratic Revolutionary Front

FECCAS: Christian Federation of the Peasants of El Salvador

FENASTRAS: National Federation of Salvadoran Workers

FMLN: Farabundo Martí National Liberation Front; founded in El Salvador in 1980; a united front of five guerrilla armies: the Popular Forces of Liberation (FPL), the Popular Revolutionary Army (ERP), the Armed Forces of National Resistance (FARN), the Salvadoran Communist Party's Armed Forces of Liberation, (FAL) and the Revolutionary Party of Central American Workers (PRTC)

FPL: Popular Forces of Liberation

FSLN: Sandinista National Liberation Front (Nicaragua)

FTC: Federation of Farmworkers

guindas: rapid community flight from approaching patrols or planes

Iglesia Popular: popular church

IMU: Institute for Research Training and Development of Women

LIC: low-intensity conflict

metate: stone for grinding corn into tortillas

milpa: cornfield

MPSC: Popular Social Christian Movement

MSM: Movement of Salvadoran Women

muchachos(as): guerrillas; literally, "boys (girls)"

MUES: Unity of Women, University of El Salvador

mujerista: Hispanic American feminist

ocote: a type of pine

ORDEN: Democratic Nationalist Organization, a paramilitary right-wing organization, precursor of today's death squads

orejas: "ears," i.e., informants

ORMUSA: Organization of Salvadoran Women for Peace

PPL: *Poder Popular Local,* local people's power, created by peasants on the war front

proceso: (revolutionary) process

PRTC: Revolutionary Party of Central American Workers

pueblo: the people

pupusas: typical Salvadoran food of tortillas filled with cheese, beans, or pork

quemada: "burned," i.e., marked by security forces

responsables: persons responsible for some aspect of communal work

repatriations: communities of refugees returned from camps in Honduras; popularly called repopulations

tatu: underground shelter

UMS: Union of Salvadoran Women for Liberation "Melida Anaya Montes"

UNHCR: United Nations High Commission on Refugees

UNTS: National Unity of Salvadoran Workers, a coalition of the popular organizations

UTC: Union of Rural Farmworkers

womanist: black American feminist

Notes

Introduction

1. Eduardo Galeano, *Memory of Fire: Century of the Wind* (New York: Pantheon, 1988), 257.

1 / The Hour of God: The Base Christian Communities

2. Ignacio Ellacuría, "Rogelio Poncelee: A Priest with the Guerrillas," photocopy, San Salvador, 1988, 10.

3. Pope John Paul II, in *The Church in the Present Day Transformation of Latin America in the Light of the Council* (Washington, D.C.: U.S. Catholic Conference, 1970), 80–82.

4. Penny Lernoux, *Cry of the People* (New York: Penguin, 1980), 429.

5. Jon Sobrino, *Archbishop Romero: Memoirs and Reflections* (Maryknoll, N.Y.: Orbis Books, 1990), 63.

6. Ibid., 255.

7. Thomas Anderson, *Matanza: El Salvador's Communist Revolt of 1932* (Lincoln: University of Nebraska Press, 1971), 17.

8. Phillip Berryman, *The Religious Roots of Rebellion* (Maryknoll, N.Y.: Orbis Books, 1984), 94.

9. Ibid., 96.

10. Tommy Sue Montgomery, *Revolution in El Salvador* (Boulder, Colo.: Westview Press, 1982), 104.

11. Pablo Galdámez, *Faith of a People* (Maryknoll, N.Y.: Orbis Books, 1986), 2.

12. Ibid., 58.

13. Berryman, *The Religious Roots of Rebellion*, 113.

14. Ibid., 115.

15. Ibid., 120.

16. Sobrino, *Archbishop Romero*, 80.

17. Ibid., 239.

18. Archbishop Romero, homily given at the Cathedral, San Salvador, February 1980.

19. Pablo Richard, *Death of Christendom: Birth of the Church* (Maryknoll, N.Y.: Orbis Books, 1989), 162.

20. Ibid., 167.

2 / The Hour of the Poor: The Peasants

21. Allan Issacman, "Peasant and Rural Protest in Africa," paper prepared for the MacArthur Interdisciplinary Program on Peace and International Cooperation, 1989, 44.

22. Quoted in Jenny Pearce, *Promised Land* (London: Latin America Bureau, 1986), 102.

23. Pearce, *Promised Land*, 144–45.

24. Ibid., 147.

25. James Scott, *Weapons of the Weak* (New Haven: Yale University Press, 1985), 345.

26. Marilyn Thompson, *Women of El Salvador* (London: Zed Press, 1986), 50.

27. Pearce, *Promised Land*, 143.

28. Ibid., 184.

29. Montgomery, *Revolution in El Salvador*, 151.

30. Four U.S. Lieutenant Colonels, "American Military Policy and the Lessons Learned from El Salvador," John F. Kennedy School of Government (Boston: Harvard University, 1988), 84.

31. Ibid., 20–21.

32. Sara Miles, "The Real War," *NACLA* (North American Congress on Latin America) 20, no. 2 (May 1986): 18.

33. Paulo Freire, *The Politics of Education* (Granby, Mass.: Bergin and Garvey, 1985), 130.

34. Alexander Cockburn, "Beat the Devil," *Nation*, September 1, 1985, 3.

35. The Commission on Integrated Long Term Strategy, "Discriminate Deterrence," classified document, Washington, D.C., 1988, 13.

3 / The Hour of Women: Women's Organizations

36. "Women's Lives in El Salvador," *Spare Rib*, reprinted in *Women and War in El Salvador*, WIRE, Washington, 19.

37. Thompson, *Women of El Salvador*, 25.

38. New Americas Press, ed., *A Dream Compels Us* (Boston: South End Press, 1989), 28.

39. Ibid., 25.

40. Ibid., 50.

41. Jean Franco, *Gender, Death and Resistance: The Ethical Vacuum*, 72.

42. Ibid., 74.

43. AMES, "Participación de la mujer salvadoreña en el proceso revolucionario" (Participation of Salvadoran women in the revolutionary process), booklet, El Salvador, 1980, 9.

44. New Americas, *A Dream Compels Us*, 87.

45. Ibid., 88.

46. Ibid.

47. Ibid., 99.

48. Joaquín Villalobos, "Interview," *Venceremos*, special report, no. 6 (Summer 1989): 7.

49. Primer Encuentro de Mujeres Salvadoreñas: Documento Final (First Encounter of Salvadoran Women: Final Document), San Salvador, September 1988.

50. Kathryn B. Ward, *Women and Urbanization in the World Economy* (New York: Academic Press, 1985), 317.

51. Ibid.

52. Ibid., 34.

53. Ibid., 309.

54. Statement of the First Assembly of Marginalized Women, unpublished

first draft of *El Salvador: A Spring That Never Runs Dry*, ed. Scott Wright, EPICA, CRIZPAZ, 1990, unnumbered text pages.

4 / The Hour of the Furnaces: The Martyrs

55. Principal sources for the story of Laura López are "Vida y testimonio de Laura (The life and testimony of Laura), photocopy published by Laura's base Christian Community, 1987, and interviews with Sister Ana, Laura's daughter, and Margarita Kling.

56. Principal sources for the story of María Cristina Gómez are interviews with Salvador Gómez, Edna Flores, Corina (president of CONAMUS), and Alicia.

57. Principal sources for the story of Silvia Maribel Arriola are interviews with Sister Emma, Sister Luisa, Magdalena, María Elena, Alfredo, and Marta.

58. Pablo Galdámez, *Faith of a People*, 48–49.

59. "¿Silvia, Dónde Vas?" ("Silvia, Where Are You Going?") from the diocesan songbook for Sunday Mass, San Salvador.

5 / The Hour of War: The Militants

60. Ana Guadalupe Martínez in New Americas Press, ed., *A Dream Compels* (Boston: South End Press, 1990), 160.

61. Ibid., 160.

62. Ibid., 177.

63. Tom Barry, *El Salvador: A Country Guide* (Albuquerque, N.M.: Inter-Hemispheric Education Resource Center, 1990), 63.

64. Interview with Salvador Somayoa, *U.S.–El Salvador Institute for Democratic Development Bulletin*, San Francisco, February 1990, 2.

65. George Vickers, "A Spider's Web," *NACLA* 24, no. 1, (June 1990): 27.

66. Rogelio Poncelee, *Muerte y vida en Morazán* (San Salvador: María Vigil López, University of San Salvador, 1987), 50.

Conclusion

67. Church of the Brethren, *Central America Working Group Report*, Washington, July 2, 1991.

68. Gene Palumbo, "Salvadoran Prelate Says Now Is 'Not the Time' for U.S. Aid," *National Catholic Reporter*, June 21, 1991, 9.

69. Noemi Ortiz, "Martyrdom Does Not Come from Death but Life," *Central America Report* 11, no.3 (June 1991): 7.

70. Eduardo Galeano, interview, *NACLA* 20, no. 5 (December 1986): 16.

71. Robin Morgan, ed., "Prefatory Notes and Methodology," *Sisterhood Is Global: The International Women's Movement Anthology* (Garden City, N.Y.: Anchor/Doubleday, 1984), xii.

72. New Americas Press, ed. *A Dream Compels Us* (Boston: South End Press, 1989), 142.

Index

Index